Clinics in Developmental Medicine No. 86

Development Screening
and the
Child with Special Needs

A Population Study of 5000 Children

CECIL DRILLIEN
Formerly Senior Lecturer in Child Health
University of Dundee

MARGARET DRUMMOND
Senior Lecturer
Department of Child Health
University of Glasgow

1983

Spastics International Medical Publications

LONDON: William Heinemann Medical Books Ltd.

PHILADELPHIA: J. B. Lippincott Co.

ISBN 0433 07810 3

Printed in England at THE LAVENHAM PRESS LTD., Lavenham, Suffolk

Contents

Acknowledgements

This longitudinal study of development screening and children with special needs, now in its eighth year, could not have been initiated or continued without the active co-operation and generous help of many different persons.

We are indebted to Dr. C.H. M. Walker, Reader in Child Health, University of Dundee and Dr. Catherine Frain-Bell, Consultant Paediatrician (Community Child Health and Educational Medicine) for inviting us to become involved in the Dundee Development Screening Programme and to Professor R. G. Mitchell for his encouragement to record the findings of our study in this book.

Miss Sandra Murray, Mr. Frank Monigatti and Mr. Jack Reid, members of the administrative staff, Community Child Health Services, Tayside Health Board, provided invaluable help in the tracing and follow-up of children included in the screening programme. We are grateful to them and to Mr. David Butterworth, Senior Systems Designer, Tayside Health Board Computer Department, who provided up-dated print-outs of all screening results for children born 1973/76 on which much of the subsequent computation was based.

The study owes much to the endeavours of community child health doctors and health visitors and their concern for children with special needs, which enabled us to demonstrate the scope and value of development screening and surveillance.

That the study continued after research-group children reached school age is due in large part to the interest and encouragement of Dr. June Cockburn, Regional Principal Educational Psychologist (Tayside Region), Mr. I. M. McNeill, Divisional Principal Educational Psychologist (Dundee Division) and Mr. D. G. Robertson, Director of Education, Tayside Region, and to the advice given by Mr. I. W. Swanson, Senior Lecturer in Educational Psychology, University of Strathclyde and by Mrs. Hilary Kennedy, Educational Psychologist (Dundee Division).

Over four years detailed information was received about all children attending Dundee primary schools. We are deeply indebted to the head teachers, assistant head teachers (early years) and class teachers of 55 schools who undertook this burden of work at a time of increasing difficulties in the educational system ,and also to educational psychologists of the Child Guidance Service and Dr. Anne C. Langlands, Senior Clinical Medical Officer, who provided on-going reports about children in need of special education.

We would like to thank Mr. and Mrs. Ronald Bonar and the other Trustees of the White Top Foundation, Dundee, who granted generous financial support for CMD (1972 to 1982) and MBD (1972 to 1980).

The senior author is particularly grateful to Dr. J. A. Macfarlane, Editor, and Merrilyn Julian, Editorial Assistant, Clinics in Developmental Medicine for their many constructive criticisms and suggestions during the preparation of the manuscript.

Finally we would like to express our appreciation of our secretary, Mrs. Nan Small (1973/82), who assisted greatly in the preparation of the manuscript and whose organisational ability and sympathetic approach contributed so much to the investigation and management of Dundee children with special needs.

CHAPTER 1

Introduction

DEVELOPMENT SCREENING AROUND THE WORLD

The concept of total population screening of young children for developmental disabilities has a long history. In 1966 a World Health Organisation working group (1967), representing six European countries stated that 'screening implies the application to *all* children born of certain procedures which can be carried out in a short time by the less specialised members of staff and which will give indication of the presence or absence of certain disabilities . . . If the result of the test is positive, indicating the actual or probable presence of the disability, the child is referred for specialist investigation and care'. The disabilities considered in this report were mental retardation, defects of hearing and vision, behaviour disorder, physical handicap and neurological disability.

The most comprehensive national development screening programmes of young children are found in Scandinavia. As in Britain, screening and surveillance are most usually undertaken in child health clinics. Where attendance is close to 100 per cent, as in Sweden and Finland, few children escape screening. In Britain, however, clinic non-attendance is reported as between 10 and 40 per cent (Robson 1978) with wide area and age differences. A high proportion of developmental problems is found amongst non-attenders (Zinkin and Cox 1976).

In Finland developmental tests are carried out at monthly intervals in the first year of life (Wynn and Wynn 1974). Each infant is examined, on average, between 10 and 11 times. 70 per cent of these examinations are carried out in clinics and 30 per cent on home visits by community (public health) nurses. The average child is seen twice by a doctor in the first year. After the age of 12 months it is the policy in Finland to have at least one developmental examination a year up to school age. Overall, a Finnish child is examined by the health service about 18 times on average from the day the responsibility is handed by the midwife to the community nurse until school entrance at seven years. Each mother is provided with a record book in which all examinations are recorded and which includes information about the child's development. A similar document, the *Mutter-Kinder Pass*, is used in the Federal Republic of Germany and in Austria.

A national health and development screening programme for children was instituted in the Federal Republic of Germany in 1972. This came under criticism, however, largely because of the widely varying quality of screening which reflected the individual training of doctors involved in the programme. In 1977 a standard developmental check list, based on child age, was established in an attempt to produce more reliable results. However, in 1980 Funke reported, 'in spite of almost

1

perfect offer of routine screening examinations to families, case finding is not nearly complete'. This was attributed to inadequate participation in the scheme, particularly of low social class and immigrant families, and to the fact that doctors in general practice, who carried out most screening examinations, rejected supervision and were opposed to the possibility that their child patients might come under the care of others. Payment by health insurance added to the reluctance of these doctors to accept alternative care for their child patients even though their own facilities and expertise might be inadequate.

Apart from Scandinavia, the most comprehensive national programme of screening and surveillance is found in Israel (Kalir 1980). Supervision of preschool children is undertaken by the maternity and child health service in 850 clinics. Examinations designed to detect deviations from normal development are offered three or four times in the first year of life, twice in the second year and yearly from three to five years. On average, clinic attendance is about 85 per cent, rather higher in the first year and rather lower thereafter. In 1973 a national plan was adopted for the establishment of child development centres, with multidisciplinary assessment and management teams, in catchment areas having populations of 100,000 to 250,000. The services of the centres are open to all but most referrals are of preschool children from the maternity and child health clinics.

Only in France is screening 'obligatory' (at eight days, nine months and two years) to the extent that since 1975 postnatal benefits have been dependent on screening attendance and reserve powers exist to discontinue family allowances for any child who is not taken for examination (Wynn and Wynn 1976). A comprehensive document, the *Carnet de Santé*, held by parents, provides information about each child from birth to 16 years. As well as recording results of the three obligatory examinations, the *Carnet* includes details about perinatal status, immunisation record, physical growth and puberty and social circumstances. The *Carnet* is compiled by both doctors and parents. In France, as in the Federal Republic of Germany, doctors, rather than community nurses, are mainly involved in developmental surveillance.

Preschool screening and intervention programmes have mushroomed in the United States since President Kennedy's statement in 1961 regarding the need for a national plan for mental retardation (United States: President's Panel on Mental Retardation 1962). In 1973 the President's Committee on Mental Retardation (United States: DHEW 1973) produced a lengthy document on screening and assessment of young children at developmental risk. The report concluded that 'the next logical steps will have to be accomplished at the local and regional level'. As might be expected across a continent with a strong tradition of state and local community independence, current programmes vary from the reasonably comprehensive to a complete absence of such provision. The opinion of one developmental paediatrician about the multiplicity of screening procedures in the United States was expressed thus: 'What can only be described as an obsession with early diagnosis has led to a proliferation of early (mostly at kindergarten level) screening instruments . . . The very proliferation of screening tests suggests an inverse Gresham's law: if any of these instruments were effective predictors, they would drive the others from the market place' (Accardo 1980). Concern has also been expressed about the range of false positive rates, amounting to 10 to 20 per cent in different studies of different screening instruments, and the morally unacceptable possibility of large numbers of normal children being 'labelled' and placed in compensatory kindergarten programmes.

In Britain preschool development screening has been successively commended by the reports of Brotherston, Court and Warnock (Great Britain: Scottish Home and Health Department 1973; DHSS 1976; Committee of Enquiry into the Education of Handicapped Children and Young People 1978; respectively). In 1981 the Education Act repealed the provisions of previous education acts relating to systems of special educational treatment for pupils formally classified in specified categories of handicap and gave effect to the Warnock committee recommendations that the concept of handicap should be replaced by one of 'special educational needs'. So far as is reasonably practical, children with special educational needs should be educated in normal schools. Section 10 of the Act places upon the health authority a duty to inform the parent and the local education authority when they form the opinion that a child under the age of five years has, or is likely to have, special educational needs. Thereafter it is proposed that assessment of such children will be by a multi-professional assessment procedure initiated by the education authority. Total population screening of infants and young children for developmental disorders and delays by the health authority could be used as the first stage in the process of early identification of children likely to have special educational needs.

Screening is now widespread in Britain and occupies much child health service time—time which questionably could be better spent on other aspects of care. That health surveillance, including development screening, should become a routine part of primary health care is subject to continuing debate (p. 274). Screening programmes have already been established, or are envisaged for the future, on the uncertain assumption of their effectiveness.

The main aim of screening is the 'earliest identification of any disabilities likely to have an educational implication in order that appropriate measures may be taken to ameliorate or minimise the disabilities detected' (Great Britain: Scottish Health Services Planning Council; Child Health Programme Planning Group 1980). By many this may be interpreted as identifying early only those 2 to 3 per cent of children with severe handicaps who, before the 1981 Education Act, would have been considered for special education. Although such children may be identified earlier when a total population is screened, it is doubtful that this objective alone could justify the time and cost of health professionals and the administrative expenses. With every child in Britain having a family doctor and a health visitor* with statutory obligations to make regular contacts with infants and

---

*In Britain, health visitors are trained general nurses who, after qualification, obtain additional obstetric experience and complete one year of college-based study and practical work leading to the Certificate of Health Visiting. They carry out regular home visiting of all preschool children. Although this is a statutory obligation, no right of entry is provided. However, access is rarely refused. Health visitors work from family doctor group practice premises and/or from local child health clinics.

young children, most children with overt handicaps should come to light early without a screening programme (p. 61). In our opinion a major aim of any screening programme should be the identification preschool of the 10 to 15 per cent of children who constitute the so-called 'learning disabilities' group and who, at present, are usually first picked up at school with educational and behavioural problems.

In 1973 the Brotherstone report recognised that there was a 'lack of firm data' on the effectiveness of total population screening as a means of early identification of children with special educational needs and recommended that 'schemes for its evaluation should be set up without delay' (Great Britain: Scottish Home and Health Department 1973). However, to date no study has attempted to confirm that total population screening does identify such children or that conventional development milestones are the best predictors of later functioning. Some studies (reviewed by Illingworth 1980) suggest that predictability of development testing results obtained from infants and young children is poor. Furthermore little is known about the way that skills measurable in an infant or young child relate to the skills needed later for formal learning in normal school, though it is probable that regular follow-up, as pertains in the screening situation, is important in ascertaining rate of development, which is likely to predict later status more accurately than a single testing (Francis-Williams 1977).

Although some approximations have been made as to the incidence and aetiology of most major handicapping conditions in young children, little has been reported on less serious impairments. Most published reports on development screening programmes are disappointing in their lack of information on the actual disabilities detected, and particularly on the assessment and management of such problems. Such data are essential in the effective prevention and amelioration of developmental and behavioural impairments of young children.

THE DUNDEE DEVELOPMENT SCREENING PROGRAMME (DDSP) RESEARCH PROJECT

The DDSP was devised and initiated by Dr. C. H. M. Walker, Reader in Child Health, University of Dundee and Dr. C. Frain-Bell, Consultant Paediatrician (Community Child Health and Educational Medicine). The programme started with a trial run in 1972 and was fully implemented in 1973. A special study of children born in 1974 and 1975 and included in the DDSP is reported here.

The DDSP was not set up with a research study in mind. Thus no 'unscreened' control group was available. Additionally, the DDSP, like all screening programmes in Britain, operates within the National Health Service and it is taken for granted that when problems are identified, efforts will be made to ameliorate them. For this reason, it was not possible to provide an 'unmanaged' control group of children. In any event it would not have been possible to retain a study group of children with developmental disabilities for long-term observation if it had been evident to parents that no attempt was being made to treat their children's problems.

This is not a true cohort study, in that children transferring into Dundee after

4

birth were included and no attempt was made to trace and follow up children who transferred out. In some of the later analyses, figures are given for the total population of 1974/75-born children who were resident in Dundee at any time during the first five years of life and for those who were born and remained in the city throughout the three-year screening period.

The main aims of the study were:

(1) to estimate the frequency of neurodevelopmental disabilities (NDD) identified in a total population of 5334 preschool children, and to describe the different types of problems presenting and their management;

(2) to relate NDD to possible causative factors, both intrinsic and extrinsic;

(3) to ascertain whether or not a development screening programme identifies preschool those children who will have educational and behavioural problems in the first two years after school entry;

(4) to ascertain whether or not preschool intervention affects the frequency of educational and behavioural problems at early school age.

Organisation of the DDSP

Every Dundee-born and resident infant, identified by birth registration, was included in the programme. Children transferring in to the city after birth but before three years, which was the last age of screening, were also incorporated into the programme. The total number of 1974/75-born children resident in Dundee at any stage from the first screening at eight weeks until school entry at four and a half to five and a half years was 5334. This number comprised the preschool research group. Of these children, 5003 were available for at least one screening examination and 331 children transferred into the city after three years (the age of the last screening examination) but before school entry.

Screening ages, examiners and procedures following failure to attend

Screening examinations were carried out at ages eight, 20 and 39 weeks, 15 months, two and three years. Appointments were made by computer for attendance at local clinic or general practitioner surgery. Infants attending hospital neonatal follow-up clinics were screened there by the authors at the same ages except that, in the case of prematurely delivered infants, examinations were made at real age (*i.e.* allowing for prematurity) rather than chronological age. All infants who were more than three to four weeks premature were asked to attend hospital clinics initially and many continued to be seen there for at least the first nine months. Appointments for screening in hospital clinics were made by the hospital and on discharge infants were incorporated into the computer appointment system for future screening locally, except for those cases who were referred for further supervision to the Child Development Centre (CDC) (p. 122).

The first screening at eight weeks was carried out by the health visitor and subsequent screenings by community child health doctors or by the few family doctors who chose to screen the children in their own practices. Initially, six of the 100 or so family doctors in the city were involved in screening. Later two more became involved and two withdrew.

5

TABLE 1.1
Screening ages, examiners and procedures following failure to attend

Screening age	Examiner	Follow-up procedure
8 weeks	Health visitor	Home screen
20 weeks		Home screen
39 weeks	Child health clinic	Home screen if:
15 months	doctor	(a) missed 2 screenings;
2 years	or	(b) previous screening doubtful;
3 years	family doctor	(c) high-risk baby.

If mother and baby did not attend at either eight or 20 weeks, a screening examination was carried out at home by the health visitor (Table 1.1). Thereafter, home screening was requested by the authors (who scrutinised all screening results weekly) if the child had missed (a) two consecutive screening appointments, (b) one appointment and had had doubtful screening results in some area/s of development or behaviour at the last screening, or (c) one appointment and was known to be included in a high-risk group due to such factors as social deprivation, severe perinatal complications or history of convulsions.

Screening schedules

The screening schedules used are shown in Appendix I. Each included items in the four main areas of development (gross motor; vision, fine motor and adaptive; comprehension and communication; social and self-help skills) as well as some aspects of behaviour, a physical examination and some indicators of neurological dysfunction. In order to minimise the number of unnecessary referrals or recalls for review, the test items selected for the first three screening examinations were appropriate for infants younger than the ages of screening. Most tests applied at eight weeks were appropriate for six-week-old infants, those applied at 20 weeks were appropriate for 16-week infants, and those applied at 39 weeks appropriate for infants of 32 to 36 weeks. Thus failures on DDSP items would suggest definite delay. At 15 months a range of items was presented, one-half appropriate for 52 weeks and one-half for 15 months.

At two years, a more detailed assessment of development was carried out with items appropriate for age. The schedule was planned thus because it was originally intended that all children who, at two years, were behaving up to age in all respects, had no physical or neurological abnormality and were not included in any high-risk group would be dropped from the programme until the age of four and a half years. Only those children not so described would be screened again at three years. Later it was decided that all children should be screened at three years and that the four-and-a-half-year examinations should be omitted. The three-year schedule included a range of items to cover responses appropriate for 30 to 36 months.

Three different schedules were designed for health-visitor screening at home at age 20 weeks or older. These covered the age ranges (a) 16 to 44 weeks, (b) 48 weeks to two years and (c) two and a half to four years (Appendix II). These schedules were also used for children attending late at screening clinics.

A manual was prepared(by CMD) giving instructions on questions to be asked and how procedures should be carried out at all screening ages, with expected responses at different ages. The manual was designed to encourage conformity in history-taking and examination, and to provide detailed guidance for less experienced screening personnel.

At neurodevelopmental component was added to the school medical examination (Appendix III) and used for all children entering school in the 1978/79 session and thereafter. For research purposes a questionnaire (Appendix IV) was designed for completion by class teachers in the third term of the school sessions, for all children attending normal primary schools in Dundee when they were aged six and a half to seven and a half years. At that age most children would be in the second class at school, having entered at four and a half to five and a half years.

Further assessment of suspect or abnormal children

Clinics for more detailed assessment of infants and young children with neuro-developmental delay or abnormality were held at CDC. Screening doctors indicated if they wished further CDC assessment on the screening card. The authors might also request referral to CDC on the basis of screening results. Alternatively, screening doctors might refer to other hospital clinics or to educational services. Notification of these referrals was also entered on screening cards.

Control groups

Two main control groups were selected for comparison with research-group children identified as having NDD preschool. (Another control group was selected later for comparison with children having schooling difficulties (p. 237)).

Control group A

These children were chosen at random to allow comparison of the frequency of certain characteristics, particularly minor abnormal neurological signs and minor congenital anomalies, with CDC-referred children with NDD. For this control group, it was also intended to compare the conclusions from one of the necessarily brief routine screening examinations with those obtained from a more detailed developmental assessment and physical and neurological examination at CDC.

Control group A was not chosen from 1974/75-born children since all these were included in the research group and were thus potentially identifiable as having NDD up to the time of school entry. Extraction of a control group from the research group at any stage during the preschool period might have disrupted this process of identification. For this reason control group A was selected from among children born in the three years subsequent to the research years, *i.e.* 1976 to 1978, inclusive.

Selection was made from the appointment lists of the 20 development screening clinics held in the city. The number of control children selected from each clinic was in proportion to the total number of children attending that clinic for screening. It was planned to include 25 children at each screening age, apart from the eight-week examination, giving a total of 125 children. The eight-week age group was excluded

7

partly because very few infants were identified as having NDD at this age and partly because it was felt that a request to include their infants in a research control group at their first screening might produce anxiety in some mothers and jeopardise subsequent screening attendance.

Over a period of two and a half years, each clinic was visited by one of the authors (MBD) as often as was necessary to enrol the pre-arranged number of children at each of the screening ages. If the chosen child was one of a twin pair, both children were included in the request. The mother was given an explanation of the research evaluation of the development screening programme. She was then asked if she would be willing for her child to be enrolled as a control in the study. This would involve one attendance at CDC. If a child whose name had been selected did not attend for screening, a letter was sent to the mother with the same explanation and request.

In order to obtain the planned number of control children it was necessary to approach a total of 162 mothers. Although the aim was to enrol 125 children as controls, the final number enrolled was 128. The enrolment of three extra children was due to the difficulty of knowing at any one point in time exactly how many more mothers should be approached. Of the 128 control children, 25 were enrolled after the 20-week screening examination, 26 after each of the 39-week, 15-month and two-year examinations, and 25 after the three-year examination.

Of the 162 mothers who were approached, 115 were interviewed at a screening clinic and 47 who had not attended the clinic were sent a letter. Of those attending their screening clinic appointments, 108 agreed to their children being used as controls but six failed to keep their appointments at CDC. Seven more did not agree to co-operate, making a total of 13 who refused either directly or indirectly and 102 who co-operated in the study. Of the 47 non-clinic attenders, 26 responded positively to the letters and all their children became controls. The remaining 21 mothers either replied negatively or did not reply. Thus, as might be expected, significantly more of the clinic-attending mothers agreed to their children becoming controls as compared with non-clinic attenders ($\chi^2 = 22.415$, p = <0.001).

SEX DISTRIBUTION

The 162 mothers approached had rather more female than male children (87 female, 75 male). The children whose mothers did not co-operate were more likely to be male (15 female, 19 male), leaving 56 males and 72 females in the final control group. In neither group, however, was the sex distribution significantly different from that in the general population of 1974/75 Dundee livebirths to Dundee-resident mothers (52 per cent male).

SOCIAL CLASS DISTRIBUTION

By choosing control children from the screening clinics in proportion to the population served by that clinic, it was hoped that the social class distribution of control group A would be representative of the general population of Dundee children. Table 1.2 shows the social class distribution by fathers' occupation, derived from mothers' histories or clinic records, of control group A children, those

TABLE 1.2

Control group A. Social class distribution derived from mothers' histories or clinic records

	Social class								
	I and II		III		IV and V		NK/Other		Total
	No.	%	No.	%	No.	%	No.	%	No.
Control group A									
Accepted	35	27	57	45	31	24	5	4	128
Refused	4	12	15	44	13	38	2	6	34
Total	39	24	72	45	44	27	7	4	162
General population*	18†		48		29		5		

*All 1974/75 Dundee livebirths to Dundee-resident mothers; †social class distribution derived from computer file; NK = not known.

whose mothers did not co-operate and the total number of mothers approached. The table also shows the percentage social class distribution (derived from computer file held by the area health board, p. 49) of all children born in Dundee in 1974 and 1975 to Dundee-resident mothers. The social class distribution for the total group of 162 mothers approached is not significantly different from that of the general population of children born 1974/75. However, there is a significant difference in distribution between the general population and those controls who attended for assessment, due to the over-representation of social classes I and II and the lower proportion of social classes IV and V in the control group ($\chi^2 = 7.240$, 2df, p = <0.05).

ASSESSMENT OF CONTROL CHILDREN

All of the 128 control children were seen at CDC for assessment within a few weeks of a screening examination. The mean screening/assessment interval was 13 days for the whole group, varying from 11 days following the 39-week screening examination to 16 days following the three-year examination. A full history was taken from the mother including family history, mother's obstetric history and details of any illnesses suffered. Hospital records were scrutinised for perinatal details and any hospital attendances by the child. A full developmental assessment was carried out by one of the authors (CMD) using the same Gesell-based scales (Drillien 1977) as for the developmental assessment of research-group children referred to CDC. A physical and neurological examination was carried out by the other author (MBD).

COMPARISON WITH SCREENING RESULTS

Development screening folders for control group A children were not seen until all children had been assessed at CDC and reports completed. Thereafter the appropriate development screening cards (with names obscured and in random order) were scrutinised by the authors and a decision reached, on the basis of information available, on what action would have been taken had the child been included in the research group. Possibilities were (a) no action, (b) screening doctor asked to take special note at next screening, or review before next screening, and

9

refer then if the problem was still present, or (c) screening doctor asked to refer forthwith. Duplicate screening cards were compiled for each child following CDC assessment (taking account of the fact that the child would be a little older) and these cards were treated in the same way.

The intention was to reproduce the circumstances which existed for the research-group children, all of whose screening cards were scrutinised by the authors. Research-group children could be referred to CDC (or to other specialist services) by screening doctors. However, referral to CDC from the screening programme was not offered as a clinical service to children born subsequent to 1974/75 and doctors reverted to the system which obtained earlier, *i.e.* referral to an appropriate hospital-based clinic or to an educational service.

Control group B

A second control group was selected for comparison with the CDC-referred children at school age. This control group was selected at the time that 1974/75-born children entered school. As mentioned above it was not considered desirable to select control children from the research group during the preschool years because of the continuing possibility throughout that period of any child being identified as having NDD. Once the children had entered school this did not apply.

Matched controls were selected for all research-group children known to be resident in Dundee at school-entry age who had been referred to CDC and identified as having moderate or more severe NDD. After excluding children with minor problems and those who had transferred out before school entry age, there remained 326 CDC-referred children. Each child known to have entered the first year of the local school was matched with the child nearest in age and of the same sex attending the same school. Children who had transferred in to the city after the end of the screening period at three years were not eligible to be controls. In those cases where entry to normal school was to be delayed by 12 months or special educational provision had been recommended, a matched control was selected from the neighbourhood school which the child would have attended had he not suffered from NDD.

The majority of the 326 children in control group B were not known to have had any developmental problems preschool. A small number had been referred to hospital clinics (six children) and in 28 cases screening examination results suggested a disability, but this was not confirmed (p. 72). None of these control children were examined at CDC.

Health visitor and hospital records of all control group B children were scrutinised and additional information obtained about social problems (p. 51) and the frequency of abnormalities of pregnancy, delivery and the neonatal period. Results of all screening examinations were known.

Control group B was selected in this way to minimise the influence of social class (which is known to have a predominant effect on educational performance and also an effect on perinatal status) and to ensure that teaching methods and expectations of teachers would be comparable for control children and research-group children with NDD. The social class distribution, derived from the computer

TABLE 1.3

Social class distribution of 1974/75-born CDC-referred children with moderate or more severe NDD and matched control group B children

Social class*	CDC-referred		Control group B	
	No.	%	No.	%
I and II	24	7	30	9
III	132	41	155	48
IV and V	124	38	115	35
Other/NK	46	14	26	8
Total	326	100	326	100

*Derived from computer file.

file, for CDC-referred children with moderate and more severe NDD and their matched controls is given in Table 1.3. There are rather more children of higher social class in the control group but the difference in distribution is not statistically significant (χ^2 = 4.345, 2df, p = <0.10). Controls were matched by sex because boys were much more likely to be referred preschool on account of NDD (p. 72). In the total population study of problems at six and a half to seven and a half years, boys were also found to have significantly more early schooling difficulties than girls (p. 229).

Summary

The Dundee Developmental Screening Programme (DDSP) is described and the aims outlined of a special study of 5334 1974/75-born Dundee-resident preschool children.

Children were screened at ages eight, 20 and 39 weeks, 15 months, two and three years. Special arrangements were made for non-attenders.

Clinics for more detailed assessment and, if necessary, subsequent management of children with doubtful or abnormal screening results were held at the Child Development Centre (CDC). Alternatively, screening doctors might refer to other hospital clinics.

Details are also given of two control groups, one randomly selected and one matched with CDC-referred children identified as having moderate or more severe developmental or behavioural disorders.

APPENDIX 1: Developmental screening schedules, eight weeks to three years

DEVELOPMENTAL SCREENING EXAMINATION AT 8 WEEKS BY HEALTH VISITOR

Name ....

Age .... weeks

Date of Examination ....

DEVELOPMENTAL EXAMINATION			CONCLUSIONS				COMMENTS
Prone posture (normal)	Yes	No	H	O	N		If abnormal—specify
Supine posture (normal)	Yes	No	H	O	D		
					A		
Intent regard of mother's face	Yes	No	H	O	N		If 'No'—specify (1) Looks around in vague staring way. (2) Shows momentary regard of face.
Follows dangling object past mid-line.	Yes	No	H	O	D		If 'No'—specify (1) Does not fixate at all. (2) Fixates and follows fractionally. (3) Fixates and follows up to but not past mid-line.
					A		
Responds vocally	Yes	No	H	O	N		If abnormal—specify
Social smile	Yes	No	H	O	D		
Responds to unseen mother's voice	Yes	No	H	O	A		

Also note:—

(1) Feeding problems:— If 'Yes' specify

(2) Response to sudden sound or movement:— Little or no response / excessive response / normal

(3) Sleep pattern:— Excessively sleepy / excessively wakeful by day; by night / normal

(4) Handling:— Floppy / stiff / normal

Appearance:

Nutritional state:

Weight—gms. .... Length—cms. .... O.F.C.—(cms.) .... Hips ....

Mother's comments:— No problems / problems (specify)

H. History   O. Observed

12

20 WEEKS EXAMINATION

Reference Number

ARR [ ]   OR [ ]   HR [ ]

If child has not been examined by doctor before, then full clinical examination should be carried out and any abnormality noted.

NAME ....

Date of examination ....   Date of Birth ....   Age .... weeks

	DEVELOPMENTAL EXAMINATION					CONCLUSION		
MOTOR	Head erect—no bobbing	Yes	No	H	O	N [ ]		
	Bears weight on legs	Yes	No	H	O			
	Pull to sit—No lag	Yes	No	H	O	D [ ]		
	Rests on forearms and pushes up when prone	Yes	No	H	O			
	Symmetric posture	Yes	No	H	O	A [ ]		
ADAPTIVE	Approaches and grasps near object	Yes	No	H	O	N [ ]		
	Hands held loosely, closed or open	Yes	No	H	O	D [ ]		
						A [ ]		
LANGUAGE & HEARING	Turns head towards sound of voice	Yes	No	H	O	N [ ]		
	Laughs	Yes	No	H	O	D [ ]		
	Variety of sounds in vocal response	Yes	No	H	O	A [ ]		
SOCIAL	Anticipates food on sight	Yes	No	H	O	N [ ]		
	Is content only for limited periods if left lying: needs entertainment	Yes	No	H	O	D [ ]		
						A [ ]		

COMMENTS

BEHAVIOUR—

MOTHER'S COMMENTS—

DIAGNOSIS—If any

PHYSICAL EXAMINATION

Appearance	N	D	A
Nutritional state	N	D	A
Weight—gms.			
Height—cms.			
O.F.C.—cms.			
Muscle tone—floppy / stiff / nil noted	N	D	A
Posture—supine normal	Yes		No
If 'No' specify			
Posture—vert. susp. normal	Yes		No
If 'No' specify			
Eyes	N	D	A
Genitals	N	D	A
Hips	N	D	A
Reflexes—moro	Present		Absent
progression (no rocking)	Present		Absent
Bicep jerks	Normal	Absent	Brisk
Knee jerks	Normal	Absent	Brisk
Ankle clonus	Present		Absent
Congenital abnormalities—specify			
Other abnormalities—specify			

CONCLUSION

N [ ]   D [ ]   A [ ]

H. History   O. Observed

39 WEEKS EXAMINATION

Reference Number

ARR ☐   OR ☐   HR ☐

Date of examination ....

NAME ....

Age.......weeks

DEVELOPMENTAL EXAMINATION

		CONCLUSION			COMMENTS
MOTOR		N	D	A	
Stands briefly, hands held, or longer with minimal axillary support	Yes No H O	☐			BEHAVIOUR—
Prone—pivots, rolls to supine	Yes No H O		☐		
Sits without support	Yes No H O			☐	
ADAPTIVE		N	D	A	
Holds cube in each hand and retains them	Yes No H O	☐			
Secures string of ring	Yes No H O		☐		
Picks up a pellet by raking—may use pincer	Yes No H O			☐	
LANGUAGE & HEARING		N	D	A	
Free and varied vocalisation	Yes No H O	☐			DIAGNOSIS—If any
Understands 'No'	Yes No H O		☐		
SOCIAL		N	D	A	
Chews stodgy food with bits	Yes No H O	☐			
Stretches for objects out of reach	Yes No H O			☐	

PHYSICAL EXAMINATION

Appearance	N	D	A
Nutritional state	N	D	A
Weight—gms.			
Height—cms.			
O.F.C.—cms.			
Muscle tone—floppy / stiff / nil noted	N	D	A
Posture—vert. susp. normal	Yes		No
If 'No'—specify			
Eyes	N	D	A
Genitals	N	D	A
Hips	N	D	A
Reflexes—righting reflex	Present		Absent
'sideways parachute'	Present		Absent
Bicep jerks	Absent	Normal	Brisk
Knee jerks	Absent	Normal	Brisk
Ankle clonus	Present		Absent
Congenital abnormalities—specify			
Other abnormalities—specify			

CONCLUSION

N ☐   D ☐   A ☐

H. History   O. Observed

14

15 MONTHS EXAMINATION

Reference Number

ARR ☐ OR ☐ HR ☐

NAME ....

Date of examination .... Date of Birth .... Age .... months

	DEVELOPMENTAL EXAMINATION				CONCLUSION			COMMENTS
MOTOR	Walks, one hand held	Yes	No	H	O	N ☐		
	Walks, alone or with minimal support	Yes	No	H	O	D ☐		
	Still mainly crawling or hitching	Yes	No	H	O			
	Upright and walking mainly	Yes	No	H	O	A ☐		
ADAPTIVE	Puts 1-2 cubes in cup after several demonstrations	Yes	No	H	O	N ☐		
	Puts 5-6 cubes in cup spontaneously or after 1 cube demonstration	Yes	No	H	O	D ☐		
	Attempts tower of 2 cubes unsuccessfully	Yes	No	H	O	A ☐		
	Attempts tower of 2 cubes successfully	Yes	No	H	O			
LANGUAGE & HEARING	Claps, waves or other parlour tricks on command	Yes	No	H	O	N ☐		
	Says 1-2 words, understands several more	Yes	No	H	O	D ☐		
	Says 3-6 words, understands many more	Yes	No	H	O	A ☐		
	Jargoning	Yes	No	H	O			
SOCIAL	Offers toys and releases	Yes	No	H	O	N ☐		
	Finds hidden toy	Yes	No	H	O	D ☐		
	Picks up cup with 2 hands, drinks, and puts cup down	Yes	No	H	O	A ☐		
	Indicates some wants by pointing and grunting	Yes	No	H	O			

PHYSICAL EXAMINATION

Appearance	N	D	A
Nutritional state	N	D	A
Weight—gms.			
Height—cms.			
O.F.C.—cms.	N	D	A
Muscle tone—floppy / stiff / nil noted	N	D	A
Posture—in vertical suspension If 'D' or 'A' specify	N	D	A
Gait If 'D' or 'A' specify	N	D	A
Eyes	N	D	A
Genitals	N	D	A
Hips	N	D	A
Bicep jerks	Absent	Normal	Brisk
Knee jerks	Absent	Normal	Brisk
Ankle clonus	Absent	Present	
Congenital abnormalities— specify			
Other abnormalities—specify			

CONCLUSION

N ☐   D ☐   A ☐

H. History   O. Observed

15

2 YEARS EXAMINATION

Reference Number ☐ ☐ ☐ ☐ ☐ ☐ ☐ ☐

ARR ☐ OR ☐ HR ☐

NAME ....

Date of examination .... Date of Birth .... Age .... months

	DEVELOPMENTAL EXAMINATION					CONCLUSION	COMMENTS
MOTOR	Walks and runs without falling	Yes	No	H	O	N ☐	**Behaviour patterns—** Sleep
	Walks downstairs alone	Yes	No	H	O	D ☐	Temper
	Turns pages singly	Yes	No	H	O	A ☐	Hyperactivity
	Kicks ball forward	Yes	No	H	O		Any other
ADAPTIVE	Builds 6-7 cube tower	Yes	No			N ☐	Record no. of cubes
	Imitates circular stroke and a straight line	Yes	No			D ☐	
	Simple formboard—success at 2nd attempt	Yes	No			A ☐	
LANGUAGE & HEARING	Joins 2-3 words	Yes	No	H	O	N ☐	Intelligibility of speech
	Names 3-5 pictures or objects	Yes	No	H	O	D ☐	Good / Fair / Poor
	Vocalises all needs	Yes	No	H	O	A ☐	
	Uses pronouns	Yes	No	H	O		
SOCIAL	Asks for toilet by day	Yes	No	H	O	N ☐	DIAGNOSIS—If any
	Uses toys meaningfully	Yes	No	H	O	D ☐	
	Pulls on a single garment	Yes	No	H	O	A ☐	
	Manages spoon efficiently	Yes	No	H	O		
	Manages cup efficiently	Yes	No	H	O		

H. History   O. Observed

PHYSICAL EXAMINATION

MEDICAL HISTORY
—Discharging ears Yes No
—Convulsions Yes No

Appearance N D A
Nutritional state N D A
Weight—gms. .... N D A
Length—cms. .... N D A
O.F.C.—cms. .... N D A
Eyes N D A
Hearing N D A
Genitals—If previous absentee N D A
Gait N D A
Congenital abnormalities— specify
Other—specify

CONCLUSION

N ☐ D ☐ A ☐

16

Reference Number

NAME ....

Age ....

ARR ☐   OR ☐   HR ☐

Date of Examination ....

DEVELOPMENTAL EXAMINATION

Category		Item	Response			CONCLUSIONS	COMMENTS
MOTOR		Runs smoothly and fast without stumbling	Yes	No	H O	N ☐	Gait, specify if abnormal
		Takes running kick at ball	Yes	No	H O	D ☐	
		Alternates feet going upstairs	Yes	No	H O	A ☐	
ADAPTIVE		Builds 7-8 cube tower	Yes	No	H O	N ☐	State no. cubes
		Imitates circle, after watching one drawn	Yes	No	H O		Intention tremor/ ataxia in reaching
		Copies circle, when shown one already drawn	Yes	No	H O	D ☐	
		Imitates cross	Yes	No	H O		Mother says 'clumsy with hands'. Yes No
		3-hole form board reversed (3 trials)	Yes	No	H O	A ☐	Preferred hand R / L / Both
LANGUAGE		Recounts experiences (what he's been doing) to mother/examiner	Yes	No	H O	N ☐	Intelligibility to strangers
		Sentence length 4-6 words	Yes	No	H O	D ☐	
		Understands prepositions (e.g. under, behind)	Yes	No	H O	A ☐	Good / Fair / Poor
SELF HELP SKILLS		Complete self feeding (not too messy)	Yes	No		N ☐	DIAGNOSIS—If any:
		Responsible for toilet by day. Asks	Yes	No		D ☐	
		Goes himself	Yes	No			
		Nappies at night	Yes	No		A ☐	
SOCIAL & BEHAVIOUR		Seperates from mother (not excessively shy)	Yes	No	H O	N ☐	
		Plays happily with other children	Yes	No			
		Sleeping problems	Yes	No		D ☐	
		Frequent temper tantrums	Yes	No	H O		
		Hyperactivity	Yes	No	H O	A ☐	

PHYSICAL EXAMINATION

Appearance	N	D	A
Nutritional state	N	D	A
Weight—Kgs.	N	D	A
Height—cms.	N	D	A
O.F.C.—cms.	N	D	A
Earache/discharging ears	Yes		No
Hearing	N	D	A
Squint	Yes		No
Peering (myopic)	Yes		No
Vision	N	D	A
Heart murmurs	Yes		No
Convulsions	Yes		No

CONCLUSION

N ☐   D ☐   A ☐

N ☐   D ☐   A ☐

H. History   O. Observed

17

APPENDIX II: Schedules for health visitor screening at home

HV1.

NAME .... D. of B. .... Examined on .... At age......... H.V. ....

ADDRESS .... G.P. ....

	16 weeks	H	O	20 weeks	H	O	24 weeks	H	O	28 weeks	H	O	32-36 weeks	H	O	40-44 weeks	H	O
Locomotion																		
Sitting	Held sitting, head steady, lumbar curve.			Held sitting, back straight, head steady, with cushions 10 mins. +			Head steady, with slight support 30 mins. +			On hard surface momentarily.			10 mins. + , topples when twists trunk.			As long as he wants		
Supine, pull to sit	Slight head lag, quickly corrects			No head lag			Helps pull up			Raises head, pulls up with little assistance			Can pull up on pram or cot...... just			Can pull up on pram or cot...... easily		
Prone	Rest on forearms, face looking forwards			Rests on partly extended arms			Rolls ⟶ supine			Rolls supine ⟶ prone			Pivots, pushes backwards			Moves forwards		
Standing	On lap, weight bears momentarily, sags			On lap, weight bears, sags			On lap, takes all weight			On lap, takes all weight and bounces			On floors, hands held shoulder high			Pulls up and holds on		
Hand manipulation:																		
Rattle (R) Cubes (C) Pellet (P)	R. Grasps, retains and regards when placed in hand.			R. Grasps when offered 1″ from fingers, retains.			R. two-handed approach, grasps when offered 6″ from fingers.			R. one-handed approach, grasps, transfers, mouths			C. Retains one in each hand. P. Secures by raking			C. Grasps 2, drops 1 to take 3rd. P. Secures by neat pincer grip		

18

Speech and Social:					
Taking notice of people, bottle, toys. Laughs	Marked interest toys, people. Requies enter-tainment when awake. Laughs, squeals.	Spontaneous vocal-social response.	Vocalises tunefully. Single and double syllables	Shy with stranger. Plays peek-a-boo. Understands 'No'.	Imitates wave, clap. Recognises own name.

Feeding:					
Accepts spoon runny foods.	Smooth semi-solids without baulking.	Smooth stodgy foods.	Stodgy foods with bits.	Chews lumpy food.	Chews biscuit, apple without choking.

ALSO NOTE:

1. OFC.....................cm.

2. **Behaviour:** Jumpy, excitable, sensitive / very placid / neither, just ordinary.

3. **Comparison with siblings:** Place in family..................... Much quicker / much slower / about the same. Same or quicker in..................... slower in.....................

4. **How baby handles:** Stiff / floppy (rag doll / about right.

5. **Posture:** Normal / Abnormal.....................

6. **Mother's opinion:** Normal / Problems.....................

7. **Response to testing:** Co-operative / apathetic / unwell / sleepy / shy / refused.

H. History   O. Observed

19

NAME .... D. of B. .... Examined on .... At age......... H.V. ....

ADDRESS .... G.P. ....

Locomotion

	48-52 weeks	H	O	56 weeks	H	O	15 months	H	O	18 months	H	O	21 months	H	O	24 months	H	O
Standing	Pulls up, falls by collapse.			Lets down gently. Stands alone.			Gets up to stand from floor.			—			—			—		
Crawling	Hands / knees, bear walk; bottom shuffling.			Still crawling mainly			Walking mainly.			—			—			—		
Cruising / walking	Side-steps holding 2 hands. Walks 2 hands held.			Side-steps, one hand. Walks one hand held. May take few staggery steps alone.			Alone across room, broad base, arms up, still falls by collapse.			Walks well, feet closer, arms down, seldom falls.			Squats in play. →			→		
Running				—			—			Trots, can't turn corners.			→			Runs smoothly and well, round obstacles.		
Stairs				—			Crawls up			and down backwards or on buttocks.			Walks up holding rail, down with hand, 2 ft/1 step.			Walks up and down alone.		
Ball				—			—			After demonstration walks into, no true kick. Throws.			After demonstration standing kick.			Kicks, no demonstration.		

Speech

	48-52 weeks	H	O	56 weeks	H	O	15 months	H	O	18 months	H	O	21 months	H	O	24 months	H	O
(also see Books)	Responds to some simple commands, words and gestures. Mamma, Dadda.			May have 3-4 words, responds to some commands without gestures.			Jargoning. 'Uh-uh' and gesture for wants. →			5-20 intelligible words, understands many more.			→ Combining words spontaneously.			Too many words to count, simple sentences, questions, speech for wants.		

Hand manipulation, adaptive, social					
Feeding	Chews and swallows household foods. Finger feeds. →	Lifts cup, two-handed, drinks. May attempt spoon, tips.	Lifts cup and replaces. Spoon into mouth without tipping. →		Complete self feeding. Up to table.
toys to mouth/drooling	Lessening →	Absent.	—		—
Rattles, cubes and other toys	Offers, releases. Casting begins.	Casting toys, one after another. Putting in / taking out games. →	Casting lessening. ↑	Using toys (cars, dolls) meaningfully. ↑	Casting absent. → Domestic mimicry. Turns handles.
Books	—	Holds upside down, pats pictures, helps turn pages.	Turns 2-3 pages, points at familiar objects. ↑		Turns single pages, names objects.
Dressing	Helps by offering arm, leg. →	Starting to pull off shoes, socks, hat, unzip. ↑	↑		Takes off all clothes except over head. Puts on shoes, socks, pants.

ALSO NOTE:

1. OFC...................cm.

2. **Behaviour:** Jumpy, excitable, sensitive / very placid / neither, just ordinary.

3. **Comparison with siblings:** Place in family.................. Much quicker / quicker / much slower / about the same. Same or quicker in.............. slower in..............

4. **Gait:** (18 months or older): Normal / Abnormal (specify)..............

5. **Speech:** (18 months or older): Intelligible / not intelligible (specify) ....

6. **Mother's opinion:** Normal / Problems ....

7. **Response to testing:** Co-operative / apathetic / unwell / shy / refused.

H. History   O. Observed

21

NAME ....   D. of B. ....   Examined on ....   At age.........   H.V. ....

ADDRESS ....   G.P. ....

	2½ Years	H	O	3 Years	H	O	3½ Years	H	O	4 Years	H	O
Gross Motor												
Running	Smoothly, fairly fast, on whole soles of feet, seldom fails			Smoothly and fast, on fore-feet (like older children)			As well as children of like age ('keeps up')			→		
Jumping	2 feet together on floor			2 feet together off low step			2 feet together off 2 steps			Broad jump from standing or running, one foot leading		
Ball	Swinging kick from standing			Running kick, may miss			Running kick, accurate			→		
Stairs	Up and down alone, 2 feet to 1 step			Alternates (1 foot to 1 step) going up			→			Alternates going down		
Standing on 1 foot	—			Momentarily			2 seconds +			4-8 seconds		
Tricycle (if he has one)	Uses pedals			and steers round wide corners			Complete control			→		
Speech												
Book	Names 5-6 of 10 pictures			Names 7-8 of 10			Names 9-10 of 12			Names 11-12 of 12		
Uses of shoe, ball, car, spoon, cup, orange	1-2 uses, usually single word replies			2-3 uses, 2-3 word reply			3 + uses →			4 + uses, replies with science		

22

Fine motor, adaptive, social

Cube tower	7-8	9-10	10
Self feeding	Uses fork efficiently	Uses spoon and fork together	Pours from jug	Uses knife
Undressing, dressing	All clothes off when unfastened. Puts on 3-4 simple garments. Tugs at buttons.	Most clothes on, help with fastenings and laces. Undoes buttons. Does up big buttons.		Complete except back fastenings and laces.
Toileting	Reliable by day, asks	Goes himself, needs help with wiping. Dry most nights.	Dry at night	

ALSO NOTE:

Behaviour: No problems, generally easy to handle / does not play well with other children (if available) / frequent, marked temper / overactive and poor concentration / sleeping problems / other (specify)

Comparison with siblings: Place in family .... Much slower / much quicker / about the same. Same or quicker in .... slower in ....

Gait: Normal / abnormal (specify) ....

Hand function: Normal / clumsy / shaky (tremor)   Mother's report / H.V. observation.   Preferred hand: R / L / both

Speech: Intelligibility to strangers.   Good / fair / poor.   Mother's report / H.V. observation

Mother's (or other caretaker's) opinion: Normal / problems (specify)

H. History   O. Observed

23

APPENDIX III

Neurodevelopmental component of the school medical examination

5-6 Year Old School Examination—Neurodevelopmental Items

Reference No. ☐☐☐☐☐☐☐☐☐ School ....

NAME: DATE OF EXAM: AGE:

Present at examination: mother / father / no-one / other (specify)

History from mother (or accompanying person)

1. Since last developmental screening:
   (a) convulsion/s
   (b) ear infection/s
   (c) other illnesses or hospital attendances
   (d) speech or other therapy (specify)

2. Does the child:
   (a) run normally   yes/no
   (b) keep up with other children of same age   yes/no
   (c) trip easily   yes/no

3. Does the child:
   (a) dress himself (apart from tie and laces)   yes/no/partially (detail)
   (b) do up small front buttons   yes/no

4. Is he clumsy with his hands   yes/no

5. Child's preferred hand   R/L/both

6. Speech:
   (a) good, clear/some words not clear/many words not clear
   (b) amount of spontaneous speech at home   normal and chatty/rather quiet/
                                                    very quiet
   (c) stammer   yes/no

7. Behaviour:
   (a) concentration   good/fair/poor
   (b) overactivity   none/moderate/severe
   (c) aggression   yes/no (specify)
   (d) accident prone   yes/no (specify)
   (e) plays well with other children   yes/no
   (f) maturity   clinging/fairly independent/independent
   (g) other problems   (specify)

8. Bedwetting   no/sometimes/frequent

9. Any other problems at all   yes/no (specify)

24

Examination

1. Hopping on each foot (count number of hops) R.   L.
    specify preferred (first used) foot   R/L

2. Copying shapes (circle, cross, square, diamond)
    Hand used   R/L/mixed
    Grip of pencil   mature/immature (specify)
    Hand function   neat/rather clumsy/very clumsy

3. Note any
    (a) fidgetiness   yes/doubtful/no
    (b) *excessive* associated or mirror movements yes/doubtful/no

    Speech
    (a) Ask child
         own name   yes/no
         address   yes/no
         age   yes/no

    (b) On above, plus spontaneous speech, comment on
         articulation   good/fair/poor

    (c) Any other comment on speech

5. Behaviour during examination
    normal/clinging to mother/withdrawn/negative/overactive/aggressive/other (specify)

6. Strabismus   yes/no

7. Gait—observe the child running if indicated (see manual)
                      normal/graceless/abnormal (expand)

8. Ask child to 'Draw-a-Man'   (Goodenough Draw-a-Man test)

9. Conclusion   N/D/A

Comments:

Signature of examiner ....

25

APPENDIX IV: **School questionnaire**

Name: School:

Date of birth: Class:

You are asked below to rate some aspects of the child's ability and attainment. Each area is subdivided into 4 categories. It is expected that in a truly representative cross-section of this age, approximately 30 per cent would be rated 1 (above average), 40 per cent 2 (average), 25 per cent 3 (below average) and 5 per cent 4 (lack of ability is a substantial handicap in school). In so far as your professional experience will allow, please rate the child in relation to **all children of this age (i.e. not just his present class or, even, school)** by ringing the number opposite the appropriate description.

Expressive language	Expresses himself very well	1
	Average for age	2
	Limited ability, uses simple word groupings	3
	Markedly poor in content and structure	4
Reading	Above average, comprehends well what he reads	1
	Average for age	2
	Sight vocabulary, 50-100 words; can blend simple three-letter words, not yet mastered all consonant blends and vowel dygraphs	3
	Non-reader or very limited sight vocabulary only	4
Number	Above average, grasps new proceses readily	1
	Average for age	2
	Can add/substract to 10 without structured apparatus, difficulty beyond this and with new processes	3
	Needs structured apparatus even for simplest processes	4
Writing	Above average, competent, neat and quick	1
	Average for age	2
	Can copy from board ± some reversals, writing still big and poorly spaced	3
	Great difficulty in copying	4

Below are a few descriptions of lack of skills and behaviour shown by some children. If the child certainly fits the description, please circle the figure 1. If it is a marginal case, or you are in some doubt about the child's inclusion under the description, circle the figure 2. If the description does not fit the child at all, circle the figure 3.

	CERTAINLY APPLIES	APPLIES SOMEWHAT	DOESN'T APPLY
Difficult to understand because of poor speech	1	2	3
Poor control of hands (e.g. in drawing, handwork, buttoning coat, tying laces)	1	2	3
Poor physical co-ordination (e.g. in running, jumping, throwing)	1	2	3
Poor attention/concentration (e.g. in listening to and remembering group instructions)	1	2	3
Poor motivation/persistence (e.g. in carrying out task without adult supervision)	1	2	3
Restless, fidgety child	1	2	3
Young for age in self-sufficiency and dependence on adults	1	2	3
Unforthcoming, shy	1	2	3
Aggressive to other children, frequent fights	1	2	3
Not much liked by other children	1	2	3

Any other problems of attainment or behaviour? Please specify overleaf.

Has the child been referred to the Child Guidance Service?		Yes	No
Has the child received extra help in reading?		Yes	No
If 'No', do you consider he should have extra help?		Yes	No
Has the child received extra help in number work?		Yes	No
If 'No', do you consider he should have extra help?		Yes	No
Has the child been retained for 2 years in P.1?		Yes	No
Will he be retained for 2 years in P.2?	Yes	Possibly	No

P.1 = Primary I

REFERENCES

Accardo, P. J. (1980) *A Neurodevelopmental Perspective on Specific Learning Disabilities. Monographs in Developmental Pediatrics No. 3.* Baltimore: University Park Press.

Drillien, C. M. (1977) 'Developmental assessment and developmental screening.' *In:* Drillien, C. M., Drummond, M. B. (Eds.) *Neurodevelopmental Problems in Early Childhood.* Oxford: Blackwell Scientific Publications.

Francis-Williams, J. (1977) 'Psychological assessment.' *In:* Drillien, C. M., Drummond, M. B. (Eds.) *Neurodevelopmental Problems in Early Childhood.* Oxford: Blackwell Scientific Publications.

Funke, E. (1980) 'Problems in organising a follow-up survey of at risk children in a developed society.' *In:* Harel, S. (Ed.) *The At Risk Infant. International Congress Series No. 492.* Amsterdam: Excerpta Medica.

Great Britain: Committee of Enquiry into the Education of Handicapped Children and Young People (1978) *Special Educational Needs. Report of the Committee* (Chairman: H. M. Warnock). London: HMSO.

—— Department of Health and Social Security (1976) *Fit for the Future. Report of the Committee on Child Health Services* (Chairman: S. D. M. Court). London: HMSO.

—— Scottish Health Services Planning Council; Child Health Programme Planning Group (1980) *Towards Better Health Care for School Children in Scotland.* Edinburgh: HMSO.

—— Scottish Home and Health Department (1973) *Towards an Integrated Child Health Service. Report of the Subgroup on Child Health Services* (Chairman: J. Brotherston). Edinburgh: HMSO.

Illingworth, R. S. (1980) *The Development of the Infant and Young Child, 7th Ed.* London: Churchill Livingstone.

Kalir, A. (1980) 'Israel national programs for "at risk" infants and children. *In:* Harel, S. (Ed.) *The At Risk Infant. International Congress Series No. 492.* Amsterdam: Excerpta Medica.

Robson, P. (1978) 'Screening for children — developmental paediatrics'. *Royal Society of Health Journal,* **98,** 231-237.

United States: Department of Health Education and Welfare; President's Committee on Mental Retardation (1973) *Screening and Assessment of Young Children at Developmental Risk. DHEW Publication No. (OS) 73-91.* Washington, DC: US Government Printing Office.

—— President's Panel on Mental Retardation (1962) *National Action to Combat Mental Retardation.* Washington, DC: US Government Printing Office.

World Health Organisation (1967) *The Early Detection and Treatment of Handicapping Defects in Young Children. Report on a Working Party Convened by the Regional Office for Europe and WHO* (Chairman: J. D. Kershaw). Copenhagen: WHO Regional Office for Europe.

Wynn, M., Wynn, A. (1974) *The Protection of Maternity and Infancy: a Study of the Services for Pregnant Women and Young Children in Finland.* London: Council for Children's Welfare.

—— —— (1976) *Prevention of Handicap of Perinatal Origin: an Introduction to French Policy and Legislation.* London: Foundation for Education and Research in Child-Bearing.

Zinkin, P. M., Cox, C. A. (1976) 'Child health clinics and inverse care laws: evidence from a longitudinal study of 1878 pre-school children.' *British Medical Journal,* **2,** 411-413.

CHAPTER 2

Acceptance (Take-up) of Development Screening

Eligibility for screening

In this analysis children considered eligible for inclusion were those who had at least one screening appointment generated or at least one screening examination carried out. Dundee-born children who died or transferred out of the city before their first appointment could be generated were excluded, as were those who were to be adopted outside Dundee. From the total 5334 1974/75-born children resident in Dundee at some time in the first five years of life, the total number of children eligible for screening was 5003. 331 children transferred into the city after the age of three years and before school entry, and were thus not eligible for screening.

Unavailability for screening

The normal population shifts which occur in any community resulted in some children being available for fewer than six screening examinations. Thus the precise totals of children offered screening differed at each screening age. Table 2.1 shows the number of children available for screening at each screening age and the percentage of available children who were screened or missed screening. The table also shows the reasons why eligible children were not available at one or more screening ages.

Transfer out

Once a child's family had moved out of the city, the child was no longer available for subsequent screening examinations. By definition there could be no children unavailable for this reason at the eight-week examination but thereafter there was a progressive increase in the number of such children, amounting to 738 (15 per cent) by the age of three years.

Transfer in

Throughout the screening period, 1974/75-born children who transferred into the city were not available until the time of their enrolment in the programme. Overall, this accounted for 461 children (9 per cent), none of whom were, of course, available for the eight-week examination.

Out of town

On 1 January 1976 the boundaries of the city of Dundee were altered to include an adjoining suburb. From that date all 1974/75-born children within that suburb were taken into the programme. With the exception of children born in November and December 1975, who were young enough to be included in the eight-week screening examination, these children were effectively transfers into the screening programme. However, as it was the whole area which transferred in rather than individual children, this group is detailed separately in Table 2.1.

Refusals

Formal permission to include their child in the screening programme was not sought from parents. Appointments were generated automatically following notification to the child health service of the child's birth or presence in the city. However, a total of 24 children were excluded from the programme by parental request. This represents 0.5 per cent of all eligible children.

The social class distribution (derived from the computer file) of the 24 families of these children differed from that of the general population. Table 2.2 shows the social class distribution, by fathers' occupation, derived from computer file, of all Dundee livebirths to Dundee-resident mothers in 1974 and 1975 compared with that of the 24 families who refused permission for screening. Nearly one-half of the refusal families were in social classes I and II compared with less than one-fifth in the general population.

Death

A total of 15 children (0.3 per cent) died within the screening period.

Handicap

The names of 20 children with severe handicap were removed from the computer appointment list once the severity of their handicap was known and arrangements for follow-up and management were well established. The names of those children who were less severely affected and those whose follow-up arrangements seemed uncertain or incomplete were retained.

Errors

Occasionally a clerical, administrative or computer programming error resulted in a child not receiving appointments for one or more screening examinations. When such errors occurred the children involved were counted as unavailable, as it was felt that the concept of availability for screening, as used here, implied that an appointment had been sent.

Place of screening

Table 2.3 details the six locations at which screenings were carried out and the percentages of children screened at each location at each screening age.

Local clinic or surgery

At each screening age the majority of children were screened at their local community child health clinic or the equivalent clinic run by their family doctor, if they were registered with one of the six practices in town participating in the screening programme. Approximately 15 per cent of all screenings were carried out by family doctors.

TABLE 2.1

1974/75-born children eligible for screening (N = 5003). Reasons for unavailability for screening and number screened at each age

	8 wks.	20 wks.	39 wks.	15 mths.	2 yrs.	3 yrs.
			Screening age			
Unavailable						
Transfer out	—	62	196	347	538	738
Transfer in	461	405	298	196	80	—
Refusal	—	13	15	17	18	24
Death	—	5	8	10	15	15
Handicap	—	—	6	9	10	20
Out of town	195	156	120	71	5	3
Error	82	77	73	43	35	12
Total unavailable	738	718	716	693	701	812
Available						
Missed *(%)*	193 (5)	234 (6)	841 (20)	732 (17)	808 (19)	762 (18)
Screened *(%)*	4072 (95)	4051 (94)	3446 (80)	3578 (83)	3494 (81)	3429 (82)
Total available	4265	4285	4287	4310	4302	4191

TABLE 2.2

Social class distribution of total Dundee livebirths and 24 families refusing screening screening

	*Social class**										*Total*	
	I		II		III		IV		V			
	No.	*%*	*No.*	*%*	*No.*	*%*	*No.*	*%*	*No.*	*%*	*No.*	*%*
General population†	304	7	509	12	2184	51	988	23	331	7	4316	100
Refusals	5	21	6	25	7	29	4	17	2	8	24	100

*Derived from computer file; †all 1974/75 Dundee livebirths to Dundee-resident mothers, excluding social class not known/other than I-V.

TABLE 2.3

Place of screening

	8 wks.	20 wks.	39 wks.	15 mths.	2 yrs.	3 yrs.	*All screenings*
			Screening age				
	%	*%*	*%*	*%*	*%*	*%*	*%*
Place of screening:							
Local clinic/surgery	75	75	72	69	68	62	71
Hospital clinic	10	6	3	1	<1	<1	3
Home	9	13	5	12	10	14	10
CDC	<1	<1	—	1	2	4	1
Day nursery	<1	<1	<1	<1	1	1	<1
Children missed	5	6	20	17	19	18	14
Total	100	100	100	100	100	100	100

31

With increasing age there was a gradual decline in the percentage of children being presented for screening at local clinic or surgery, from 75 per cent at eight weeks to 62 per cent at three years. It is well recognised that use of services offered to young children decreases with increasing age. In a Ministry of Health report on child welfare centres (Great Britain: Ministry of Health, Central Health Services Council Standing Medical Advisory Committee 1967), the proportions of children attending local authority child welfare centres in 1965 decreased from 77 per cent of those up to the age of one year, to 70 per cent of one- to two year olds and 21 per cent of two- to five year olds.

Hospital clinic
Children whose adverse perinatal circumstances merited continued supervision at the hospital infant clinic did not require separate arrangements for development screening as their development was checked routinely at each hospital visit. However, to ensure completion of screening records for these high-risk infants, development screening examinations were carried out by the authors in the hospital follow-up clinics at the usual ages. This arrangement allowed for prematurely delivered infants (most of whom attended hospital clinics in the first year) to be screened at conceptional rather than chronological age.

Home screening
Health visitors attempted to carry out home screening for all clinic non-attenders at the eight-week and the 20-week examinations. At later ages home screening was carried out only in certain circumstances at the request of the authors (p. 6). As will be seen from Table 2.3, 10 per cent of all screenings were carried out at home, ranging from 5 per cent at 39 weeks to 14 per cent at three years. The most common reason for requesting home screening at any age subsequent to 20 weeks was two consecutive missed appointments. Since only 6 per cent of children missed their 20-week screening, there were relatively fewer children for whom home screening was requested at 39 weeks than at later screening ages.

Child Development Centre
Although most children with severe handicapping conditions were removed from the screening programme once the diagnosis and follow-up arrangements were well established, this did not apply to children with less severe neurodevelopmental disabilities (NDD), most of whom were assessed and followed up at the Child Development Centre (CDC). Any screenings falling due during the period of follow-up at the Centre were carried out by the authors. The proportions of such screenings increased from 1 per cent at the eight- and 20-week screening ages to 4 per cent at the three-year examination.

Day nursery
Children attending day nurseries were called to the local clinic for screening. In the event of non-attendance, and if day nursery placement was known, a request might be made for screening to be carried out there. At the two- and three-year

TABLE 2.4

Children missing screening for whom home screening was and was not requested

	Screening missed							
	39 wks.		*15 mths.*		*2 yrs.*		*3 yrs.*	
	No.	*%*	*No.*	*%*	*No.*	*%*	*No.*	*%*
Home screening:								
Requested	34	4	110	15	121	15	213	28
Not requested	807	96	622	85	687	85	549	72
Total	841	100	732	100	808	100	762	100

screening ages, 1 per cent of examinations were carried out in day nurseries. Later it was found that arrangements for screening children attending day nurseries were not entirely satisfactory and it was considered that more formal arrangements should have been devised to ensure development screening for day nursery children, particularly because it is likely that, by virtue of the reasons for day nursery attendance (*e.g.* single parent family, both parents working, depriving social circumstances), these children are both less likely to be taken for their routine appointments and more likely to have the problems that screening seeks to identify.

Take-up at the eight- and 20-week screening examinations

The proportion of infants screened at eight weeks and 20 weeks was high at 95 per cent. Theoretically, however, take-up should have been 100 per cent in view of the standing arrangement that home screening should be carried out on all non-attenders at these screening ages. Examination of reasons for non-screening at eight weeks indicated that in one-third of cases non-screening was unavoidable, in one-third circumstances existed which were amenable to correction and in one-third no obvious reason for failure to obtain home-screening could be discovered.

Take-up at 39 weeks, 15 months, two and three years

Take-up dropped to 80 to 83 per cent in the examinations subsequent to eight and 20 weeks. Unlike the earlier two screening ages, no attempt was made to aim for 100 per cent take-up and home screening for non-attenders was only requested in certain circumstances (p. 6). Table 2.4 shows, for those children who were not screened, the number and percentage who were not screened despite a request for home screening and those for whom no such request was made. At each screening age, the majority of children were not screened because, after due consideration of the circumstances, home screening was not considered necessary.

It could be argued that, for the 39-week and subsequent screening examinations only those for whom a home screening had been requested but not carried out should be considered to have missed that screening. Those clinic-attenders for whom home screening was not requested form an intermediate group. Presumably most would have been screened had a home request been made, as 78 per cent of all requests for home screening throughout the study were successfully completed by health visitors. Expressed as a percentage of the total available children at each screening age, those who were not screened despite a request for home screening represent 1 per cent of the 39-week total, 3 per cent of the 15-month and two-year total and 5 per cent of the three-year total, percentages more in keeping with the 5 to 6 per cent who were not screened at the eight-week and 20-week examinations where the aim was 100 per cent take-up.

Availability throughout the screening period

Table 2.5 details the attendance patterns of children, grouped according to the number of screening examinations for which they were available. Of the 5003 eligible children, 52 per cent attended all screenings for which they were available. After excluding the 220 children who were only available for one screening, 80 per cent of the remaining 4783 children had all, or all but one, possible screenings.

Children who were never screened

Two per cent (108) of the total 5003 eligible children evaded all screenings. Of these, 66 were only available for one screening and 22 for two. The remaining 20 children were never screened, despite having been available for between three and six examinations. In nine cases parents asked for the child's name to be removed from the screening programme at some time. In a further case, the parents effectively refused permission by never allowing the health visitor into the house. In three cases, administrative or clerical errors were responsible. In the remaining seven cases, the families of the children concerned moved around within the town so frequently that the health visitors could never locate them for home screening although, in each case, the child was thought still to be in town and it was felt inappropriate to remove his name as a transfer out.

Minimum acceptable frequency of screening

Although, ideally, a development screening programme should aim for 100 per cent take-up at each screening age, this was not considered practical in the DDSP, other than at the eight- and 20-week examinations, mainly in order to keep within manageable limits the burden of home screening which fell on health visitors. By applying the guidelines used to determine whether or not home screening would be requested in any particular case (p. 6), it was possible to define, somewhat arbitrarily, a minimum acceptable frequency of screening and to say, for each child, whether this was achieved or not.

For the purposes of this study children were considered to have achieved this minimum acceptable frequency when they had at least:
(1) two out of the three possible examinations in the first year of life, *i.e.* at eight, 20 and 39 weeks;
(2) one out of the two possible examinations in the second year of life, *i.e.* at 15 months and two years;
(3) either the two- or the three-year examination with the proviso that, if the two-year screening result had been doubtful or abnormal, then the three-year screening must be carried out.

TABLE 2.5

Attendance pattern of 5003 children eligible for screening

No. examinations for which children available	Available children		Eligible children (N = 5003) No. examinations carried out						
			6	5	4	3	2	1	0
	No.	%	%	%	%	%	%	%	%
6	3429	69	52	26	16	4	1	<1	<1
5	445	9		44	33	19	3	1	<1
4	305	6			49	32	16	3	<1
3	295	6				56	33	9	2
2	309	6					61	32	7
1	220	4						70	30

This definition could only be applied to the 69 per cent (3429) of total eligible children who were available for all six screenings. Minimum acceptable frequency of screening was achieved in 90 per cent (3087) of these children.

Comparison with 1973- and 1976-born children

As mentioned earlier (p. 4), the screening programme began in Dundee with a running-in period in 1972, but the initial problems were largely solved by the time the first of the 1973-born children were entering the programme. Instructions given to health visitors for those children who did not attend for the eight- or 20-week screening were the same as were later given for the research group; there was a standing request for the health visitor to attempt home screening in all cases. At later screening ages there were no formal arrangements for non-attenders although screening doctors might organise recall appointments if they wished.

Table 2.6 shows, in similar format to Table 2.1, the overall total of 1973-born children eligible for screening (2216), the number and percentage of available children screened at each age and the reasons why children were unavailable at particular screening ages. An additional category of unavailability, 'cancelled', covers the 18 per cent of children who were not sent appointments for the three-year screening, which was selective for 1973-born children (p. 6). Children who were developmentally and behaviourally normal at two-year screening and were not included in any high-risk group were not sent appointments for screening at three years.

A comparison of take-up with 1974/75-born children is shown in Table 2.7. The overall take-up for all three years of birth was roughly similar for the eight-, 20- and 39-week screening examinations. Thereafter there was an increasing divergence in overall take-up between 1973-born children and those born 1974/75. The table suggests that the improved take-up of screening for the research group, amounting to 14 per cent at the 15-month examination, 19 per cent at two years, and 27 per cent at three years, was largely due to the availability of home screening for 1974/75-born children. The biggest discrepancy was noted at three years, but take-up at that age for 1973-born children may be somewhat deflated by the selective exclusion of

TABLE 2.6

1973-born children eligible for screening (N = 2216). Reasons for unavailability for screening and number screened at each age

| | Screening age | | | | | |
	8 wks.	20 wks.	39 wks.	15 mths.	2 yrs.	3 yrs.
Unavailable						
Transfer out	—	37	104	170	222	292
Transfer in	173	140	115	80	30	—
Refusal	1	1	1	1	—	1
Death	—	2	6	7	7	7
Handicap	—	—	—	2	2	5
Out of town	3	2	2	2	1	—
Error	85	86	52	42	36	14
Cancelled	—	—	—	—	—	398
Total unavailable	262	268	280	304	298	717
Available						
Missed *(%)*	144 (7)	236 (12)	399 (21)	593 (31)	684 (36)	681 (45)
Screened *(%)*	1810 (93)	1712 (88)	1537 (79)	1319 (69)	1234 (64)	818 (55)
Total available	1954	1948	1936	1912	1918	1499

TABLE 2.7

Take-up of screening for 1973- and 1974/75-born children

| | 1973 | | 1974/75 | |
| | Total | Missed | Total | Missed |
	No.	%	No.	%
Screening age				
8 wks.	1954	7	4265	5
20 wks.	1948	12	4285	6
39 wks.	1936	21	4287	20
15 mths.	1912	31	4310	17
2 yrs.	1918	36	4302	19
3 yrs.	1499	45	4191	18

TABLE 2.8

Minimum acceptable frequency of screening by year of birth

| | Frequency of screening | | | | | |
| | Acceptable | | Not acceptable | | Total | |
	No.	%	No.	%	No.	%
Year of birth						
1973	927	60	607	40	1534	100
1974	1448	92	122	8	1570	100
1975	1414	92	131	8	1545	100
1976	1129	77	330	23	1459	100

18 per cent of the population. Since these children were excluded on the basis, amongst others, of having no adverse social factors, it is reasonable to infer that as a group they would have tended to have a higher attendance rate than that of the total population.

For children born in 1976 and subsequently, routines established for 1974/75-born children continued but the authors no longer monitored take-up of screening or scrutinised screening cards weekly. This responsibility fell on community child health doctors. When 1976-born children were medically examined after school entrance, development folders were seen and the opportunity existed of comparing minimum acceptable frequency of screening (p. 78) for 1976-born children who had been resident in the city throughout the screening period, with that of similar 1973- and 1974/75-born children (Table 2.8). The fall-off in take-up of screening in 1976-born children suggests that there may be an advantage in a central monitoring system for take-up of screening, particularly as it later turned out (p. 239) that children who are not taken for screening examinations form a high-risk group for schooling difficulties.

COMPARISON WITH OTHER STUDIES

Take-up results for eight other development screening programmes are available for comparison with DDSP. These results are shown in Table 2.9.

The highest take-up, with virtually total coverage at each screening examination, occured in the primary-care programmes described by Starte (1972) and Curtis Jenkins *et al.* (1978). Both programmes were similar in their organisational detail in that all the children in a group practice were screened by one partner who was particularly interested and experienced in development screening. Attendance rates at clinics were high. Only 3 per cent of Starte's cases were described as non-clinic attenders and only 4 per cent of Curtis Jenkins' cases failed to attend the clinic after two or more appointments. However, despite the high spontaneous take-up, both programmes included special arrangements for non-attenders. In the former practice these were followed up by health visitor and family doctor and screening was carried out at home. In Curtis Jenkins' practice the health visitor called at the home, taking a third appointment card with her, whenever two clinic appointments had been missed. If this did not result in clinic attendance, the child's own family doctor wrote a personal letter to the parents. These two studies set the standard for all development screening programmes in the primary-care setting.

Other attempts by family doctors to screen children in their practices have been less successful. Bain (1974) reported the attendance rates at screening clinics in his group practice during the course of one year. Each partner was responsible for screening children on his own list. Take-up ranged from 77 per cent at the six-month examination to 62 per cent at three years. A maximum of three appointments was sent for each examination but, because of pressure of work, only persistent non-attenders were visited at home by the health visitor to investigate the reason for failure to attend and to encourage later clinic attendance. No home screenings were

TABLE 2.9

Comparison of take-up percentages in nine screening programmes

Author(s)	No. of children	Period of study	≤12 mths.			Screening ages 13-24 mths.		>2-3 yrs.	>3-5 yrs.
			%	%	%	%	%	%	%
Paterson 1972	9690	1 yr.	78 (1.5)*	78 (6)	78 (12)		70 (24)	52 (3)	45 (4)
Starte 1972	276	1 yr.		99 (7)			98 (24)		
Bain 1974	1524	1 yr.	71 (1.5)	77 (6)		75 (16)		62 (3)	76 (4.5)
Zinkin and Cox 1976	1878	Completed cohort study	85 (1.5)	92 (6)	96 (12)	93 (18)	94 (24)	93 (3)	
Barber et al. 1976	600	1st. 2 yrs. of programme	86 (1.5)	75 (6)	68 (10)	60 (18)			
Barber 1982	281	1st. 2 yrs. of revised programme	97 (1.5)	97 (9)			91 (24)		
Jacobs and Hall 1976	20,00	6½ yrs.	66 (1)	56 (9)				44 (2.5)	60 (4.25)
Curtis Jenkins et al. 1978	1100	2 yrs.	100 (0.75)	98 (7)	98 (12)		95 (24)	98 (3)	97 (4.5)
Dundee DSP	5003	Completed cohort study	96 (2)	95 (5)	80 (9)	83 (15)	81 (24)	82 (3)	

*Figures in parentheses indicate age at screening examination in mths. or yrs.

carried out. Bain estimated that 6 per cent of non-attendances could be due to families moving from the area but despite this he expressed disappointment in the results. He was aware that many of the non-attenders were children of 'problem families' and thus more likely to be in need of developmental surveillance than many of those who attended.

Barber *et al.* (1976) published the results of the first two years of a screening programme used at the Woodside Health Centre in Glasgow. Five of the eight group practices using the Centre participated in screening, one doctor from each practice being involved. In the studies mentioned above, health visitors assisted at screening clinics but did not carry out developmental examinations themselves. In the Woodside project it was planned that health visitors would carry out some of the developmental examinations although physical examination would remain the responsibility of the family-practitioner. Children were taken into the programme at birth; thus results from the first two years of the scheme (1973/74) included only the first four of the projected seven examinations. Take-up fell off fairly rapidly from 86 per cent at six weeks to 60 per cent at 18 months. Second appointments were sent to non-attenders but it was seldom possible for the health visitor to screen these at home, as had been intended, because of pressure of work. A revision of the programme took place in 1975 with the production of new charts on which the child's development could be plotted, allowing visual comparison with the normal range and with the child's previous development. The health visitors became responsible for the majority of the developmental examinations, with the doctors carrying out the two physical examinations within the screening period. The first year of this new system was reviewed by Freer and Ogunmuyiwa (1977) who examined the attendance rates for one of the five group practices. The results were disappointing, the highest attendance rate at three months being only 69 per cent, dropping to 49 per cent at the two-year examination. Subsequently further changes in the Woodside programme were made with the number of recommended examinations being reduced to four: at six weeks, seven to nine months, two years and four years. At each age the developmental part of the examination was to be completed by the health visitor and at three of the four ages a physical examination was to be carried out by the family doctor. Under the most recent scheme health visitors carry out home examinations of clinic non-attenders. At the six-week and seven-to ten-months examination, 97 per cent of infants were screened (16 and 63 per cent, respectively, were screened at home) and at two years, 91 per cent were screened (32 per cent at home). This marked reduction of 'default rate' was attributed principally to an active policy of follow-up examination at home (Barber 1982).

Screening all children within a defined area was adopted by some community child health services (formerly called the local health authorities) from as early as 1968. Meadows and Keating (1970) published the results of a trial period during which two of Bournemouth's infant welfare clinics were altered in function to become development screening clinics. Take-up figures by screening age were not given but it was reported that, of the first 574 appointments at screening clinics, 89 per cent of children either attended the first appointment or their parents requested and attended a subsequent appointment.

39

A much larger study involving the total under-five population of the City of Westminster was reported by Paterson (1972). This was largely a local authority programme, although three family doctors and one hospital-based child welfare clinic were also involved. The work carried out by medical officers in local authority clinics in 1971 was surveyed. Take-up at each screening age is shown in Table 2.9. Unfortunately the figures are not completely accurate and the total number of children at each screening age is only an estimate. Paterson calculated that probably most infants of one year and under were screened but that almost certainly no more than 50 per cent were screened at the three and four-and-a-half-year examinations. No mention is made of any second appointment for clinic non-attenders and health visitors did not carry out home screening.

Jacobs and Hall (1976) published the results of seven years' experience of development screening in the Newham health district of London, where the population of under-fives was approximately 20,000, making this the largest study published in terms both of population and length of period reviewed. All examinations were carried out by local authority medical officers. Overall take-up percentages are shown in Table 2.9. Over the seven years of the programme (1968/75), neighbouring boroughs reported falling attendance rates at their infant welfare clinics, thought to be due to an increase in the number of working mothers and to population mobility. In contrast, attendance rates in Newham were not only maintained but rose slightly. Jacobs and Hall felt this was attributable to the popularity of the screening programme with Newham mothers. Nevertheless the overall take-up was disappointingly low, the highest being less than 70 per cent at the one-month examination. Pressure of work did not allow routine recall of non-attenders and there was no provision for home screening by health visitors. The particularly poor attendance at the nine-month examination prompted the introduction of recall appointments at this screening only from 1974 onwards. This resulted in an increase in mean uptake from 52 per cent in the years prior to 1974 to 67 per cent in subsequent years. Overall take-up figures are little different from figures for the last two years of the study when 68 per cent were screened at one month, 63 per cent at nine months, 45 per cent at two and a half years and 59 per cent at four and a half years. The medical records of one-year cohort of children were scrutinised in the first year of infant school. 8 per cent failed to attend for any screening examination. This compares with 2 per cent of Dundee 1974/75-born children.

The Zinkin and Cox study (1976), carried out in the London Borough of Hounslow, stands on its own in that it was planned as a research project. This was a true cohort study of all children born from October 1970 to February 1973. Children who transferred in to the area were not included, while an attempt was made to trace and screen children who moved out of the catchment area. Local authority medical and health visiting staff were involved but the development screening examinations offered were not part of an ongoing service to the local population. Clinic non-attenders were all sent second appointments. If these were not kept the situation was assessed by a health visitor who either encouraged clinic attendance or arranged a home screening by one of the project's doctors. As would be expected from a highly

40

TABLE 2.10

Comparison of Hounslow and Dundee home screening rates

Hounslow	Home screenings	Dundee	Home screenings
	%		%
6 wks.	2	8 wks.	9
6 mths.	4	5 mths.	13
12 mths.	7	9 mths.	5
18 mths.	9	15 mths.	12
2 yrs.	11	2 yrs.	11
3 yrs.	11	3 yrs.	14

motivated research team, the take-up results achieved were impressive (Table 2.9). Despite automatic second appointments for non-attenders, home screening was still required in approximately 10 per cent of children from the 12-month examination onwards.

Table 2.10 compares the percentage of home screenings carried out at each of the six screening ages in the Hounslow and Dundee studies. Overall the necessity for home screening was higher in the Dundee study, although this was associated with a higher take-up only at the first two examinations. However after this age, home screening in Dundee was selective and not routine as in Hounslow. The refusal rate in the Hounslow study was 1.6 per cent compared with 0.5 per cent in Dundee.

Shortly after birth all Hounslow infants were assigned to one of two groups, depending on whether they were considered to be at high or low risk of delayed and aberrant development, which might be associated with medical or educational handicap. The criteria used were those found to be most predictive in the National Child Development Study (Davie *et al.* 1972). In order of importance these were: birthweight under 2500g; gestational age of 37 weeks or less; parity five or more; neonatal illness; adverse delivery and social class V. 22 per cent of cohort infants were considered high-risk.

Overall, 40 per cent of cohort children had moved out of the catchment area by the time they were three years old and 12 per cent had moved more than once. No significant difference was found in the proportion of high-risk children between families who did not move from the catchment area and those who made one move (22 per cent and 19 per cent respectively), but the proportion of high-risk children rose significantly with increasing numbers of moves, from 24 per cent of those who moved twice to 50 per cent of those who moved four times. It was also shown that high-risk children amongst the families who moved were concentrated in those who moved within the borough and not those who moved to other parts of the country or abroad. These findings underline the need for all screening programmes to identify families who move around frequently and make special efforts to screen their children.

A feasibility study carried out in Grampian Region (Robinson 1982) selected a 2.7 per cent sample of all children under four years of age in the region. Over a six-month period, all children who were eligible for screening at the four ages selected (six weeks, eight months, 18 months and three years) were enrolled in one of six locations, chosen to allow comparison between urban and rural communities and variations in participating staff (general practitioners, health visitors and child health service doctors). Thus a total 804 children were enrolled, 87 per cent of whom were brought for screening after the first appointment and 10 per cent after the second appointment. Only two children were never contacted. The study group considered that the high acceptance rate was due partly to self-selection of screening personnel (and their subsequent enthusiasm) and partly to extra work undertaken by health visitors. This study estimated the time for each mother/child consultation to be approximately 35 minutes and calculated that, allowing for second appointments and recalls, 40 hours in a 50-week year would be required to cover the screening requirements of 100 children. It was thought unlikely that many family doctors would be prepared to accord such priority to a development screening programme, although they might be willing to carry out a programme where only the essential medical elements were performed by a doctor while a health visitor shouldered the main burden, as in the Glasgow Woodside programme.

Summary

The analysis of take-up of screening included all children who had had at least one screening appointment and/or one screening examination. The number of eligible 1974/75-born children was 5003.

Place of screening

At each age the majority of children were screened at their local child health clinic or equivalent family doctor clinic. With increasing age there was a decline in attendance for clinic screening from 75 per cent of the total population at eight weeks to 62 per cent at three years, with an increase in home screening by health visitors from 9 to 14 per cent.

Overall, 15 per cent of screenings were carried out by family doctors, 10 per cent by health visitors and 75 per cent by clinic doctors. 14 per cent of all examinations were missed.

Take-up of screening

Take-up at different screening ages was: eight weeks, 95 per cent; 20 weeks, 94 per cent; 39 weeks, 80 per cent; 15 months, 83 per cent; two years, 81 per cent; three years, 82 per cent.

Requests for home screening were made for all non-attenders at eight and 20 weeks. Thereafter request for home screening was selective. Those who missed screening despite such a request were: 1 per cent of the total population at 39 weeks; 3 per cent at 15 months and two years; and 5 per cent at three years.

Screening was refused by parents of 0.5 per cent. 2 per cent totally evaded all screening.

Minimum acceptable frequency of screening

A minimum acceptable frequency was defined. Of the 69 per cent of the total population who were available for all screenings this frequency was achieved in 90 per cent.

Comparison of take-up with 1973- and 1976-born children

The improved take-up in 1974/75-born as compared with those born in 1973 was attributed to the reduced availability of home screening in 1973. A fall-off in take-up in 1976 was attributed to the discontinuation of the central monitoring system available for the 1974/75-born children.

REFERENCES

Bain, D. G. B. (1974) 'The results of developmental screening in general practice.' *Health Bulletin,* **32,** 189-193.

Barber, J. H. (1982) 'Preschool developmental screening: the results of a 4-year period.' *Health Bulletin,* **40,** 170-178.

—— Boothman, R., Paget-Stanfield, J. (1976) 'A new visual chart for pre-school developmental screening.' *Health Bulletin,* **34,** 80-91.

Curtis Jenkins, G. H., Collins, C., Andren, S. (1978) 'Developmental surveillance in general practice..' *British Medical Journal,* **1,** 1537-1540.

Davie, R., Butler, N., Goldstein, H. (1972) *From Birth to Seven.* London: Longman for the National Children's Bureau.

Freer, C. B., Ogunmuyiwa, T. A. (1977) 'Pre-school developmental screening in a Health Centre: the problem of non-attendance.' *Journal of the Royal College of General Practitioners,* **27,** 428-430.

Great Britain: Ministry of Health, Central Health Services Council Standing Medical Advisory Committee (1967) *Child Welfare Centres, Report of the Sub-Committee.* London: HMSO

Jacobs, R., Hall, C. J. (1976) 'Periodic developmental assessment of pre-school children in Newham.' *Public Health,* **90,** 179-186.

Meadows, J. G., Keating, P. J. H. (1970) 'A pilot scheme in developmental screening clinics.' *Medical Officer,* **124,** 270-271.

Paterson, M. T. (1972) 'Developmental screening of pre-school children.' *Community Medicine,* **128,** 423-424.

Robinson, H. G. (Chairman) (1982) *Pre-school Health Surveillance Feasibility Study Report.* Aberdeen: Grampian Health Board.

Starte, G. D. (1972) '"Child's play" or paediatric developmental assessment in general practice.' *Practitioner,* **209,** 84-89.

Zinkin, P. M., Cox, C. A. (1976) 'Child health clinics and inverse care laws: evidence from longitudinal study of 1,878 pre-school children.' *British Medical Journal,* **2,** 411-413.

CHAPTER 3

Definitions, Categorisations and Ascertainment

Definitions of the words 'impairment', 'disability' and 'handicap' have been established for international use by the World Health Organisation (1980). An impairment is defined as 'any loss or abnormality of psychological, physiological or anatomical structure or function', a disability as 'any restriction or lack (resulting from an impairment) of ability to perform an activity in the manner or within the range considered normal for a human being' and handicap as 'a disadvantage for a given individual resulting from an impairment or a disability that limits or prevents the fulfilment of a rôle that is normal (depending on age, sex and social and cultural factors) for that individual'. In this study the simpler definitions of disability and handicap suggested by Mitchell (1977) and Holt (1977) have been adopted. A disability is defined as a measurable functional impairment (due to a neurodevelopmental or behavioural abnormality) which may also be described as a handicap if it causes the child to be disadvantaged in his particular environmental circumstances. The details of those conditions which we considered should be included under the general heading of neurodevelopmental disability (NDD) are discussed later (p. 46).

An attempt was made to ascertain the total number of 1974/75-born children identified by whatever means as having NDD before school entry. In addition to the 5003 children included in the screening programme, 331 children transferred into the city after the age of three years and before school entry. Some of these children were identified before school entry as having NDD and are included in figures of frequency of NDD given in Chapter 4.

The term 'identified' implies not only that suspicion of disability was raised by, for example, parent, family doctor or screening programme, but that the disability was confirmed following referral to a recognised specialist service such as a paediatric outpatient department, speech therapy clinic or Child Development Centre (CDC). Identification depends on the recognition by both parents and doctor that a problem exists: the mother may refuse referral if she is satisfied with the child's progress and the doctor, while recognising sub-optimal performance, may consider this to be appropriate for the family and pass the child as acceptably normal.

Sources of ascertainment information

Clinics and services responsible for children with NDD

Table 3.1 lists the health service clinics and educational services to which preschool children with suspected or confirmed neurodevelopmental disorders might be referred or, in the case of the hospital infant clinic, might be attending. The majority of children whose development appeared doubtful on screening and who were considered to require further assessment were referred to CDC. Details of the

TABLE 3.1

Clinics and services holding information on children with NDD

Hospital infant clinic
Hospital children's medical outpatient clinics
Children's hearing assessment clinic
Children's orthopaedic service
Child psychiatry
Clinical psychology
Speech therapy
Occupational therapy
Strathmartine Mental Deficiency Hospital
Child Development Centre
Community child health services—handicap register
—deaths of cohort children
Educational psychology department
Nursery class for the physically handicapped
Assessment class

NDD of these children and the circumstances of identification were readily available for ascertainment. The card index system or records of the other clinics and services were scrutinised and details of other children with NDD who were not known to the Centre were obtained.

Information recorded on screening cards and held in screening folders

Most Dundee hospital specialist services dealing with children send copies of all hospital discharge letters and many outpatient clinic letters to doctors in the community child health service. These copies are filed in the children's development screening folders, which were sent to the authors after each screening examination of 1974/75-born research-group children. At each screening examination the doctor or health visitor was also asked to record details of any hospital referral or attendance since the last screening and details of any such referrals arising from the current examination.

All screening folders of children entering school were seen again after the first school medical examination and further scrutinised. Details about problems of health and development recorded at the time of the medical examinations allowed up-dating of information on hospital referrals and conditions associated with NDD occurring between the time of the final screening examination and school entry.

The number of children transferring into the city after the age of three years and before school entry was ascertained at this stage. Some children may have transferred in after three years and removed again before school entry, but there was no way that the number of such children could be ascertained.

Circumstances of identification

In order to assess the part played by the screening programme in identifying children with NDD the circumstances of identification were investigated. Each child was assigned to one of six groups:

(1) *Identified on screening* This implied not only that suspicion of delay or deviation in some area of development or behaviour was raised during a screening

examination but that this resulted directly, or after review by the screening doctor, in the child being referred for further investigation with subsequent confirmation of the disability.

(2) *Missed on screening*   When a child with NDD was identified by some means other than the screening programme and when inspection of the relevant screening card gave no indication of delay or disorder sufficient to have caused concern, the child's condition was judged to have been missed by the screening programme.

(3) *Missed through non-attendance*   A child was placed in this category when NDD was identified by some means other than the screening programme and the relevant screening examination was found not to have taken place, either at the clinic or by the health visitor at home.

(4) *Suspected on screening but not identified*   This applied when NDD was subsequently identified by some means other than the screening programme, but where a degree of suspicion sufficient to have warranted concern or referral for further assessment was noted on the relevant screening examination card. In some cases referral to CDC had been requested by the authors. The reasons why referrals did not occur are discussed in Chapter 4 (p. 72).

(5) *Known*   Disabilities were classified as 'known' when they were (a) identified before the first screening examination at eight weeks, (b) identified before transfer into the city, (c) suspected because of a similar genetic condition in a sibling or (d) diagnosed in hospital following postnatal accident or infection.

(6) *Other*   This is a miscellaneous group of children whose common circumstances were that identification took place by means other than by screening and that such identification would not have been influenced by the screening programme, *e.g.* NDD presenting and identified between screening ages or after the last screening examination at three years.

Categories of identified NDD

The categories of NDD which are used in this study and to which children were assigned after referral and assessment are detailed below. Many children had more than one developmental problem at intial referral or their problems changed over a period of time. The categories used in the calculation of frequency of disabilities refer to what seemed to be the major problem at the time of initial diagnosis and at a later date if problems changed.

The difficulty of assigning to a young child an exact developmental level was recognised throughout. The developmental quotients (DQs) and ranges quoted below must be considered as approximations only and should not be equated with results of standardised tests of intelligence and of specific abilities appropriate for older children. The majority of children with NDD were assessed at CDC according to agreed criteria as to what was considered within or without the normal range. In some instances of referral and identification elsewhere, it was difficult to ascertain that the child had been assessed according to similar criteria. This applied particularly to children with speech disorders, the only category of NDD, apart from specific conditions, for which a substantial number of children were not assessed at the Centre. It could be that some of these children would have been passed as within normal limits by the authors (p. 144), especially as over one-half of the speech disorders referred elsewhere were described as mild expressive delays or minor problems of articulation only.

Global delay

Using the developmental schedules described by Drillien (1977), which are based on those of Gesell (Knobloch and Pasamannick 1974; Knobloch *et al.* 1980), a child was considered to show global delay when DQs for adaptive, speech and language and self-help skills lay in the mid-70s and mid-80s range, *i.e.* well below average but not borderline or mildly mentally retarded. In many of these children motor development was also delayed, but this was not invariable.

Mental retardation

This category included those globally delayed children whose DQs were below 50 to 55 (severe) or between 55 and 75 (mild or borderline). There is no clear-cut distinction between mild or borderline mental retardation and global delay. However, younger children and those for whom a considerable deprivational element, likely to respond to improvement in the child's environment, was noted, tended to be categorised as globally delayed rather than borderline mentally retarded if DQs were in the range 70 to 75.

Motor disorder

Children in this category showed delay in gross and/or fine motor function (DQ on motor scale at or below the mid 80s) with other abilities considered to be within the normal range, or with other NDD of minor severity compared with the motor disorder. Most exhibited minor abnormal neurological signs but none were thought to be suffering from even mild cerebral palsy. Children with motor delay due to specific physical or neurological disorder were not included in this category.

Cerebral palsy

Thirty-nine per cent of the children in this category were mildly affected according to classification derived from Ingram (1964) as outlined in Chapter 7 (p. 129, see also Appendix VI, p. 137), but all were considered to be cases of definite cerebral palsy. The children in this group were subdivided into those who were or were not mentally retarded.

Minor neurological abnormality only

This category does not define a neurodevelopmental disability but was included because of the authors' interest in the significance of such signs in young children. The few children in this category (apart from one first seen in the hospital infant clinic) were all referred to CDC from the screening programme on account of delays in various areas of development. When the children were seen for assessment the delays were not confirmed. Nevertheless, the finding of unequivocal minor abnormal neurological signs made us unwilling to classify these children as being within normal limits. The frequency of these signs among children with NDD and in a control group is discussed in Chapter 5 (p. 95).

Speech disorder

Children were considered to have problems of speech or language when their DQs in this area lay in the mid-80s or below. Delay in speech development was most usually in expressive language but a few children, not considered to be globally delayed, were equally slow in both comprehension and expression. Children whose language development was within the normal range but who had significant articulatory problems (p. 145) were also included in this category.

Behaviour disorder

Behaviour problems were more difficult to quantify. With severe disturbances there was no difficulty in including a child in this category but exactly when a less serious deviation from the normal behaviour patterns of young children should be classified as a problem is often a matter of individual clinical judgement. Most behaviour problems identified in the preschool period were exaggerations or inappropriate prolongations of normal behaviour patterns. They were categorised as problems when they were socially unacceptable, resulted in a degree of family disruption or appeared to be affecting the child's developmental progress.

Severe hearing loss

This category was reserved for children whose hearing loss was so severe as to require a hearing aid and/or attendance at a nursery school or special school for the hearing-impaired.

Severe visual handicap

This category included children considered, after ophthalmological assessment, to be blind or partially sighted and certain or very likely to require special educational facilities on account of visual handicap.

Specific conditions

Specific conditions included those which are invariably or likely to be associated with global delay or mental retardation (*e.g.* fetal alcohol and Down's syndromes) or likely to be associated with delay in specific areas of development (*e.g.* cleft palate with speech disorder, severe congenital talipes with motor delay). Children with specific conditions were subdivided into those who were or were not mentally retarded.

Severity grading

An overall severity grading was applied to each child's disability or disabilities based on the likely implication for educational progress and behaviour at early school age. Although social and economic factors are recognised as having a major influence on school progress, home circumstances were not included in the prediction of probable or possible continuing effects of preschool NDD. The accuracy of these predictions is discussed in Chapter 14 (p. 256).

Severity of disability was graded as:

Minor These disabilities were considered to be transient or easily remediable before school entry and unlikely to affect school progress or behaviour in Primary 1 classes of ordinary schools.

Very severe Cases of severe mental retardation, with or without additional physical handicaps, were graded as very severe. Such children would need special education or institutional care.

Severe In the majority of disabilities graded as severe it seemed unlikely that the child would be able to enter a Primary 1 class at the usual age. Most would require special education, at least initially. Those who were accepted into normal school were unlikely to be able to participate in normal physical activities and/or to progress in lessons at the same rate as their classmates.

Moderately severe Disabilities graded as moderately severe were thought likely to pose considerable problems in the early school years, though it was expected that most children would enter normal school at age five to five and a half years. Children in this category eligible by date of birth to start in Primary 1 before their fifth birthdays were likely to be retained in nursery classes or admitted to a special assessment class for a further 12 months.

Moderate Disabilities which could not be described as transient or easily remediable and yet were thought unlikely to pose considerable problems in school were graded as moderate.

Disabilities detected in control group A children were also graded by severity, although this could only be on the basis of a single CDC examination and not on a period of observation (often prolonged) and is not therefore strictly comparable with severity gradings applied to CDC-referred children (p. 7).

Sources of social information

Social class

Information about the social class of the child's father, based on the Registrar-General's classification of occupations, 1970 (Office of Population Censuses and Surveys 1971), was available from two sources. Details of social class recorded at birth are held on the computer files of the Tayside Health Board for all children born in the area. In addition details about social class were obtained from parents (most usually mothers) of the 414 CDC-referred children.

In 56 of the CDC-referred children, social class of the father was other than I to V (five cases) or was not held on the computer file (51 cases). In three more cases the mother could not provide social class details although these were held on computer. After the exclusion of these 59 children, social class appeared to have changed between birth and attendance at the Centre in 124 cases (35 per cent). The social class distribution of CDC-referred children derived from these two sources differs, as is shown in Table 3.2. When social class was obtained from parents, more fathers appeared in social classes I and II, largely due to the disproportionate number of such families amongst transfers in to Dundee, birth record details of whose children were not known to the computer. This accounted for 35 per cent of social class I fathers and 19 per cent of social class II fathers (as reported by parents). 10 per cent of children with fathers in social classes III, IV and V were not known to the computer.

According to parents, the largest proportion of fathers (one-half) appeared in social class III, although the computer spread this number more evenly over classes III and IV. The proportion of children with fathers in social classes IV and V combined is roughly similar when derived from either source, but when examined individually the proportions are reversed. Although it is not difficult to recognise a skilled occupation from the mother's description, it is more difficult to differentiate between semi-skilled and unskilled work. Many unemployed men, described as having had a number of short-lived jobs, were designated as social class V because mothers had little idea about the nature of the employment. In most of the subsequent analyses social classes IV and V are combined (as are social classes I and II) and errors in assigning fathers to social class V rather than to social class IV do not affect the conclusions.

In comparisons of the social class distribution of CDC-referred children with those referred to hospital or with the general population, social class held by computer is used. When comparing social class distribution within the group of CDC-referred children, information given by the parent is used.

Social grade

According to parents, one-half of fathers of CDC-referred children were in social class III. In this social class group (and to a lesser extent in other social classes) patterns of child-rearing and the aspirations and expectations of families show considerable variation. The inadequacy of social class as an index of social disadvantage was demonstrated in the Newcastle Child Development Study (p. 245) in which a normal control group matched by age, sex and postal district was selected for comparison with a speech-retarded subgroup. No significant difference in social class distribution was found between control and speech-retarded subjects but there were highly significant differences in other measures of social inadequacy and disadvantage (Fundudis *et al*. 1979). The authors concluded that occupational social class was a relatively crude index of social disorganisation and malaise and that other measures of 'social-environmental risk' were more sensitive in assessing or reflecting adverse factors.

In many studies social class is the only measure available but in this study an alternative social grading classification was also used (Drillien 1964). With emphasis on socio-economic background, child-rearing practices and aspirations, particularly as regards education, the families were divided into (1) middle class, (2) superior working-class, with child-rearing practices and aspirations very similar to those found in middle-class homes, (4) poor working-class, with standards of care and management well below acceptable levels, and (3) average working-class, homes which came neither into grade (2) or grade (4).

Two- and one-parent families

Irrespective of marital status, a two-parent family was taken to be one containing two parents or parent-substitutes who might or might not be the natural parents of the child. Two-parent families were those in which the parents were married or remarried and in which the parents were unmarried but living in a stable

TABLE 3.2

CDC-referred children, social class distribution derived from parents' history and computer file

	Social class (parents' history)						Total	
	I	*II*	*III*	*IV*	*V*	*Other/NK*	No.	%
Social class (computer file)								
I	9	2	—	—	—	—	11	3
II	1	25	—	—	—	—	26	6
III	—	3	138	10	19	—	170	41
IV	—	4	40	32	33	3	112	27
V	—	—	10	2	27	—	39	9
Other/NK	5	8	21	5	10	7	56	14
Total (%)	15 (4)	42 (10)	209 (50)	49 (12)	89 (22)	10 (2)	414 (100)	

NK = not known.

TABLE 3.3

Social problem groups

1. Unstable parental relationship, *e.g.* temporary separations, verbal and physical violence
2. One or both parents handicapped, *e.g.* mental retardation, severe physical handicap, blindness, deafness
3. Mental retardation or severe physical handicap in a sibling
4. Psychiatric illness in one or both parents, under the care of a psychiatrist either as an in- or out-patient
5. Father chronically unemployed, described as 'seldom/never works', 'won't work'
6. One or both parents with criminal record
7. Very poor social conditions, *i.e.* likely to provide an unstimulating and depriving atmosphere
8. One or both parents described as alcoholic or having 'a drinking problem'
9. Severe financial problems, *e.g.* leading to eviction, disconnection of electricity
10. Child taken into care
11. Non-accidental injury (not counted as an additional problem if taken into care on account of NAI)

long-term relationship with each other. One-parent families included unmarried mothers living alone without a steady co-habitee and mothers (occasionally fathers) who lived alone following separation from or death of the spouse.

Social problems

Details were recorded about specific social problems listed in Table 3.3 for all children attending CDC. In 1976 health visitors provided similar information on items 1 to 9 for all but 11 per cent of 1974/75-born children. The figures derived from this source will underestimate the frequency of these problems as those arising for the first time when the child was older were not recorded routinely. Health visitor details were held by computer, coded as no social problems, single-parent family without problems or with, one specified social problem only or, if more than one, the total number of problems. Information provided on screening cards or through contact with health visitors, mainly about non-clinic attenders, was written into the computer file. Information was also available for CDC-referred children about involvement with social agencies. Social problems for control group B are likely to be more completely recorded as health visitor and hospital records of these children were scrutinised. No social details, other than social class of father, were known for control group A children.

Deprivation

As well as social grade of home and specific social problems, other estimates of deprivation were employed based on discussions with health visitors, social workers, inspectors from the Royal Scottish Society for the Prevention of Cruelty to Children (RSSPCC), day nursery matrons and nursery class teachers as well as personal observations made by the authors. All children coming from social grade 4 homes were exposed to a degree of socio-economic deprivation but in some families material neglect was more considerable, the children being dirty, poorly fed and clothed and reared in highly disorganised households, 66 CDC-referred children (16 per cent) came into this category which comprises 55 per cent of all those classified as coming from social grade 4 homes.

Other children were judged to be suffering from emotional deprivation which was graded as moderate, moderately severe or severe. In one-third of families where the child was classified as emotionally deprived there was considerable material deprivation as well. In two-thirds of families material care of the child was less inadequate although specific social problems existed in most cases.

The most common cause of moderate and moderately severe emotional deprivation was psychiatric illness, depression or other personality disorder in the mother, who was so concerned with her own problems that she was unable to respond to the emotional needs of her child. In other cases the mother was unable to respond to her child because of violence and disruption in the home. In cases of severe emotional deprivation these sorts of problems were compounded and one-half of such children had been taken into care.

An example of a severely emotionally deprived child was the younger (by three years) of two sisters. The mother, married to a regular solider, died in childbirth. The maternal grandmother took charge of both children until the younger was returned to the father in Germany at age 10 months after his remarriage. Following the birth of a half-sister the older child was increasingly neglected both physically and emotionally. The army authorities confirmed that on many occasions battering was suspected. The parents asked for the child to be removed and she was fostered in another army family before being returned to her grandmother at age three and a half years.

An example of moderately severe emotional deprivation was the case of an only child of an average working-class couple, born before marriage and regarded as a 'mistake' from conception. Initially mother was working and the baby provided with a full-time day nursery place. From the time he was transferred to part-time nursery class both parents complained bitterly about his behaviour to family and clinic doctors, health visitor and teacher. Parental handling was strict and lacking in

TABLE 3.4

Material and emotional deprivation among CDC-referred
children

Deprivation		CDC-referred children	
Emotional	Material		
		No.	%
—	+	29	7
Moderate	—	39	10
"	+	5	1
Moderately severe	—	16	4
"	+	18	4
Severe	—	9	2
"	+	14	3
Total		130	31

affection or understanding. Household organisation was very rigid and allowed no deviations to accommodate the interests of the child. The head teacher of his nursery school described any behavioural problems as being 'entirely of mother's making'. A number of referrals were initiated but the parents disregarded all advice.

An example of moderate emotional deprivation was the case of the second child of a basically caring average working-class mother who suffered from severe and prolonged post-natal depression, necessitating psychiatric treatment. She confessed that she had 'never been able to talk naturally' to her son.

Table 3.4 gives the numbers of CDC-referred children exposed to considerable material deprivation and/or varying degrees of emotional deprivation. Overall, these depriving circumstances existed in 31 per cent of families. 16 per cent of children suffered from considerable material neglect and 24 per cent from emotional deprivation.

Summary

An attempt was made to ascertain the total number of 1974/75-born Dundee children who were identified by whatever means as having NDD before school entry. The sources of ascertainment information and the circumstances of identification are given.

All children identified as having NDD could be included in one of nine main clinical categories which were: global delay, mental retardation, motor disorder, cerebral palsy, speech disorder, behavioural disorder, severe hearing loss, severe visual handicap and specific conditions. These categories of NDD are defined.

A severity grading was applied to each child's disability based on what was considered to be the likely implication for educational progress and behaviour at early school age, ranging from minor to very severe. These gradings are defined.

Various social indicators were used. Social class of father and specified severe social problems were known for most children in the total population. A social grade classification was applied to the families of CDC-referred children (middle-class, superior, average, poor working-class) and also other measures of material and emotional deprivation.

REFERENCES

Drillien, C. M. (1964) *The Growth and Development of the Prematurely Born Infant.* Edinburgh: Livingstone.
—— (1977) 'Developmental assessment and development screening.' *In:* Drillien, C. M., Drummond, M. B. (Eds.) *Neurodevelopmental Problems in Early Childhood.* Oxford: Blackwell Scientific Publications.
Fundudis, T., Kolvin, I., Garside, R. F. (1979) *Speech Retarded and Deaf Children: Their Psychological Development.* London: Academic Press.
Holt, K. S. (1977) *Developmental Paediatrics.* London: Butterworth.
Ingram, T. T. S. (1964) *Paediatric Aspects of Cerebral Palsy.* Edinburgh: Livingstone.
Knobloch, H., Pasamanick, B. (Eds.) (1974) *Gesell and Armatruda's Developmental Diagnosis, 3rd Ed.* New York: Harper & Row.
—— Stevens, F., Malone, A. F. (1980) *Manual of Developmental Diagnosis.* New York: Harper & Row.
Mitchell, R. G. (1977) 'The nature and causes of disability in childhood.' *In:* Drillien, C. M., Drummond, M. B. (Eds.) *Neurodevelopmental Problems in Early Childhood.* Oxford: Blackwell Scientific Publications.
Office of Population Censuses and Surveys (1971) *Classification of Occupations 1970.* London: HMSO.
World Health Organisation (1980) *International Classification of Impairments, Disabilities and Handicaps.* Geneva: WHO.

CHAPTER 4

Frequency and Distribution of Neurodevelopmental Disability

FREQUENCY OF NEURODEVELOPMENTAL DISABILITY IDENTIFIED PRESCHOOL

Table 4.1 gives the total numbers and percentages of all 1974/75-born children identified in the preschool period as having neurodevelopmental disability (NDD) after referral for assessment of the Child Development Centre (CDC) or elsewhere, for the total population of children resident in Dundee at any time during the first five years of life and for those who lived in the city during the three-year screening period. The table also indicates the number and percentage of children whose disabilities were graded as moderate and more severe in these two groups.

Twelve per cent of the total population were identified as having NDD before school entry (9 per cent moderate or more severe). 14 per cent of the more stable population were identified preschool as having NDD (12 per cent moderate or more severe). Even for the more stable population, these figures cannot be equated with true incidence of NDD as children transferring out of the city after the three-year screening may have been identified elsewhere as having NDD before school entry.

Distribution by clinical category

Tables 4.2 and 4.3 detail what was considered to be the principal problem for each child with NDD referred to CDC or to other hospital clinics, at initial assessment and diagnosis (Table 4.2) and at discharge, or at school entry age if the child was still in attendance (Table 4.3). Table 4.3 also shows the frequency per 1000 of these disabilities among the total preschool population and the more stable population of children who remained in the city throughout the screening period. The frequency of disabilities considered to have probable or possible educational implications (*i.e.* excluding minor NDD) is also shown.

Among the children referred to CDC, the principal problem changed over the period of attendance in 76 cases (18 per cent). Five children (2 per cent) attending other hospital clinics changed category. Table 4.4 details the changes in principal problems for CDC-referred children.

Age at which NDD was identified and by what means

Table 4.5 details the circumstances of identification for children with NDD referred to CDC and to hospital clinics. After excluding children in the known and other categories for whom screening was irrelevant (p. 46), 97 per cent of children referred to CDC and 42 per cent of children referred to hospital clinics came through the screening programme.

TABLE 4.1

**Frequency of NDD identified preschool in total population and
more stable population**

	Total population* (N = 5334)		More stable population[†] (N = 3667)	
	No.	%	No.	%
All children with NDD referred to:				
CDC	414	7.8	356	9.7
Hospital	206	3.9	169	4.6
Total	620	11.6	525	14.3
Excluding minor NDD:				
CDC	359	6.7	345	9.4
Hospital	132	2.5	109	3.0
Total	491	9.2	454	12.4

*1974/75-born children resident in Dundee at any time during the
first five years of life; [†]1974/75-born children who lived in Dundee
throughout three-year screening period.

TABLE 4.2

Clinical categories at initial diagnosis of children with NDD

	Children with NDD					
	CDC		Hospital		Total	
	No.	%	No.	%	No.	%
Clinical category:						
Global delay	81	20	2	1	83	13
Mental retardation mild	12 }	4	— }	—	12	3
Mental retardation severe	5 }		— }		5	
Motor disorder	72	17	14	7	86	14
Cerebal palsy not MR	12 }	4	— }	—	12 }	3
Cerebal palsy with MR	6 }		— }		6 }	
Minor neuro. abnorm.	6	1	1	<1	7	1
Speech disorder	135	33	114	55	249	40
Behaviour disorder	70	17	38	18	108	17
Specific conditions not MR	5 }	3	28 }	15	33 }	7
Specific conditions with MR	6 }		2 }		8 }	
Hearing loss	4	1	5	2	9	1
Visual handicap	—	—	2	1	2	<1
Total	414	100	206	100	620	100

MR = mental retardation.

TABLE 4.3

Clinical categories at final diagnosis of children with NDD and frequencies of disabilities in total and more stable populations

| | Children with NDD | | | | | | NDD frequency per 1000 | | Excluding minor NDD, frequency per 1000 | |
| | CDC | | Hospital | | Total | | Total population* | More stable population† | Total population* | More stable population† |
Clinical category:	No.	%	No.	%	No.	%	No.	No.	No.	No.
Global delay	77	19	2	1	79	13	15	17	14	17
Mental retardation mild	27	8	—	—	27 }	5	6	8	7	8
Mental retardation severe	6 }		— }		6					
Motor disorder	59	14	14	7	73	12	14	18	11	17
Cerebral palsy not MR	13 }	4	— }	—	13 }	3	3	4	3	4
Cerebral palsy with MR	5		—		5					
Minor neuro. abnorm.	4	1	2	1	6	1	1	1	1	2
Speech disorders	125	30	116	56	241	39	45	57	29	42
Behaviour disorder	83	20	36	17	119	19	22	26	20	25
Specific conditions not MR	5 }	3	27 }	14	32 }	6	7	9	5	7
Specific conditions with MR	6		2		8					
Hearing loss	4	1	5	3	9	1	2	2	2	2
Visual handicap	—	—	2	1	2	<1	<1	—	<1	—
Total	414	100	206	100	620	100	116	143	92	124

*1974/75-born children resident in Dundee at any time during the first five years of life; †1974/75-born children who lived in Dundee throughout three-year screening period; MR = mental retardation.

TABLE 4.4

CDC-referred children, principal problem at initial referral and at discharge or school-entry age

Final category:	Initial category									Total	Changed category No.	%
	Global delay	Mental retardation	Motor disorder	Cerebral palsy	Minor neuro. abnorm.	Speech disorder	Behaviour disorder	Specific conditions	Hearing loss			
Global delay	60	5	4	—	—	6	2	—	—	77	17	22
Mental retardation	13	11	4	—	1	3	—	—	1	33	22	67
Motor disorder	3	1	50	—	1	2	2	—	—	59	9	15
Cerebral palsy	—	—	—	18	—	—	—	—	—	18	—	—
Minor neuro. abnorm.	—	—	—	—	4	—	—	—	—	4	—	—
Speech disorder	3	—	7	—	—	115	—	—	—	125	10	8
Behaviour disorder	2	—	7	—	—	8	66	—	—	83	17	20
Specific conditions	—	—	—	—	—	—	—	11	—	11	—	—
Hearing loss	—	—	—	—	—	1	—	—	3	4	1	25
Total	81	17	72	18	6	135	70	11	4	414	76	18
Changed category (%)	21 (26)	6 (35)	22 (31)	— (—)	2 (33)	20 (15)	4 (6)	— (—)	1 (25)			

58

TABLE 4.5

Circumstances of identification of children with NDD

| | \multicolumn{2}{c}{Children with NDD} | | | | |
| Circumstances of identification: | CDC | | Hospital | | Total | |
	No.	%	No.	%	No.	%
Screening programme	374	90	59	29	433	70
Missed	—	—	31	15	31	5
Missed, non attendance	2	1	12	6	14	2
Suspected, not identified	9	2	39	19	48	8
Known	20	5	23	11	43	7
Other	9	2	42	20	51	8
Total	414	100	206	100	620	100

Table 4.6 shows the number of children available for screening at each age, those actually screened, and of these, the proportion subsequently identified as having NDD as a result of screening. The screening ages after which children were first referred and the clinical categories at initial diagnosis are also given. 10 per cent of those available for screening and 12.3 per cent of those actually screened were identified as having NDD (N = 433) following a referral from the screening programme. As the table indicates, most referrals (just over two-thirds) followed screening at ages two and three years.

Of the 374 children referred to CDC from the screening programme, 60 per cent were spontaneous referrals by screening doctors or health visitors, 32 per cent were referred at the request of the authors on the basis of screening schedule results and 8 per cent were transferred to the Centre from the hospital infant clinic (where their routine development had been carried out by the authors). Table 4.7 details the number and proportion of spontaneous and author-requested referrals at each screening age.

Table 4.8 shows the year of life, from birth to five years, in which all children with NDD (including those identified by means other than screening) were identified. The frequency of the different clinical categories of NDD (initial diagnosis) is also shown. These figures also include those cases in which diagnosis was known before referral to CDC or to Dundee hospital clinics (*i.e.* children who transferred into the city with the diagnosis already made, and children under supervision of the authors at the hospital infant clinic whose disability was diagnosed before transfer to CDC).

Distribution of NDD by severity grading

Table 4.9 shows the severity grading of children with NDD referred to CDC and to hospital clinics, judged according to the likely implications at early school age of the total impairments suffered by each child. Of the 414 CDC-referred children it was anticipated that 13 per cent would not have problems in school, 38 per cent would be certain or very likely to have problems and that, for 49 per cent, the prognosis was less clear.

TABLE 4.6

Screening age after which children were first identified as having NDD and clinical category at initial diagnosis

	8 wks.	20 wks.	39 wks.	15 mths.	2 yrs.	3 yrs.	Total
Available for screening	4265	4285	4287	4310	4302	4191	
% NDD	<0.1	0.8	1.1	1.2	3.4	3.5	
Actually screened	4072	4051	3446	3578	3494	3429	
% NDD	<0.1	0.9	1.4	1.5	4.2	4.3	

Age at screening

	8 wks.			20 wks.			39 wks.			15 mths.			2 yrs.			3 yrs.			Total		
	CDC	Hosp.	All	CDC	Hosp.	All	CDC	Hosp.	All	CDC	Hosp.	All	CDC	Hosp.	All	CDC	Hosp.	All	CDC	Hosp.	All
Initial category:																					
Global delay	—	—	—	3	—	3	13	—	13	10	1	11	32	—	32	20	—	20	78	1	79
Mental retardation	—	—	—	—	—	—	1	—	1	6	—	6	3	—	3	1	—	1	11	—	11
Motor disorder	—	—	—	13	2	15	20	6	26	21	—	21	8	—	8	6	—	6	68	8	76
Cerebral palsy	1	—	1	3	—	3	2	—	2	4	—	4	3	—	3	—	—	—	12	—	12
Minor neuro. abnorm.	1	—	1	2	—	2	1	1	2	1	—	1	—	—	—	1	—	1	6	1	7
Speech disorder	1	—	1	8	1	9	—	—	—	2	—	2	76	8	84	53	28	81	131	36	167
Behaviour disorder	—	—	—	—	2	2	1	—	1	3	1	4	16	—	16	31	4	35	60	6	66
Specific conditions	—	—	—	1	1	2	1	1	2	1	1	2	—	1	1	1	1	2	4	6	10
Hearing loss	—	—	—	—	—	—	1	—	1	1	—	1	1	—	1	—	—	—	4	1	5
Total	3	—	3	30	6	36	40	8	48	49	3	52	139	9	148	113	33	146	374	59	433

60

TABLE 4.7
Spontaneous and requested referrals for children referred to CDC from
screening programme

	Referrals				Total
	Spontaneous		Requested		
	No.	%	No.	%	No.
Screening examination					
8, 20 and 39 wks.	64	88	9	12	73
15 mths.	34	69	15	31	49
2 yrs.	82	59	57	41	139
3 yrs.	73	65	40	35	113
Total	253	68	121	32	374

It was more difficult to assign a severity grading to children who were not assessed at the Centre (N = 206). Some confidence was felt in assigning children to the following gradings: minor (36 per cent), moderately severe (16 per cent) and severe or very severe (4 per cent). In nine cases (4 per cent) it was not possible to make a grading. The remaining 82 cases (40 per cent) were graded as moderate.

Table 4.10 details the severity gradings of disabilities detected in each year of life. As would be expected, children with less severe disabilities were more likely to be identified at later ages. Of the 59 children with severe or very severe disabilities, only 14 per cent were identified after the age of three years, compared with 33 per cent of the 141 children with moderately severe disabilities, 37 per cent of the 282 children with moderate disabilities and 40 per cent of the 129 children with minor NDD.

Since most CDC-referred children came from the screening programme, very few (5 per cent) were first seen later than the fourth year of life. In contrast, 27 per cent of hospital-referred children were seen after that age. Over three-quarters of these late referrals were on account of speech disorders or delays (Table 4.8).

Very severe disabilities

Of the 15 children with very severe disabilities, all (apart from four who died) are now in special school or residential institutions. All but four were identified in the first year of life. One child with severe mental retardation and a neurogenic club foot, under supervision at an orthopaedic clinic, appeared developmentally within the normal range until his 15-month screening examination. A deaf child with autistic-type behaviour and mental retardation (probably mild) born to a mildly retarded mother, was suspected by the health visitor and the screening doctor as having a significant hearing loss at nine months: the mother could not be persuaded to accept referral until the child was 16 months old, at which age she was referred to CDC. The third child suffered a severe Coxsackie B meningo-encephalitis at the age of four and a half years leaving him severely mentally retarded as a result of cerebral atrophy. The fourth child transferred into Dundee shortly before his second birthday and was referred by the family doctor to a hospital clinic (and thereafter to CDC) on account of slow development. He is severely mentally retarded with very marked hyperactivity.

TABLE 4.8
Year of life in which children were first identified as having NDD

Clinical category:*	Year of identification																	
	1st yr.			2nd yr.			3rd yr.			4th yr.			5th yr.			Total		
	CDC	Hosp.	All	CDC	Hosp.	All	CDC	Hosp.	All	CDC	Hosp.	All	CDC	Hosp.	All	CDC	Hosp.	All
Global delay	16	—	16	12	1	13	33	1	34	16	—	16	4	—	4	81	2	83
Mental retardation	3	—	3	8	—	8	4	—	4	1	—	1	1	—	1	17	—	17
Motor disorder	34	8	42	23	4	27	7	—	7	6	—	6	2	2	4	72	14	86
Cerebral palsy	7	—	7	8	—	8	3	—	3	—	—	—	—	—	—	18	—	18
Minor neuro. abnorm.	4	1	5	1	—	1	—	—	—	1	—	1	—	—	—	6	1	7
Speech disorder	—	—	—	6	4	10	81	36	117	44	31	75	4	43	47	135	114	249
Behaviour disorder	10	6	16	5	6	11	17	9	26	30	8	38	8	9	17	70	38	108
Specific conditions	10	24	34	—	3	3	—	2	2	1	1	2	—	—	—	11	30	41
Hearing loss	2	1	3	2	—	2	—	1	1	—	2	2	—	1	1	4	5	9
Visual handicap	—	2	2	—	—	—	—	—	—	—	—	—	—	—	—	—	2	2
Total	86	42	128	65	18	83	145	49	194	99	42	141	19	55	74	414	206	620

*Initial diagnosis.

62

TABLE 4.9

Distribution of NDD by overall severity grading

| | Children with NDD | | | | | |
| | CDC | | Hospital | | Total | |
	No.	%	No.	%	No.	%
Overall severity grading*						
Minor	55	13	74	36	129	21
Moderate	200	49	82	40	282	45
Moderately severe	108	26	33	16	141	23
Severe	38	9	6	3	44	7
Very severe	13	3	2	1	15	3
Not known	—	—	9	4	9	1
Total	414	100	206	100	620	100

*According to likely implications of total impairments at early school age.

Apart from the first child mentioned above, only one other child with a very severe disability was identified on screening. This child had a severe dystonic cerebral palsy and mental retardation and was noted to be abnormal by the health visitor at the eight-week screening. Overall, it appears that the screening programme had little relevance to the identification of children with very severe disabilities.

Severe disabilities

In contrast, 34 of the 44 children with disabilities graded as severe were referred for further assessment from the screening programme. The severity of the final diagnosis was not always apparent at initial assessment. Table 4.11 details the clinical conditions of these children, the circumstances of identification and, for those identified on screening, the screening ages after which they were referred.

Overall, 30 (68 per cent) of these 44 children required special education, 26 being placed initially in special schools. 11 children (25 per cent) entered normal school following deferment of school entrance and one or two years' attendance at an assessment class for children who may require special education (p. 122). One child was removed from this class and enrolled in the neighbourhood school against advice. She was transferred to special education after one year, as was another child who did not take up the place offered in the assessment class. Four other children were admitted to normal schools without prior attendance at the assessment class: no vacancies existed in three instances and the parents refused in the other. The two remaining children, both likely to require special education, transferred out of town before final school placement.

Of the 34 children identified through the screening programme, 18 were referred after the 15-month examination or earlier. 11 children were referred after the two-year screening: of these, referral had been requested, but not carried out, for one child following the 15-month screening, four children had not attended for screening at 15 months and one had transferred into the city after that age. Five children appeared developmentally and behaviourally within normal limits at 15 months, but this number includes two children who presented later with severe

63

TABLE 4.10

Distribution by overall severity grading and year of life in which NDD was first identified

	1st yr. CDC	1st yr. Hosp.	1st yr. All	2nd yr. CDC	2nd yr. Hosp.	2nd yr. All	3rd yr. CDC	3rd yr. Hosp.	3rd yr. All	4th yr. CDC	4th yr. Hosp.	4th yr. All	5th yr. CDC	5th yr. Hosp.	5th yr. All	Total CDC	Total Hosp.	Total All
Overall severity grading:																		
Minor	14	10	24	6	2	8	21	24	45	10	16	26	4	22	26	55	74	129
Moderate	32	23	55	26	12	38	72	14	86	60	14	74	10	19	29	200	82	282
Moderately severe	17	4	21	21	4	25	42	7	49	24	9	33	4	9	13	108	33	141
Severe	14	3	17	9	—	9	10	1	11	5	1	6	—	1	1	38	6	44
Very severe	9	2	11	3	—	3	—	—	—	—	—	—	1	—	1	13	2	15
Not known	—	—	—	—	—	—	—	3	3	—	2	2	—	4	4	—	9	9
Total	86	42	128	65	18	83	145	49	194	99	42	141	19	55	74	414	206	620
No. children identified by (%)	86 (21)	42 (20)	128 (21)	151 (36)	60 (29)	211 (34)	296 (71)	109 (53)	405 (65)	395 (95)	151 (73)	546 (88)	414 (100)	206 (100)	620 (100)			

TABLE 4.11

Circumstances of identification of children with severe NDD (N = 44)

	Known	Screening 20 wks.	Screening 39 wks.	Screening 15 mths.	Screening 2 yrs.	Screening 3 yrs.	Other	Missed	Total
Clinical category:*									
Mental retardation	1	2	3	6	6	2			20
Cerebral palsy	2	1		1			1		5
Communication disorder			1		2				3
Behaviour disorder					3	3	1	1	8
Specific conditions	2		1						3
Hearing loss		2		1					3
Visual handicap	2								2
Total	7	5	5	8	11	5	2	1	44

*Final diagnosis.

TABLE 4.12

CDC-referred children, social class distribution derived from computer file by clinical category

Clinical category:*	I and II No.	I and II %	III No.	III %	IV and V No.	IV and V %	Other/NK No.	Other/NK %	Total No.
Global delay	5	6	25	33	37	48	10	13	77
Mental retardation mild	1	3	7	30	14	49	5	18	27
Mental retardation severe	—		3		2	32	1	7	6
Motor disorder	4	7	32	54	19	32	4	7	59
Cerebral palsy not MR	3	22	7	50	—		3	28	13
Cerebral palsy with MR	1		2	50	—		2		5
Minor neuro. abnorm.	—		2	50	2	50	—		4
Speech disorder	10	8	58	46	44	35	13	10	125
Behaviour disorder	12	14	30	36	27	33	14	17	83
Specific conditions not MR	—	9	2	36	3	9	—	18	5
Specific conditions with MR	1		2		1		2		6
Hearing loss/visual handicap	—	—	—	—	2	50	2	50	4
Total (%)	37 (9)	18	170 (41)	48	151 (36)	29	56 (14)	5	414 (100)
% General population†	18		48		29		5		100

*Final diagnosis; †all 1974/75 Dundee livebirths to Dundee-resident mothers; NK = not known; MR = mental retardation.

TABLE 4.13

Hospital-referred children, social class distribution derived from computer file by clinical category

Clinical category:*	Social class								Total
	I and II		III		IV and V		Other/NK		
	No.	%	No.	%	No.	%	No.	%	No.
Global delay	1	50	—	—	1	50	—	—	2
Motor disorder	4	28	5	36	5	36	—	—	14
Minor neuro. abnorm.	—	—	2	100	—	—	—	—	2
Speech disorder	21	18	51	44	29	25	15	13	116
Behaviour disorder	5	14	17	47	11	31	3	8	36
Specific conditions not MR	4 } 14		9 } 31		10 } 41		4 } 14		27
Specific conditions with MR	—		—		2		—		2
Hearing loss/visual handicap	—	—	3	43	1	14	3	43	7
Total (%)	35	(17)	87	(42)	59	(29)	25	(12)	206 (100)
% General population†	18		48		29		5		100

*Final diagnosis; †all 1974/75 Dundee livebirths to Dundee-resident mothers; NK = not known; MR = mental retardation.

66

communication disorders (p. 152) which would not have been apparent at the earlier screening. Of the five children referred after the three-year screening, two had transferred in after two years, parents had refused earlier referral in two cases, and one child, who had been suspect at the 15-month screening, did not attend again until three-year screening.

Only one of these 44 children appears to have been missed on screening. He was referred to the Child Guidance Service (in Scotland, the educational psychology service of the local authority education department) from nursery class with severely disturbed behaviour at four and a half years. At three-year screening, his behaviour had been reported as normal although history given later belied this.

Children identified as in need of special education after school entry are discussed in Chapter 14 (p. 265).

Distribution by social factors

Social class

Table 4.12 details the distribution by social class, derived from computer file, for the general population of 1974/75 live-births (Dundee-born and resident) and for NDD children referred to CDC by clinical category (final diagnosis). Table 4.13 gives the same details for children referred to hospital clinics.

The social class distribution of children referred to hospital clinics was very close to that of the general population. However, among the CDC-referred children, there were fewer with fathers in social classes I and II and more in social classes IV and V than in the general population. The difference in social class distribution between all CDC- and hospital-referred children, after exclusion of the other/not known categories, is significant at a p value of <0.01 (2df, χ^2 = 11.272). The difference is particularly obvious for children with speech disorders suggesting that parents from social classes I, II and III are more likely to take the initiative in seeking advice from family doctors if they are concerned about their children's speech, whereas children from social classes IV and V are more likely to be referred following a screening examination.

Table 4.14 details the social class distribution, derived from parents' histories, for CDC-referred children by clinical category. As would be expected, there was an excess of children from social class IV and V homes amongst those who were globally delayed or mentally retarded when compared with the general population. In contrast, children with cerebral palsy and specific conditions were over-represented in social classes I and II. Apart from specific conditions, there were more children than would be expected from social class IV and V homes in all clinical categories except speech disorders. This suggests that speech delay and articulatory problems may be accepted as within normal limits by both parents and medical personnel when the child comes from a low socio-economic background.

Social grade

It is likely that social grade is a more sensitive index of social disadvantage than social class (p. 50). Table 4.15 gives the social grade distribution by clinical category

TABLE 4.14

CDC-referred children, social class distribution derived from parents' histories by clinical category

	Social class							
	I and II		III		IV and V		Total		Other/NK
Clinical category:*	No.	%	No.	%	No.	%	No.	%	No.
Global delay	6	8	35	49	31	43	72	100	5
Mental retardation mild	1	3	12	50	13	47	26	100	1
Mental retardation severe	—		4		2		6		—
Motor disorder	11	19	28	48	19	33	58	100	1
Cerebral palsy not MR	3	33	5	33	5	33	13	100	—
Cerebral palsy with MR	3		1		1		5		—
Minor neuro. abnorm.	—		4	100	—		4	100	—
Speech disorder	15	12	76	61	33	27	124	100	1
Behaviour disorder	14	17	37	45	31	38	82	100	1
Specific conditions not MR	3	30	3	60	1	10	4	100	1
Specific conditions with MR	3		3		—		6		—
Hearing loss	1	25	1	25	2	50	4	100	—
Total (%)	57	(14)	209	(52)	138	(34)	404	(100)	10
% General population†	18		48		29		100		5

*Final diagnosis; †all 1974/75 Dundee livebirths to Dundee-resident mothers; MR = mental retardation; NK = not known.

TABLE 4.15

CDC-referred children, social grade distribution by clinical category

Clinical category*	Social grade								Total
	1		2		3		4		
	No.	%	No.	%	No.	%	No.	%	No.
Global delay	2	3	3	4	31	40	41	53	77
Mental retardation mild	1	3	2	15	8	27	16	55	27
Mental retardation severe	—		3		1		2		6
Motor disorder	7	12	11	19	28	47	13	22	59
Cerebral palsy not MR	3	33	3	22	5	33	2	11	13
Cerebral palsy with MR	3		1		1		—		5
Minor neuro. abnorm.	—		4	100	—		—		4
Speech disorder	12	10	18	14	75	60	20	16	125
Behaviour disorder	10	12	10	12	41	49	22	27	83
Specific conditions not MR	—	18	—	—	4	64	1	18	5
Specific conditions with MR	2		1		3		1		6
Hearing loss	—	—	1	25	1	25	2	50	4
Total (%)	40	(10)	56	(13)	198	(48)	120	(29)	414 (100)

*Final diagnosis; MR = mental retardation.

TABLE 4.16

CDC-referred children, severity of NDD by social grade

	1		2		3		4		Total	
	No.	%	No.	%	No.	%	No.	%	No.	%
Overall severity grading										
Minor	8	20	8	14	29	14	10	8	55	13
Moderate	17	43	28	50	105	53	50	42	200	48
Moderately severe	8	20	14	25	49	25	37	31	108	26
Severe	6	15	2	4	11	6	19	16	38	10
Very severe	1	2	4	7	4	2	4	3	13	3
Total	40	100	56	100	198	100	120	100	414	100

for CDC-referred children. The predominance of globally delayed and mentally retarded children from poor working-class homes is more clearly demonstrated by social grade than by social class distribution: 54 per cent of such children came from social grade 4 homes in contrast to 44 per cent from social class IV and V homes. In contrast, the occurrence of motor disorders, including cerebral palsy does not appear to be affected by social background: over one-third of such children (36 per cent) come from homes graded 1 or 2 (22 per cent from social class I and II homes).

The small number of children from poor homes referred on account of speech disorders is more evident by social grade (16 per cent social grade 4) than by social class distribution (27 per cent social class IV and V). Similarly, fewer children from social grade 4 homes were referred on account of behaviour disorders (33 per cent) than were children from social class IV and V homes (38 per cent). Again, it seems likely that degrees of behaviour disturbance that would be considered unacceptable in children from average and superior working-class and middle-class homes may not be thought to merit referral when the child is known to come from a poor and disorganised background.

Severity and social grade

Table 4.16 details the social grade distribution of CDC-referred children by severity grading of NDD. The proportion of children with very severe disabilities is roughly similar in all social grades. There is little difference in distribution by severity among children coming from middle-class or from superior and average working-class homes, but there is an excess of more severe disabilities among children from poor working-class homes. After excluding the small number of children with very severe disabilities, the distribution by severity of the 116 children from poor homes is significantly different from that of the 285 children from better homes ($\chi^2 = 14.290$, 3df, p = <0.01). There are two possible explanations for this: children from poor homes may be more likely to suffer from more severe degrees of NDD, or children from poor homes with minor or moderate NDD may be less likely to be detected and referred on account of NDD. The latter explanation seems more reasonable.

TABLE 4.17

**Social problems among families of CDC-referred and
control group B children**

	CDC-referred (N = 414)		Control group B (N = 326)	
	No.	%	No.	%
Specific social problems				
1. Unstable parental relationship	32	8	18	6
2. Parent/s handicapped	22	5	5	2
3. Sibling handicapped	7	2	1	<1
4. Psychiatric illness	32	8	6	2
5. Chronic unemployment	65	16	7	2
6. Criminal record	18	4	8	3
7. Very poor social conditions	66	16	28	9
8. Alcoholism	8	2	3	1
9. Financial problems	8	2	7	2
10. Child taken into care	20	5	5	2
11. Non-accidental injury	10	2	3	1
None of the above	256	62	267	82
Involvement of:				
Social work	74			
RSSPCC	3	} 23		
Social work and RSSPCC	20			

RSSPCC = Royal Scottish Society for the Prevention of Cruelty to Children.

Specific social problems

Table 4.17 details the specific social problems known to be operating among the families of CDC-referred and all but four control group B children. There were severe social problems in over one-third of the CDC group: social workers and inspectors of the Royal Scottish Society for the Prevention of Cruelty to Children (RSSPCC) were involved with 23 per cent of these children. The figure for social work involvement does not include routine involvement with families with handicapped children but no other problems, or those families seeking day nursery placements with no social problems other than the need for the mother to find employment.

Table 4.18 details the distribution, by number, of specific social problems among CDC-referred and control group B children and that reported in the total population of the 5334 research-group children, excluding from the last group 808 children for whom this information was not available. Four children from control group B were also excluded. A total of 278 control group B children were reported preschool as having no severe social problems; scrutiny of hospital and health visitor records at school entry revealed that an additional 11 children (4 per cent of all controls) had experienced severe social problems which had not been recorded earlier.

Although it was recognised that information about control group B children and the total population was incomplete, it seemed certain that there were significantly more CDC-referred children with one or more social problems (38 per cent) than pertained in control group B (17 per cent known) or the general population (14 per cent known). The social class distribution of control group B children was not significantly different from that of CDC-referred children with moderate or more severe disabilities (see Table 1.3). The difference in distribution of social problems among control group B children and matched CDC-referred children is, however, highly significant ($\chi^2 = 35$, p = <0.001). This emphasises the limitations of social class, based on father's occupation, as an indicator of social circumstances operating within the home.

Two- and one-parent families
   Table 4.19 shows the distribution of two- and one-parent families for CDC-referred children. 16 per cent were living in one-parent families compared with 9 per cent of the total research-group population.

Distribution by sex
   Table 4.20 details the numbers of boys and girls with NDD referred to either CDC or to hospital clinics by clinical category. Nearly two-thirds (64 per cent) of all children with NDD identified before school entry were male. This compares with 52 per cent male children in the general population of 1974/75 children born and resident in Dundee.
   Sex distribution differed by clinical category. 54 per cent of the children with global delay and mental retardation were male, which is very close to the sex distribution in the general population. The sex distribution of specific conditions and hearing and visual defects (55 per cent male) was also comparable to that in the general population. In contrast, 64 per cent of children with behavioural disorder and with motor disorders (including cerebral palsy) were male, as were 71 per cent of those referred on account of speech delays and deviations.

CHILDREN WITH NEURODEVELOPMENTAL DISABILITY
SUSPECTED BUT NOT IDENTIFIED
BY DIAGNOSTIC ASSESSMENT

   In any screening programme failure to identify children with NDD may be due to two main factors: (1) the programme itself may have poor validity or give inconsistent results depending on the expertise of screening personnel (p. 276), and (2) deviations and delays may be noted on screening but no action taken to confirm the presence of NDD. Confirmation (or 'identification') is essential to the amelioration of disabilities detected on screening.
   In addition to those children referred from the screening programme to hospital clinics and to CDC, other children were suspected of having NDD but this was not identified by diagnostic assessment.
   As mentioned earlier, all screening cards were scrutinised by the authors weekly. On some cards screening doctors referred to CDC. On the basis of information

TABLE 4.18

**Social problems among families of CDC-referred and control group B
children and total research-group population**

	CDC		Control group B*		Total population*	
	No.	%	No.	%	No.	%
No. social problems						
0	256	62	267	83	3907	86
1	89	21	30	9	496	11
2	45	11	17	5	92	2
3	15	4	5	2	26 }	1
≥ 4	9	2	3	1	5 }	
Total	414	100	322	100	4526	100

*Excluding those for whom information unavailable (4 in control group B, 808 in total population).

TABLE 4.19

Parenting of CDC-referred children

	No.	%
Child cared for by:		
Two parents married	329	79
Two parents unmarried	15	4
One parent	66	16
In care long-term or fostered	4	1
Total	414	100

TABLE 4.20

Children with NDD; distribution of clinical categories by sex

	Male			Female			Total	% Male
	CDC	Hosp.	All	CDC	Hosp.	All		
Clinical category:*								
Global delay	42	2	44	35	—	35	79	56
Mental retardation	17	—	17	16	—	16	33	52
Motor disorder	36	8	44	23	6	29	73	60
Cerebral palsy	13	—	13	5	—	5	18	72
Minor neuro. abnorm.	2	1	3	2	1	3	6	50
Speech disorder	92	80	172	33	36	69	241	71
Behaviour disorder	52	25	77	31	11	42	119	65
Specific conditions	9	13	22	2	16	18	40	55
Hearing loss	1	3	4	3	2	5	9	44
Visual handicap	—	2	2	—	—	—	2	100
Total	264	134	398	150	72	222	620	64

*Final diagnosis.

TABLE 4.21

Children with NDD suspected but not identified by diagnostic assessment (N = 203)

Review/referral recommended (N = 177)		
(a) Review before next screening examination (N = 107)		
Children attending	32	
Improved		27
Not improved		5
Children not attending	75	
Attended subsequent screening examination—Improved		31
Not improved		17
Other problem		6
Did not attend any subsequent screening examination		21
(b) Review at next screening examination (N = 20)		
Children attending	20	
Improved		13
Not improved		7
(c) Referral (N = 50)		
No response		24
Mother unwilling		16
Doctor unwilling		7
Child transferred out		3
Review/referral not recommended (N = 26)	26	
Attending hospital for other problem		5
Mother unwilling		8
Doctor unwilling		3
Screening card not submitted		3
No obvious reason		7

available on other cards one of the following was suggested:

(1) no action, for routine screening at next screening age;

(2) screening doctor asked to take special note at the next screening examination and refer if problem still present;

(3) screening doctor asked to recall for review before next screening and refer if problem still present or, if the screening doctor had indicated on the card an intention to review, to refer than if the problem still existed;

(4) refer the child to CDC.

Of the 374 NDD children referred to CDC from the screening programme, referral was requested by screening doctors or health visitors in 68 per cent of cases and by the authors in 32 per cent (Table 4.7). In a further 24 instances, the mother agreed to a CDC referral but did not attend.

No ongoing record was kept by the authors of those children for whom review or referral had been suggested. Information about such children was collected retrospectively when development screening folders were seen again at the time of the child's school medical examination. At that time it was found that a request for review or referral had been made, at some stage, for 177 children in addition to the 121 who were referred following such suggestions. For 26 more children, screening results had been sufficiently suspect to merit such action, but for various reasons this had not been suggested. Thus, overall, 203 children were suspected of having some deviation or delay at some point on screening in addition to the 620 children with identified NDD known to CDC or hospital clinics. At a later date a few more children, whose folders had not been sent in after school entry, were found to have been suspect preschool (p. 263). These children are not included here.

Circumstances following request to review or refer

Table 4.21 details the circumstances following request for review or referral for the 177 children with suspected NDD who were not followed up with diagnostic assessment. In 52 cases, a review took place, either before or at the next screening examination. In 40 of these children, the problem was resolving or had resolved; in 12 it was still present. 75 children did not re-attend for review, but of these, 31 were found to be acceptably normal at a later screening examination, 23 had the same or a different problem at later screening and 21 were not seen again.

Referral had been requested for 50 children: in 24 cases, there was no response to this request, in 16 cases mothers were unwilling for referral as were doctors in a further seven cases. Three children left the city before appointments could be arranged. 17 of these 50 children were considered normal at their next screening.

Thus in 88 cases (50 per cent) the child was considered significantly improved or within normal limits at a later examination by the screening doctor or health visitor. In 35 children (20 per cent), the problems were still evident at the last screening examination. For the remaining 54 children (30 per cent), the outcome was not known.

Suspected NDD, no request for review or referral

Table 4.21 also details why no request was made for review or referral of 26 children with suspected NDD on screening. Five children were attending children's medical outpatient clinics with other conditions and it was not considered desirable to duplicate screening clinics. In eight cases, it was stated on the screening cards that mothers would not accept a referral and in three cases, that doctors did not consider referral necessary. In three cases screening cards were not submitted and came to light too late for referral to be requested. In seven cases, no reason for failure to request referral was found due, presumably, to error on the part of the authors.

Overall, 48 mothers were unwilling for referral to CDC or did not attend appointments there. This number comprises 10 per cent of all those with NDD identified after screening (433 children) and those sufficiently suspect on screening for immediate referral to be suggested (50 children).

Categories of suspected NDD

The distribution of suspected problems among the 203 children with doubtful or abnormal screening results who were not seen at CDC, and the 24 who did not attend their CDC appointments, is given in Table 4.22.

Children with suspected motor disorder or minor abnormal neurological signs only were most likely to be reported as normal at later examination. These

TABLE 4.22

Distribution by clinical category of suspect children who did not attend/were not referred to CDC

	Suspect at screening examination		Still suspect last screening examination	
	No.	%	No.	%
Suspected disability:				
Global delay	61	27	22	22
Motor disorder	23	10	3	3
Minor neuro. abnorm.	11	5	2	2
Speech disorder	94	40	41	41
Behaviour disorder	38	17	31	32
Total	227	100	98	100

TABLE 4.23

Social class distribution of 203 children with suspected NDD and that of CDC-referred children in the same clinical categories

	Social class								Total
	I and II		III		IV and V		Other/NK		
	No.	%	No.	%	No.	%	No.	%	No.
Suspected disability:									
Global delay	5	9	21	38	21	38	8	15	55
Motor disorder	3	14	9	41	8	36	2	9	22
Minor neuro. abnorm.	1	10	3	30	6	60	—	—	10
Speech disorder	13	15	35	40	32	36	8	9	88
Behaviour disorder	5	18	11	39	9	32	3	11	28
Total	27	13	79	39	76	37	21	10	203
CDC-referred	31	9	147	42	129	37	41	12	348

TABLE 4.24

Children with suspected NDD found to be within normal limits

	1974		1975		Total	
	CDC	Hospital	CDC	Hospital	CDC	Hospital
Suspected disability:						
Global delay	2	—	2	—	4	—
Motor disorder	4	1	6	4	10	5
Speech disorder	8	3	1	5	9	8
Behaviour disorder	—	2	2	—	2	2
Specific conditions	4	3	—	20	4	23
Other	2	—	1	—	3	—
Total	20	9	12	29	32	38

problems were mostly recognised at the 15-month or earlier screening examinations and a longer period was available for subsequent screening observation. Global delay, speech delay and behaviour disturbance were usually detected at the two- or three-year screening, with a shorter period for continued observation. The most common reason for not identifying disability was that the last screening had taken place and the child was not seen again.

Distribution by social class and sex

Table 4.23 shows the social class distribution (derived from the computer file) of these 203 children by their suspected clinical categories and the social class distribution of CDC-referred children with identified NDD in the same clinical categories. There were rather more children from social classes I and II amongst those who were not referred to CDC, but this is not statistically significant (χ^2 = 2.626, p = >0.10). There is no evidence that social background of families influenced the decisions of screening doctors on referral.

The school problems of children with suspected NDD who were not referred for assessment are discussed in Chapter 14 (p. 263).

CHILDREN WITH SUSPECTED NEURODEVELOPMENTAL DISABILITY FOUND TO BE WITHIN NORMAL LIMITS

Not all children referred from screening were found to have NDD. There were 70 false positive referrals, 16 per cent of the total number of children (433) referred to CDC or to hospital clinics for diagnostic assessment following a screening examination. Table 4.24 details the categories of suspected NDD for these children, where they were referred and their years of birth. The categories are the same as those used throughout with the exception of three children who could not be so classified and are included here under 'other'. Two children were referred for apparent delay in visual following after eight-week screening and one for reported hyperacusis at 15 months. In the last case, both parents were extremely worried about their own illiteracy, particularly as their eldest child was about to enter school. The complaint about the baby (and the anxiety of the parents evident to the screening doctor who referred the child) appeared to be a 'cry for help' with their own problems. Both parents were referred to the adult literacy scheme with satisfactory outcome.

Nearly twice as many false positives were recorded for CDC-referred children born in 1974 as for those born in 1975, presumably because of the increasing expertise and confidence of screening personnel with the passage of time. The much larger number of false positives amongst 1975-born children referred to hospital clinics is accounted for by 18 children referred because of suspected congenital dislocation of the hip (CDH). Most of these children were referred after the late diagnosis of CDH in two 1974-born children. The community child health service had been alerted by the children's orthopaedic service and had become particularly vigilant about this disorder.

TABLE 4.25
1976 births, NDD identified before entry to normal school

Clinical category:	Referred to: Paediatrician	Others		Total	
	No.		No.	No.	%
Global delay	8	Educational psychologist	3	11	7
Motor disorder	3		—	3	2
Cerebral palsy	7		—	7	5
Minor neuro. abnorm.	7		—	7	5
Speech disorder	7	Speech therapist	71	78	50
Behaviour disorder	34	Psychologist/ psychiatrist	17	51	32
Total (%)	66 (42)		91 (58)	157	(100)

FREQUENCY OF NEURODEVELOPMENTAL DISABILITY IDENTIFIED PRESCHOOL AMONG 1976-BORN CHILDREN

Facilities at CDC for more detailed assessment of children suspected of having NDD of any degree of severity were only available on a routine basis for children born in 1974/5. Thereafter, arrangements for further investigations and management of such children reverted to what had obtained previously, *i.e.* children were referred initially to appropriate hospital clinics from whence those with more severe or complicated disabilities could be transferred to CDC, the function of which changed from development to handicap centre.

The development screening folders and health visitor records were scrutinised for all 1976-born children after the school-entry medical examination. Both contained copy letters from hospital specialist services and others dealing with children with NDD (p. 45).

The referral rate for 1976-born children who had been included in the screening programme (*i.e.* had not transferred into the city after the age of three years) and had entered normal Dundee primary schools, was compared with that for similar 1974/75-born children. Overall, 10 per cent (N = 157) of these 1574 1976-born children were identified as having NDD preschool compared with 13 per cent (N = 427) of 3260 1974/75-born children who had also been included in the screening programme and admitted to normal Dundee schools. A bigger difference was noted when comparing the proportions of children identified as having NDD after a screening examination: 49 (31 per cent) of the 157 1976-born children and 295 (69 per cent) of the 427 1974/75-born children.

There was also a difference in the types of preschool problems referred and identified (Table 4.25). One half of the 1976-born children were referred on account of speech disorder. One-third had behaviour disorders, the most common complaint being eneuresis and/or encopresis which was the presenting disorder in one-half of those children referred to paediatricians. Of 427 comparable 1974/75-

born children identified as having NDD at CDC or other clinics, 38 per cent had speech disorders and 16 per cent had behaviour disorders. The low frequency of global delay and motor disorder identified preschool among 1976-born children may be of some importance as 1974/75 born research-group children in these clinical categories referred to CDC were found to have the highest incidence of schooling difficulties at ages six and a half to seven and a half years. The lowest incidence of schooling difficulties was found among children with preschool speech disorders (p. 262).

Overall, only 43 per cent of 1976-born children with NDD (excluding those with severe or very severe disabilities necessitating special education) were assessed preschool by paediatricians. 45 per cent were only assessed by speech therapists.

NEURODEVELOPMENTAL DISABILITY IN CONTROL GROUP A

Frequency of NDD

Selection procedures for control group A are outlined in Chapter 1 (p. 7). For each of these 128 control children, the results from one of the screening examinations were compared with those of a more detailed developmental assessment and neurological examination at the same age at CDC. As a result of assessment, it was considered that 102 children (80 per cent) were within normal limits developmentally and behaviorally and that 26 (20 per cent) showed developmental disorder or delay. Seven children, all seen following the 20-week screening, were normal developmentally, but showed minor abnormal neurological signs (p. 96).

Details of the number of NDD control group A children in each clinical category by screening age are shown in Table 4.26. (Figures in parentheses indicate the number of occasions when NDD was considered of minor severity.)

The number of children categorised as having NDD is high (20 per cent) compared with the frequency of NDD identified preschool among 1974/75-born children (14 per cent, see Table 4.1). Several factors should be taken into account when considering this difference:

(1) Control group A children were assessed at one of five different ages associated with the five screening examinations and are not directly comparable with a population of children who have had a number of screening examinations. Children with NDD in the 1974/75 research group were 'identified' once only, although they may well have had the same, or a different, form of NDD at more than one screening examination. In a discontinuous group such as control group A, it is the number of disabilities rather than the number of children which is being measured.

(2) The frequency of NDD in the 1974/75 research group, ascertained at the time of school entry, is almost certainly an underestimate. Other children were suspected of having NDD on the basis of their screening examinations but, for a variety of reasons, were not seen for assessment (p. 72).

TABLE 4.26
Control group A, NDD identified at different screening ages

			Screening age			
	20 wks.	39 wks.	15 mths.	2 yrs.	3 yrs.	Total
Clinical category:						
Global delay	—	1	1	—	5 (1)*	7 (1)
Mental retardation	—	—	—	—	1	1
Motor disorder	2 (1)	1	1	3 (2)	2 (2)	9 (5)
Speech disorder	—	—	—	3	1 (1)	4 (1)
Behaviour disorder	1	—	1	1	2 (1)	5 (1)
Total	3 (1)	2	3	7 (2)	11 (5)	26 (8)

*In parentheses, number of occasions when NDD was considered of minor severity.

(3) 'Identified' NDD in the 1974/75 research group implied that both doctors and parents agreed that a problem existed. 13 per cent of the 1974/75 CDC-referred children had problems considered mild or transitory in nature, compared with 31 per cent of control group A children with NDD. Despite the small number of cases (8) in the latter group, the excess of minor NDD among control children was statistically significant (χ^2 = 6.097, p. = <0.02). It is likely that some of the minor problems detected after the two- and three-year screenings among control children would not have been considered problems at routine development screening.

Comparison of screening results with CDC assessments

Of the 128 control group A children who attended CDC, 26 had not attended a screening examination (p. 8). 102 children attended both CDC and local screening but the development folders (and results of local screening) could not be traced for four children. This left 98 cases for comparison.

Table 4.27 details what action would have been taken, following scrutiny of screening cards and CDC duplicates, had these been submitted for 1974/75 research-group children.

In only two children considered within normal limits at CDC did local screening results suggest that review or referral was indicated. One boy at 20 weeks showed some delay in head control and was described as slightly floppy, easily startled and jumpy. On assessment at CDC at 23 weeks, gross motor development was up to age and he was neurologically normal. Had he been a research-group child, referral would have been recommended if motor delay or abnormal neurological signs persisted at the 39-week screening. One girl at 20 weeks had not acquired head control, made no attempt to reach or grasp a rattle and was described as hypertonic. At 24 weeks she was performing up to age in all areas of development and was neurologically normal. Referral would have been requested in this case.

Screening results agreed in all other cases considered within normal limits at CDC. Thus the *specificity* of screening results (*i.e.* the ability of the screening

TABLE 4.27

**Control group A, recommendations indicated by scrutiny of screening cards
and CDC duplicates**

	CDC assessment			
	No action:		Review	Refer	Total
	WNL	Minor			
Screening clinic					
No action, normal	73	6	—	6	85 ⎫
" minor	—	1	2	—	3 ⎭
Review	1	—	2	—	3
Refer	1	—	1	5	7
Total	75	7	5	11	98

WNL = within normal limits.

examination to identify correctly children without developmental delay or disorder)
was satisfactory at 97 per cent.

The *sensitivity* of screening examinations (*i.e.* the ability to identify correctly
those children found to have delay or disorder) was less satisfactory. CDC
assessment showed 15 children to have NDD, and one child to have neurological
abnormality of sufficient severity to merit review or referral. Only eight of these
16 children were recorded as being sufficiently suspect on screening for the
authors to have recommended review or referral. Thus one may say that
sensitivity of the tests was only 50 per cent. This disappointing result was
examined in more detail.

Review at next screening would have been recommended for two children
who were seen at CDC after the 20- and 39-week screenings respectively. Minor
deviations on screening had been recorded in both cases.

Six children had problems meriting referral. The circumstances were as
following:
(1) The three-year screening card was incomplete for one globally delayed girl
who, on assessment at CDC, was found to be performing little better than would
be expected of a two year old. The child had attended all previous screenings and
had been consistently slow. In making the decision whether or not to ask for
review or referral of children in the 1974/75 research group, the authors had the
benefit of information on all previous screening cards. Referral would have been
requested for this child after the 15-month screening examination. Thus she
cannot be said to have been missed on screening.
(2) Three girls were developmentally up to age but had (at 15 months, two and
three years respectively) moderately severe problems of behaviour other than those
specified on screening cards. The mother of the 16-month-old girl reported feeding
battles, refusal to sleep without mother with her and constant attention-seeking to
the extent that she (the mother) often felt like battering her. 'No problems' for
behaviour was recorded on the 15-month screening card. Another girl had
vomited from birth and by two years was able to induce vomiting whenever
frustrated, which was often. No mention of vomiting appeared on any screening

card although weight gain was noted to be poor at 15 months and at two years. Persistent pica was reported for the three-year-old girl: she was said to chew crayons, matches, paper, wood, armchair covers and other household articles. Presumably none of these problems had been reported to the screening doctors, possibly because of the limited time available.

(3) Two boys who appeared to have significant global delay at three years were passed as within normal limits at local screening. Both were particularly poor on adaptive tests although these items were said to have been passed at previous screening. Speech and locomotor function at screening had been assessed largely on mothers' histories and recorded as normal, although both boys were considered significantly delayed in these areas of development when examined at CDC. The failure to identify developmental delay was the more regrettable as this was their final screening examination. These two cases suggest inadequate training of screening personnel and failure to adhere to instructions in the manual, as well as undue reliance on mother's histories. It may be significant that three of the five children with unsuspected moderate or more severe problems (categories 2 and 3 of the above) had been screened by one doctor of limited experience.

None of the 10 children whom the authors suspected, on the basis of routine screening cards, of having NDD had been referred for diagnostic assessment or advice on management, although continued surveillance of children recognised to have problems may have been planned by some screening doctors. The effectiveness of any screening programme is totally dependent on the training and expertise of those who carry out the screening examinations and on appropriate actions being taken when problems are recognised. These points should be borne in mind when considering who should be responsible for screening in the future and the organisation of follow-up assessment and management facilities (pp. 274; 281; 282).

COMPARISON WITH OTHER STUDIES

Frequency of NDD in studies of total population

The frequency of NDD in the preschool Dundee population (14.3 per cent) is very similar to that reported in other published studies. In the National Child Development Study follow-up at seven years of age, 13.4 per cent of children were either attending special school (0.4 per cent), receiving remedial help in ordinary school (5 per cent), or were considered by their teachers to be in need of such help (8 per cent) (Kellmer Pringle et al. 1966). Webb (1967) found that 80 (16 per cent) of 500 five to seven year olds attending an infants' school in the south of England presented with behaviour and learning problems. In the Isle of Wight study, Rutter and colleages (1970) found 354 (16 per cent) of 2199 nine to eleven year olds to be handicapped in one or more of the four areas studied: intellectual, educational, psychiatric and physical. Exclusion of physically handicapped children suffering only from such non-neurodevelopmental conditions as asthma and diabetes reduces the handicap rate in this study to approximately 12 to 13 per cent. Chazan and colleagues (1980) found 1145 (16 per cent) of 7320 children aged between three years nine months and four years three months in two counties of England and Wales who were screened for handicap by health visitors, teachers and play-group leaders to have some developmental problem, rated mild in one-third.

A survey of the health and development of 922 four-year-old children was carried out in Adelaide preschools during 1976/77. 75 per cent of all children in this age group attended such schools (Johnston 1980). Schools were selected in equal numbers from suburbs rated low in socio-economic status and average to high. The sample comprised 52 per cent boys and 48 per cent girls. There were fewer fathers in professional classes (15 per cent) and fewer Australian born (60 per cent) than in the general population (18 per cent and 72 per cent respectively). Development was tested by nurses using an 11-item test derived from the Denver Developmental Screening Test (Frankenburg and Dodds 1967), Sheridan (1973), Sundelin and Vuille 1975 and DIAL (Developmental Indicators for Assessment of Learning, Mardell and Goldenberg 1975). The children were also assessed by teachers using DIAL alone. Of the total number of children assessed on the nurse inventory, 20 per cent appeared to have developmental delay of six months or more, double the percentage found to be delayed by the teachers using DIAL. Nearly one-half of children found to be delayed by teachers on DIAL were classified as having no delay on the nurse inventory. It was concluded that both the false negative and false positive rates in the nurse inventory were unacceptably high: 10 per cent of the total number of children were referred for full psychological assessment on the basis of DIAL results; 5 per cent were confirmed as being developmentally delayed; 5 per cent as having delay or disorder of speech and language and 4 per cent as having significant behaviour disorder (percentages refer to numbers of disabilities). The number of children with any disability is not given.

It is not known whether the majority of children having problems in the school studies quoted could have been identified before school entry. This must be one of the aims of any developmental screening programme. In the Dundee study we had the opportunity to demonstrate the relationship, if any, between preschool identification of NDD and problems in school, and to test the hypothesis that the 10 to 12 per cent of children with moderate or more severe problems identified in the preschool period would form a majority of children with later educational difficulties. Alternatively, adverse environmental factors, which are recognised to have a major influence on school progress, might not have the same effect on development and behaviour in the first three years of life, potential school failures remaining unidentified on developmental norms. It could be that high-risk indicators in early life other than developmental delay or behaviour disorder are more effective in predicting school failure. This is discussed in Chapter 13.

Frequency of NDD detected in other developmental screening programmes

A number of published reports give figures for developmental delays and more obvious disabilities detected on developmental screening. However, it is difficult to make comparisons between these studies or between other reported studies and the Dundee project for the following reasons:

(1) Definitions of what are considered to constitute developmental disabilites are seldom given and may differ between studies.

(2) The suspicion of delay raised on screening may be equated with definitive identification of disability, rather than being the first stage in a process requiring further diagnostic assessment, the importance of which is stressed by writers on the philosphy of screening (*e.g.* Egan *et al.* 1969, Frankenburg 1973, Holt 1977). In most of the reported studies, such diagnostic assessment occurred only for children suspected of having the more serious neurodevelopmental disorders such as mental retardation, cerebral palsy and visual or hearing loss. There is seldom any evidence that the suspicion of disability raised at screening has been confirmed, apart from those cases of children with suspected handicap and specified conditions (such as squint and congenital dislocation of the hip) who are referred to appropriate specialist services and children with speech disorders referred for speech therapy assessment.

(3) Few of the published studies attempt to ascertain the number of children in the given population who are identified as having NDD by means other than screening, *i.e.* those missed on screening and those to whom screening was irrelevant.

(4) Numbers of children found to have NDD are usually given by screening age and are not directly comparable with a population study.

Most reports come from family doctors screening children in their own or in group practices. Starte (1976) reported that of 815 children screened at seven months, 112 (14 per cent) had developmental abnormalities defined as being 'below the normal range of achievement at this age'. Nine children were referred for further assessment, of whom four had squints and defective vision. Of the total 112 delayed or deviant children, 67 (60 per cent) were found to be normal on review at nine months. At two years, 17 children (3.3 per cent) were still showing delay. Of 633 children screened at two years, 106 (17 per cent) showed abnormalities of development, of whom 14 were referred for assessment. By four and a half years, the development of 23 children (3.6 per cent) was still doubtful. It is not stated what proportion, if any, of the 815 children screened at seven months were among the 633 children screened at two years or if any of the doubtful or 'identified' children were counted more than once.

Bain (1974) details the total number of disorders suspected throughout the course of one year. Most children listed had only minor physical disorders and insufficient detail is given to estimate the number of children with NDD.

In the Woodside group practice (Barber 1982), 281 children were included in a screening programme from six weeks to four years. Only seven children were eligible for the final examination: one had a physical abnormality, one showed 'delayed' development and one had 'abnormal' development. Overall, 41 children (15 per cent) showed physical abnormality, 31 (11 per cent) were delayed and three (1 per cent) were described as abnormal. What action was taken about the disabilities detected is not stated, apart from suggestions made to mothers by most health visitors about ways in which the abilities of delayed children might be helped.

In a report on their practice screening programme, Curtis Jenkins and his child health colleagues (1978) detail the total number of suspected disorders found at each screening age over a period of two years. The study lists all the disorders found or suspected and the number of children referred for specialist opinion. It appears that Curtis Jenkins was more concerned to show the number of specialist referrals generated by a screening programme (with a view to advocating an increase in these services) than to ascertain the frequency of NDD, since he gives the number of disorders rather than the number of children with disorders and does not state whether or not disorder was confirmed. Assuming that no child was counted more than once and that disorder was confirmed in all children referred, the proportions of identified disorder following seven-month, one-year and two-and-a-half-year examinations are similar to the proportions of children found to have NDD at roughly equivalent screening ages in the Dundee programme. At the three-year examination, 21 per cent of those screened were referred for specialist opinion, mostly for suspected speech delay. This three-year examination was only for selected children, based on the results of the two-year examination or by request of parents, health visitor or other agency. In an earlier report on the programme (1977), Curtis Jenkins stated that, on this selective basis, 44 per cent of all possible three-year-old children were screened. Assuming this proportion to be correct for the later series, children referred for specialist opinion would constitute 9 per cent of all the three year olds. This is almost three times the proportion of children identified as having NDD after the three-year examination in Dundee (Table 4.6). A further 20 children (5 per cent of those screened) were referred for specialist opinion after the four-and-a-half-year screening. However, many of the disorders listed by Curtis Jenkins (*e.g.* squint, myopia, battered baby) are not included as separate categories of NDD in the Dundee study.

Table 4.28 shows the frequencies per 1000 of those clinical categories in the Dundee and Curtis Jenkins studies which are comparable and the social class distribution of the two populations. Assuming that the children from the Curtis Jenkins study are only included in one category and counted once, it appears that the frequency of speech disorders in the two populations is not dissimilar in view of the fact that there are disproportionately fewer children from social classes I and II and more from social classes IV and V in the Dundee population. The frequencies of motor disorders and cerebral palsy were twice as high in the Dundee group, behaviour disorders three times and global delay four times as high.

All these reports of development screening programmes come from family doctor practices and do not refer to total populations. In a review of 3000 children up to the age of four years seen in a one-year period of screening in Westminster, Paterson (1972) found that screening led to the identification of 54 children (2 per cent) with disabilities severe enough to warrant placement on a handicap register. No mention is made of children with less serious impairments.

In a preliminary report of an infant screening programme undertaken by health visitors, Morris and Hird (1981) describe screening examinations carried out for 2692 children (3483 examinations) over a period of two years. 16 children

TABLE 4.28

TABLE 4.28

Frequency of certain categories of NDD and social class distribution in Dundee
and Curtis Jenkins studies

	Dundee *(N = 5003)*	*Ashford (Curtis Jenkins)* *(N = 2157)**	
	per 1000		*per 1000*
Global delay	16	Developmental delay	4
Motor disorder	14	Motor delay/lack of fine motor co-ordination	6
Cerebral palsy	4	Cerebral palsy	2
Speech disorder	48	Speech/language delay	32
Behaviour disorder	24	Behaviour disturbance/depression	6
	%		*%*
Social class			
I and II	18		25
III	48		53
IV and V	29		18
NK	5		5

*Preschool children screened in a general practice (Ashford, Middlesex); NK = not known.

(1 per cent) were classified as abnormal, of whom four suffered from severe congenital handicaps and had been under surveillance since birth. The proportion of children considered doubtful at different screening ages was 5 per cent at eight weeks, 11 per cent at 10 months, 7 per cent at 15 months and 8 per cent at two years.

Of the 804 children in the Grampian feasibility study (Robinson 1982), 127 (16 per cent) were recorded as having a doubtful or abnormal finding after physical examination and 75 (9 per cent) after developmental examination. 6 per cent of children were referred for a specialist opinion as a result of screening.

Social class distribution

None of the reports quoted above give social class distribution of children with and without NDD. Such population studies as have been published are concerned with school age children.

In the Isle of Wight study (Rutter *et al.* 1970), social class distribution amongst the nine to eleven year olds with handicaps are discussed separately for those children with intellectual retardation, reading retardation, psychiatric disorder and physical handicap. There was a significant increase of children in social classes IV and V amongst those with intellectual retardation and a significant association between specific reading retardation and social class III (manual). Prevalence of psychiatric disorder was not related to social class, apart from a slight non-significant trend for fewer children with anti-social and mixed anti-social/neurotic disorders to come from social classes I, II and III (non-manual). Amongst physically handicapped children with cerebral palsy and other 'brain disorders', social class distribution was similar to that of the general population.

In the follow-up at seven years of the National Child Development Study (Kellmer Pringle *et al.* 1966), there was a significant association with social class with an excess of children in social classes III (manual), IV and V among the 13 per cent of children attending normal school who were receiving (or were considered to be in need of) special educational help.

Sex distribution

The larger number of male children with NDD in the Dundee study is consistent with the findings in most other studies. In the Isle of Wight study, the male:female ratio was 0.9:1 for children with intellectual handicap. However, in all other groups, boys were more frequently represented than girls as follows: reading backwardness, 2.0:1; specific reading retardation 3.3:1; psychiatric disorder 1.9:1; physical handicap 1.2:1.

Amongst seven year olds attending normal school in the National Child Development Study follow-up, twice as many boys as girls were considered by their teachers to be in need of special educational treatment. In the study of children with problems in an infant school (Webb 1967), boys outnumbered girls by 3:1.

In the preschool study of four year olds (Chazan *et al.* 1980), 20 categories of 'problems' are listed, in 17 of which boys were more commonly affected than girls. The most marked excess of boys was found in the categories relating to language, hand-eye co-ordination, self-help skills and restless, destructive and aggressive behaviour. Visual problems and dependent and withdrawn behaviour were more common among girls.

Summary

Frequency of NDD identified preschool

Twelve per cent of all children were identified as having NDD before school entrance and in 9 per cent NDD was moderate or more severe. The frequencies in those who remained in Dundee throughout the screening period were 14 and 12 per cent.

Distribution of NDD by clinical category, severity and age at identification

Major problems at initial assessment and discharge are listed and the frequency of different clinical categories identified in each year of life from birth to five years. Of all children included in the screening programme, 10 per cent were identified as having NDD following a screening examination, two-thirds following screening at two or three years. Children with more severe disabilities were identified at earlier ages. Circumstances of identification are discussed.

Distribution by social factors and sex

Children with fathers in social classes IV and V and those from poor working-class homes (social grade 4) were over-represented in all clinical categories except motor disorder and cerebral palsy, specific syndromes and speech disorders. It is suggested that speech disorder (and to a lesser extent behaviour disorder) is more likely to be considered acceptable in children from a low socio-economic background. It also appeared that children from these homes with minor or moderate NDD were less likely to be referred for assessment.

Two-thirds of children with identified NDD were male. Males predominated in the clinical categories of motor disorder, cerebral palsy, behaviour and speech disorder.

Children with NDD suspected but not identified or not confirmed
In addition to the 620 children with identified NDD, a further 203 children were suspected of having developmental or behavioural disorders on the basis of screening results. 70 other children were referred for assessment and found to be within normal limits.

NDD in a randomly selected control group
20 per cent of a control group were categorised as having NDD but in one-third of these the problems were considered to be mild or transitory.

REFERENCES

Bain, D. G. B. (1974) 'The results of developmental screening in general practice.' *Health Bulletin,* **32,** 189-193.
Barber, J. H. (1982) 'Pre-school developmental screening: the results of a 4-year period.' *Health Bulletin,* **40,** 170-178.
—— Boothman, R., Paget-Stanfield, J. (1976) 'A new visual chart for pre-school developmental screening.' *Health Bulletin,* **34,** 80-91.
Chazan, M., Laing, A. F., Bailey, M. S. Jones, G. (1980) *Some of our Children: The Early Education of Children with Special Needs.* London: Open Books.
Curtis Jenkins, G. H. C. (1977) 'Surveillance of pre-school children in general practice.' *In:* Drillien, C. M., Drummond, M. B. (Eds.) *Neurodevelopmental Problems in Early Childhood.* Oxford: Blackwell Scientific Publications.
—— Collins, C., Andren, S. (1978) 'Developmental surveillance in general practice.' *British Medical Journal,* **1,** 1537-1540.
Egan, D., Illingworth, R. S., MacKeith, R. C. (1969) *Developmental Screening 0-5 Years. Clinics in Developmental Medicine No. 30.* London: SIMP with Heinemann Medical; Philadelphia: Lippincott.
Frankenberg, W. K. (1973) 'Pediatric screening.' *Advances in Pediatrics,* **20,** 149-175.
—— Dodds, J. B. (1967) 'The Denver Developmental Screening Test.' *Journal of Pediatrics,* **71,** 181-191.
Holt, K. S. (1977) 'Some thoughts on developmental screening.' *Child: Care, Health and Development,* **3,** 275-282.
Johnstone, O. (1980) 'Ill health and developmental delays in Adelaide four-year-old children.' *Australian Paediatric Journal,* **16,** 248-254.
Kellmer Pringle, M. L., Butler, N. R., Davie, R. (1966) *11,000 Seven-Year-Olds.* London: Longman for the National Children's Bureau.
Mardell, C. D., Goldenberg, D.S. (1975) 'Pre-kindergarten screening information DIAL.' *Journal of Learning Disabilities,* **8,** 18-25.
Morris, J. B., Hird, M. D. (1981) 'A neurodevelopmental infant screening programme undertaken by health visitors.' *Health Bulletin,* **39,** 236-250.
Paterson, M. T. (1972) 'Developmental screening of pre-school children.' *Community Medicine,* **128,** 423-424.

Rutter, M., Tizard, J., Whitmore, K. (1970) *Education, Health and Behaviour.* London: Longman.

Robinson, H. G. (Chairman) (1982) *Pre-school health surveillance feasibility study report.* Aberdeen: Grampian Health Board.

Sheridan, M. D. (1973) *Children's Developmental Progress from Birth to 5 Years.* Windsor: National Foundation for Educational Research.

Starte, G. D. (1976) 'Results from a developmental screening clinic in general practice.' *Practitioner,* **216,** 311-316.

Sundelin, C., Vuille, J. C. L. (1975) 'Health screening of four-year-olds in a Swedish County: II. Effectiveness in detecting health problems.' *Acta Paediatrica Scandinavica,* **64,** 801-806.

Webb, L. (1967) *Children with Special Needs in the Infant's School.* London: Fontana.

CHAPTER 5

Perinatal Complications, Minor Neurological Abnormality and Multiple Minor Congenital Anomalies

PERINATAL COMPLICATIONS

The frequency and severity of perinatal complications were compared between children referred to the Child Development Centre (CDC) with moderate or severe neurodevelopmental disability (NDD) who remained in Dundee until after school age and their matched controls (group B).

The social class distribution, by father's occupation, of CDC-referred and control group B children was similar (p. 10). 26 CDC-referred children and 18 control children were born outside Dundee. Perinatal records were unobtainable for two CDC-referred children and four controls, leaving 324 CDC-referred and 322 control children for comparison.

Complications of pregnancy and delivery were graded by an additive scoring method: one point was allotted to complications of pregnancy and one point to complications of delivery.

Complications of the neonatal period were scored 1 to 3 and graded as:

Minor This category included such problems as a few minutes of initial resuscitation, jaundice responding quickly to phototherapy, and mild respiratory problems not requiring specific treatment (Scored 1).

Severe The infant's condition causing major anxiety over a period of one to two weeks or longer on account of combinations of apnoeic attacks, respiratory distress requiring specific therapy, severe metabolic disturbances, cardiac arrest and prolonged neurological abnormality (Scored 3).

Moderate Infants with postnatal complications not sufficiently severe to justify inclusion in previous category but more than minor in severity (Scored 2).

The children were also divided by birthweight and intra-uterine growth. Those considered small for date (SFD) were at or below the 5th centile of birthweight by gestation for Aberdeen births (Thomson *et al.* 1968).

At a later date, pregnancy and delivery records will be subjected to more detailed scrutiny by obstetric colleagues.

Table 5.1 details for CDC-referred and control group B children perinatal complications, numbers of low birthweight (LBW) and SFD infants and the number who had no complications, were of birthweight >2500g and of normal weight for gestational age.

Using the scoring method CDC-referred children appeared to have had rather more complications than had control children, but the difference in distribution was not statistically significant. However, there were highly significant differences in the proportions of children who had been LBW/SFD ($\chi^2 = 23.445$, p = <0.001).

TABLE 5.1

CDC-referred and matched control group B children. Complication score, low birthweight and retarded intra-uterine growth

	CDC		Control group B	
	No.	%	No.	%
Complication score				
0	118	36	127	40
1	102	31	99	31
2	70	22	72	22
3	19	6	14	4
≥4	15	5	10	3
Total	324	100	322	100
Birthweight (g)/ intra-uterine growth				
≤2000	13 }	6	4 }	2
≤2000 SFD	7 }		2 }	
2001-2500	20 }	12	6 }	4
2001-2500 SFD	20 }		8 }	
>2500 SFD	13	4	8	2
All LBW/SFD	73	23	28	9
BW/IUG normal	251	77	294	91
No complications	101	31	143	44

SFD = small for date; LBW = low birthweight; BW = birthweight; IUG = intra-uterine growth.

18 per cent of CDC-referred children weighed ≤2500g at birth and 4 per cent were above that birthweight but at or below the 5th centile of birthweight for gestational age. 6 per cent of control children were LBW (which is close to what would be expected in the general population of Dundee births) and an additional 2 per cent were SFD.

The proportions of infants in the two groups who were without any complications, and were of birthweight >2500g and of normal weight for gestational age is also statistically significant: 31 per cent of CDC-referred children and 44 per cent of controls ($\chi^2 = 12.043$, p = <0.001).

Table 5.2 gives the breakdown of complications by type and indicates that the differences in complication scores are largely accounted for by neonatal complications. There was no significant difference between the groups in frequency of pregnancy and delivery complications but there was a highly significant difference in distribution of neonatal complications scored as 0,1,2 and 3 ($\chi^2 = 24.516$, 2df, p = <0.001). This is not entirely due to the excess of LBW/SFD infants among the CDC-referred children as neonatal complications were more common among CDC-referred children of normal birthweight and in those LBW/SFD. This is discussed below (p. 105).

Although there were no significant differences in the frequency of pregnancy and delivery complications between CDC-referred and control children, within the CDC-referred group taken as a whole there was a significant association of

TABLE 5.2

CDC-referred children and matched control group B children.
Complications of pregnancy, delivery and the neonatal period

	CDC		Control group B	
	No.	%	No.	%
Complications				
None	149	46	168	52
Pregnancy	53	16	44	14
Delivery	73	23	63	20
Both	49	15	47	15
Total	324	100	322	100
Neonatal period				
0	231	71	277	86
1	56	17	35	11
2	28	9	9	3
3	9	3	1	<1
Total	324	100	322	100

TABLE 5.3

CDC-referred children (N = 386), neonatal complications by complications of pregnancy and delivery

	Complications									
	Nil		Pregnancy		Delivery		Both		Total	
	No.	%	No.	%	No.	%	No.	%	No.	%
Neonatal period										
0	149	83	55	76	51	63	35	65	290	75
1	18	10	13	18	18	22	8	15	57	15
2	8	4	2	3	11	14	8	15	29	7
3	4	2	2	3	1	1	3	5	10	3
Total	179	100	72	100	81	100	54	100	386	100

neonatal complications with complications of delivery (but not with complications of pregnancy). This is detailed in Table 5.3. There was no difference in the distribution of neonatal scores between those with no complications of pregnancy or delivery and those with complications of pregnancy only ($\chi^2 = 3.065$, 2df, p = >0.30), but there were significant differences between those with no complications and those with complications of delivery only ($\chi^2 = 12.915$, 2df, p = <0.01) and also with those having complications of both pregnancy and delivery ($\chi^2 = 10.480$, 2df, p = <0.02).

Although major handicapping conditions such as mental retardation and cerebral palsy were seldom attributed primarily to low birthweight, retarded intra-uterine growth or neonatal complications (pp. 203; 208), the marked excess of these circumstances among all CDC-referred children with moderate or more severe NDD, as compared with a matched control group, suggests that these adverse perinatal factors may be important in rendering a child more vulnerable to other adverse postnatal influence.

MINOR NEUROLOGICAL ABNORMALITY

All children referred to CDC with NDD were examined carefully for evidence of minor neurological abnormality, as were control group A children.

Different categories of minor neurological abnormality

An attempt was made to divide the combinations and permutations of minor abnormal neurological signs detected among CDC-referred children into broad groupings. This is detailed in Table 5.4. All children could be included in one of five groups, and their neurological status categorised as normal, doubtful or abnormal.

Dystonia

This was by far the most common early abnormal neurological presentation, being presented by 74 (67 per cent) of the 110 CDC-referred children examined in the first year of life. It was seldom seen in the second year of life and never after the age of 18 months. The dystonic infant shows variable increase in extensor tone on changes of posture, exaggeration and prolongation of primitive reflexes, brisk tendon jerks and often marked irritability. Dystonic posturing of legs and arms is well seen with the infant held in vertical suspension when legs are held extended and adducted with plantar flexion of ankles and arms extended, abducted and internally rotated or flexed across the chest. In both postures, hands are usually fisted and frequently thumbs are held across the palms. Extension of first toes is often seen when the infant is lowered to the floor and there is a strong extensor thrust when the infant's feet touch the floor. He may also begin to walk forward on toes because of a retained walking reflex and at later ages, when walking reflexes have disappeared, may still be up on toes. The presentation may be less obvious than described and the abnormal neurological signs vary in number and severity.

The majority of children with dystonic signs were categorised as neurologically abnormal; a few who presented with a small number of the signs described were categorised as doubtful. Of the 80 infants with dystonic signs, eight (10 per cent) were discharged from CDC before the age of 18 months and their later neurological status was not known, in 27 cases (34 per cent) the dystonia resolved and the children appeared neurologically normal between 18 months and three years, and in 45 cases (56 per cent), the dystonia resolved but the children developed other abnormal or doubtful neurological signs.

Hypotonia

Mild hypotonia was disregarded. Moderate hypotonia without other abnormal signs was considered of doubtful significance. Hypotonia with increased tendon jerks and/or hand tremor was considered abnormal (these children were often

TABLE 5.4

CDC-referred children, patterns of minor neurological abnormality by clinical category (N = 370)

Minor neurological abnormality	Global delay					Mental retardation					Motor disorder					Speech disorder					Behaviour disorder					Total
	Abnormal <1 yr	Abnormal >1 yr	Doubtful ≤1 yr	Doubtful >1 yr	All	Abnormal <1 yr	Abnormal >1 yr	Doubtful ≤1 yr	Doubtful >1 yr	All	Abnormal <1 yr	Abnormal >1 yr	Doubtful ≤1 yr	Doubtful >1 yr	All	Abnormal <1 yr	Abnormal >1 yr	Doubtful ≤1 yr	Doubtful >1 yr	All	Abnormal <1 yr	Abnormal >1 yr	Doubtful ≤1 yr	Doubtful >1 yr	All	
Dystonia	9	1	—	—	10	—	3	—	—	3	6	1	—	—	7	7	—	—	—	7	11	—	—	—	11	35
→HJ ± CT	1	—	—	—	1	—	—	—	—	—	7	1	—	—	8	3	—	—	—	3	1	—	—	—	1	15
→H + C and/or T	1	—	—	—	1	6	—	—	—	6	10	3	—	—	13	2	—	—	—	2	4	—	—	—	4	26
→Other	—	—	—	—	—	1	—	—	—	1	1	—	—	—	1	1	—	—	—	1	1	—	—	—	1	4
Hypotonia	2	1	—	—	3	1	—	—	—	1	1	—	1	—	1	8	1	—	—	9	4	—	—	—	4	17
+ J ± C and/or T	2	—	2	—	7	1	1	—	—	3	5	5	—	—	6	6	1	—	—	6	2	2	—	—	4	24
+ C, T, or other	1	5	—	—	7	1	1	2	2	3	2	2	4	2	12	2	1	1	2	5	2	2	—	—	6	33
Clumsiness	—	4	—	—	4	—	—	2	2	2	—	—	—	—	—	12	1	—	—	15	4	1	—	—	5	26
+ T	—	—	—	—	—	2	—	—	—	2	3	3	—	—	3	—	—	1	2	2	—	1	—	—	1	6
+ Other	2	2	—	—	2	—	—	—	—	—	1	1	—	—	2	2	2	—	—	2	—	—	—	—	2	6
Increased jerks/tone	—	—	2	—	3	—	—	2	—	2	—	—	—	—	—	1	1	—	1	—	2	2	—	—	2	5
+ C, T, or other	—	—	—	2	2	2	—	2	—	—	—	—	—	—	—	1	1	—	—	1	—	—	—	—	—	3
Other	1	2	—	—	3	1	—	—	1	1	—	—	—	1	1	4	—	—	4	5	—	2	2	2	2	12
Total	14	10	3	14	41	10	6	6	6	22	30	16	6	2	54	16	8	2	30	56	18	7	1	13	39	212
Neuro. normal	4	30	—	—	34	1	6	—	—	6	1	4	—	—	5	4	64	—	—	68	—	44	—	—	44	158

H = hypotonia; J = increased tendon jerks; C = clumsy gait and/or hand function; T = hand tremor; NK = not known; NA = not applicable.

94

clumsy), but hypotonia with clumsy gait and/or hand function only was considered of doubtful significance. One-half of dystonic infants went on to present with combinations of hypotonia, increased tendon jerks, clumsiness and hand tremor. Thus it is possible that some children, seen after the age of 18 months with hypotonia and clumsiness, might have been categorised as neurologically abnormal had they been examined at younger ages.

Clumsiness

Children who were definitely clumsy in gait and/or hand function after the age of two years were categorised as neurologically doubtful unless the clumsiness was associated with more than a mild hand tremor in which case they were categorised as abnormal.

Increased tendon jerks ± increased tone

After the age of two years this finding was often associated with clumsiness, hand tremor or other minor abnormal signs. The child was categorised as abnormal or doubtful on the basis of the total presentation.

Other

This was a miscellaneous group of minor abnormal signs, usually categorised as of doubtful significance, comprising such signs as asymmetries, exaggeration and prolongation of primitive reflexes without dystonic signs, dystonic posturing of arms only, chewing difficulties often associated with sluggish tongue movements and absent gag reflex, crossed adductor responses, extensor plantar responses after the age of two years, brisk tendon jerks with tone unexceptional and spreading fingers on reach.

This classification of minor abnormal neurological signs seen among CDC-referred children was based on several examinations carried out over a period of months or years. Because control group A children were examined on one occasion only (p. 7), it was not possible to fit the abnormal neurological presentations seen into this classification.

Distribution of minor neurological abnormality

Table 5.5 details the neurological status of control group A children with and without NDD and of CDC-referred children (N = 414), after excluding from the latter group: 18 children with cerebral palsy; four with minor abnormal neurological signs only; 15 with specific conditions and hearing loss; four with severe mental retardation and abnormal neurological signs resulting from postnatal infection or injury and (in one case) from an associated specific condition, and three children who were not adequately examined on their first attendance (because of lack of co-operation) and did not re-attend subsequently. Of the remaining 370 children, 43 per cent were considered to be neurologically normal throughout their attendance at CDC, and at the hospital infant clinic if they had been supervised there, 36 per cent to show definite neurological abnormality and 21 per cent to show abnormality of doubtful significance. The distribution of neurological abnormality detected among

TABLE 5.5

TABLE 5.5

Neurological status of CDC-referred children (N = 370) and of control group A children

	Normal		Neurological status Doubtful		Abnormal		Total
	No.	%	No.	%	No.	%	No.
CDC-referred children, clinical category*							
Global delay	34	45	17	23	24	32	75
Mental retardation	7	24	6	21	16	55	29
Motor disorder	5	8	8	14	46	78	59
Speech disorder	68	55	32	26	24	19	124
Behaviour disorder	44	53	14	17	25	30	83
Total	158	43	77	21	135	36	370
Control group A, WNL	77	75	18	18	7	7	102
Control group A, with NDD	10	38	7	27	9	35	26
Total	87	68	25	20	16	12	128

*Final diagnosis; WNL = within normal limits.

control children with NDD was very similar. In contrast there was a highly significant excess of neurological abnormality among all children with NDD as compared with control children who were considered developmentally and behaviourally within normal limits. The difference in distribution between CDC-referred children and normal control children was significant at a p value of <0.001 (χ^2 = 41, 2df). The difference in distribution between control children with and without NDD was also significant at the same level (χ^2 = 33, 2df).

It was immediately obvious that children examined in the first year of life were much more likely to exhibit definite abnormal neurological signs than were those examined for the first time at later ages, for which reason children were divided into those who were first examined at 12 months or younger and those who were examined after their first birthday. Some children who were referred to CDC in the second or subsequent years of life had been examined by the authors in the hospital infant clinic. Overall, 82 CDC-referred children (20 per cent) were examined in the first year of life in that clinic. 31 of these with NDD were referred directly to CDC for further supervision; for the remaining 51 cases no developmental or behavioural problem was evident at the time of their discharge from the infant clinic but problems developed later. A few children had been examined by other paediatricians during the first year of life and reported by them as being neurologically abnormal. All these children are included as examined in the first year of life even if their referral to (and examination at) CDC was at an older age.

Table 5.6 shows the neurological status of these 370 CDC-referred children and of control group A children with and without NDD by age of first examination. Of CDC-referred children examined in the first year of life, 9 per cent were neurologically normal and 80 per cent abnormal, compared with 57 per cent normal and 18 per cent abnormal of those examined for the first time after that age. Of six control children with NDD examined in the first year, five were neurologically abnormal compared with four of 20 children examined later. No developmentally

TABLE 5.6
Minor abnormal neurological signs among CDC-referred children (N = 370) and control group A children

	CDC referrals		WNL		Control group A NDD		All	
	No.	%	No.	%	No.	%	No.	%
Neurological status								
Examined 1st year								
Normal	10	9	28	61	—	—	28	54
Doubtful	12	11	11	24	1	17	12	23
Abnormal	88	80	7	15	5	83	12	23
Total	110	100	46	100	6	100	52	100
Examined later								
Normal	148	57	49	75	10	50	59	78
Doubtful	65	25	7	25	6	30	13	17
Abnormal	47	18	—	—	4	20	4	5
Total	260	100	56	100	20	100	76	100

WNL = within normal limits.

normal control child examined after one year was considered neurologically abnormal although seven (15 per cent) of those examined earlier did show definite abnormality in the absence of any developmental or behavioural problem at that time. This does not exclude the possibility of NDD presenting later.

Minor neurological abnormality and complications of pregnancy, delivery and the neonatal period

The perinatal status of control group A children was compared with that of 368 of these 370 CDC-referred children for whom perinatal information was available. Perinatal complications were graded by the scoring method described earlier (p. 90).

Table 5.7 details the complications of pregnancy, delivery and the neonatal period and the numbers of LBW and SFD infants for CDC-referred children in different clinical categories considered to be neurologically normal, doubtful or abnormal. The distribution of complications score (from 0 to ≥ 3) was compared between children with NDD who were neurologically normal or abnormal. There was a significant excess of complications reported for the neurologically abnormal children ($\chi^2 = 12.181$, 3df, p = <0.01). Similarly there was a significant excess of LBW and/or SFD infants in the group with definite neurological abnormalities ($\chi^2 = 7.376$, p = <0.01).

Complications were also more common among control group A children who were neurologically abnormal or doubtfully so as compared with those who were neurologically normal. This is shown in Table 5.8. However, the difference in distribution was not statistically significant ($\chi^2 = 6.954$, 3df, p = >0.05).

Table 5.9 gives a breakdown of complications by type for CDC-referred children who were neurologically normal, doubtful or abnormal. Neurologically normal

TABLE 5.7

CDC-referred children (N = 368), neurological status by complication score, low birthweight and retarded intra-uterine growth

	Neurological status — Normal						Neurological status — Doubtful						Neurological status — Abnormal					
	Global delay/MR	Motor disorder	Speech disorder	Behaviour disorder	Total No.	Total %	Global delay/MR	Motor disorder	Speech disorder	Behaviour disorder	Total No.	Total %	Global delay/MR	Motor disorder	Speech disorder	Behaviour disorder	Total No.	Total %
Complication score																		
0	16	3	37	16	72	46	8	3	13	3	27	36	12	18	11	6	47	35
1	16	2	16	18	52	33	9	4	11	5	29	38	13	10	5	7	35	26
2	6	—	10	6	22	14	4	1	7	5	17	22	9	8	6	8	31	23
3	1	—	3	3	7	} 7	1	—	1	1	3	} 4	5	7	1	2	15	} 16
≥4	2	—	2	—	4		—	—	—	—	—		1	3	1	2	7	
Total	41	5	68	43	157	100	22	8	32	14	76	100	40	46	24	25	135	100
Birthweight (g)//intra-uterine growth																		
≤2000	1	—	—	1	1		3	—	—	—	3		4	—	2	1	7	
<2000 SFD	1	1	1	1	2		—	—	—	3	—		4	2	—	—	6	
2001–2500	3	1	2	—	6		2	1	3	3	9		3	5	1	—	9	
2001–2500 SFD	5	—	2	2	9		—	—	—	—	—		4	1	3	1	9	
>2500 SFD	1	1	1	—	3		—	1	1	2	4		3	1	—	—	4	
All LBW/SFD	11	1	5	4	21	13	5	2	4	5	16	21	18	9	6	2	35	26
BW/IUG normal	30	4	63	39	136	87	17	6	28	9	60	79	22	37	18	23	100	74

SFD = small for date; LBW = low birthweight; IUG = intra-uterine growth; BW = birthweight; MR = mental retardation.

TABLE 5.8

Control group A. Neurological status by complication score, low birthweight and intra-uterine growth

	Normal		Doubtful		Abnormal	
	No.	*%*	*No.*	*%*	*No.*	*%*
Complication score						
0	31	36	7	28	5	31
1	35	40	11	44	8	50
2	19	22	4	16	1	6
3	1 }	2	3 }	12	2 }	13
≥4	1		—		—	
Total	87	100	25	100	16	100
Birthweight(g)/intra-uterine growth						
≤2000	—	—	—	—	—	—
<2000 SFD	—	—	2	—	—	—
2001-2500	—	—	—	—	—	—
2001-2500 SFD	—	—	2	—	—	—
>2500 SFD	1	—	1	—	—	—
All LBW/SFD	1	1	5	20	—	—
BW/IUG normal	86	99	20	80	16	100

LBW = low birthweight; SFD = small for date; BW = birthweight; IUG = intra-uterine growth.

children had rather fewer complications of pregnancy and delivery than had those who were doubtful or abnormal. However, the difference in distribution of complications (none, pregnancy or delivery, both) between neurologically normal children and the rest is not statistically significant (χ^2 = 4.617, 2df, p = 0.10). Neonatal complications were similar in number and severity for the neurologically normal and doubtful children but significantly increased among neurologically abnormal children (χ^2 = 17.548, 2df, p = <0.001). This analysis indicates that neonatal complications, rather than complications of pregnancy and delivery, are significantly associated with later minor neurological abnormality. The more detailed scrutiny of pregnancy and delivery factors proposed may reveal a relationship not evident with the rather crude scoring for pregnancy and delivery complications used here.

The relationship of perinatal factors to school problems and to motor dysfunction at six and a half to seven and a half years is discussed later (p. 235).

Neurological status and sex

The neurological status of CDC-referred children differed for boys and girls (Table 5.10). The proportions of boys and girls who were neurologically normal were very similar (43 per cent boys, 42 per cent girls). However, there was an excess of boys amongst those with neurological signs of doubtful significance and an excess of girls amongst those who had definite abnormal neurological signs. The difference in distribution was statistically significant (χ^2 = 8.230, 2df, p = <0.02). This could be explained by the hypothesis that a more serious insult is needed to produce an

99

TABLE 5.9

CDC-referred children (N = 368), neurological status by complications of pregnancy, delivery and the neonatal period

	Normal		Doubtful		Abnormal		Total	
	No.	%	No.	%	No.	%	No.	%
Complications								
None	84	54	30	39	60	45	174	47
Pregnancy	25	16	18	24	23	17	66	18
Delivery	30	19	16	21	30	22	76	21
Both	18	11	12	16	22	16	52	14
Total	157	100	76	100	135	100	368	100
Neonatal period								
0	126	80	64	84	87	64	277	75
1	23	15	8	11	25	19	56	15
2	6	4	3	4	19	14	28	8
3	2	1	1	1	4	3	7	2
Total	157	100	76	100	135	100	368	100

TABLE 5.10

CDC-referred children (N = 370), neurological status by sex

	Normal		Doubtful		Abnormal		Total	
	No.	%	No.	%	No.	%	No.	%
Male	100	43	58	25	75	32	233	100
Female	58	42	19	14	60	44	137	100

TABLE 5.11

CDC-referred children (N = 370), neurological status by severity of clinical condition

	Normal (N = 158)	Doubtful (N = 77)	Abnormal (N = 135)	Total (N = 370)
	%	%	%	No.
Overall severity grading				
Minor	61	17	22	54
Moderate	45	23	32	194
Moderately severe	33	19	48	89
Severe	27	18	55	33

100

TABLE 5.12
CDC-referred children (N = 370), neurological status by social grade

| | Neurological status | | | |
	Normal (N = 158)	Doubtful (N = 77)	Abnormal (N = 135)	Total (N = 370)
	%	%	%	No.
Social grade				
1 and 2	34	19	47	76
3	46	21	33	183
4	43	23	34	111

overt disability meriting referral in girls than in boys. The examination of a total population at school age indicated that boys were more likely to be reported as 'clumsy' than were girls (p. 229).

Neurological status by severity of the clinical condition and social grade

CDC-referred children with more severe degrees of NDD were more likely to be neurologically abnormal than those whose NDD was considered of minor or moderate severity. This is shown in Table 5.11. The difference in distribution of neurological status by severity of clinical condition was highly significant (χ^2 = 18.027, 3df, p = <0.001).

Although children from less favourable environments were more likely to suffer from more severe disabilities (p. 70), neurological abnormality among CDC-referred children was not affected by the social grade of the home (Table 5.12). The neurological status was very similar for children coming from social grade 3 and 4 homes. There was an excess of abnormality among children coming from social grade 1 and 2 homes. The difference in distribution was not statistically significant (χ^2 = 5.220, 2df, p = >0.05), but there was a significant excess of definite neurological abnormality among children with NDD from social grade 1 and 2 homes (χ^2 = 5.150, p = <0.05). Again it could be that a more serious innate insult is needed to produce an overt disability among children reared in the best homes. Certainly the excess of NDD among children from poor homes was not associated with an increase in neurological dysfunction among these children.

MULTIPLE MINOR CONGENITAL ANOMALIES

All children with NDD referred to CDC and control group A children were carefully examined for the presence of minor congenital anomalies. Note was taken of the minor anomalies detailed by Drummond (1977) (Appendix V). Epicanthic folds, pigmented or vascular naevi and partial syndactyly of toes, all very common among young children, were not counted as anomalies. The presence of one or two of the other anomalies listed was accepted as normal, but note was taken of children showing multiple anomalies (three to five, and six or more).

TABLE 5.13

Minor congenital anomalies detected among CDC-referred and control group A children

	CDC	Control group A		CDC	Control group A
	No.	No.		No.	No.
Skull			**Face and jaws**		
big head (OFC >90th centile			asymmetric face/jaws	6	—
not hydrocephalic)	27	5	malocclusion	9	—
brachycephaly	14	1	hypomandibulosis	9	1
plagiocephaly (marked)	3	—			
			Neck		
Hair			thyroglossal cyst	2	—
fine electric	11	3	short neck/webbing	2	—
sparse	6	2			
low hairline	6	2	**Spine**		
			midline anomalies	10	—
Ears					
low set	18	8	**Chest**		
slanting	2	1	pectus excavatum	1	2
simple	11	6	shield shaped	1	—
lack of lobule	2	1	pigeon	5	—
prominent ('bat')	7	2			
dissimilar	6	—	**Hands**		
pre-auricular tags/sinuses	1	—	abnormal palmar creases	38	21
narrow external canals	2	—	incurving fifth fingers	9	3
			ulnar deviation fingers	2	—
Eyes and eyebrows			broad palms, short stubby		
wide-set eyes	77	32	fingers	5	2
slanting palpebral fissures	3	1	proximally placed thumbs	4	3
Brushfield spots	4	1	hypoplasia of nails	1	—
heterochromia	2	1			
small and/or deepset	10	2	**Feet**		
bushy eyebrows	4	4	wide separation first and		
			second toes	20	5
Nose			long (often broad) first toe	49	21
snub	4	—	misplaced toes	14	5
broad root	3	1	lateral deviation toes	2	—
beaked	1	—			
anteverted nares	4	1	**Hands and feet**		
			small podgy hands/feet	9	2
Mouth and lips			long/thin fingers/toes	8	2
long upper lip	5	1			
macro/microstoma	9	1	**Skin**		
triangular (fish shaped)	7	—	skin dimpled/creased	11	2
			(over/around joints)		
Teeth			other unusual creases	3	1
enamel dysplasia	7	1	unusual fat distribution	7	1
abnormal shape or spacing	12	—	hirsuitism	5	1
Tongue			**External genitalia**		
macroglossia	1	—	minor hypospadias	3	1
			hypoplasia of scrotum		
Palate			and/or penis	11	3
high-arched	21	1	small soft testes	10	—
bifid uvula	5	—	undescended testes	10	—

OFC = Occipitofrontal circumference.

TABLE 5.14

Minor congential anomalies among CDC-referred children (N = 401) and in control group A

	Minor congenital anomalies						Total
	≤2		3-5		≥6		
	No.	%	No.	%	No.	%	No.
Clinical category:							
Global delay	54	71	15	20	7	9	76
Mental retardation, mild	14 }	48	6 }	18	7 }	34	27
Mental retardation, severe	2 }		— }		4 }		6
Motor disorder	41	69	15	26	3	5	59
Cerebral palsy, not MR	7 }	35	6 }	39	— }	6	13
Cerebral palsy with MR	3 }		1 }		1 }		5
Minor neuro. abnorm. only	4	100	—	—	—	—	4
Speech disorder	106	86	15	12	3	2	124
Behaviour disorder	69	83	11	13	3	4	83
Hearing loss	3	75	1	25	—	—	4
Total	303	76	70	17	28	7	401
Control group A, WNL	89	87	13	13	—	—	102
with NDD	13	50	10	38	3	12	26

MR = Mental retardation; WNL = within normal limits.

Two CDC-referred children were not adequately examined and were thus excluded from this analysis, as were the 11 children suffering from specific conditions. This left a total of 401 CDC-referred children. Frequency of multiple minor congenital anomalies was not affected by social grade of children's homes.

Table 5.13 details the numbers of minor congenital anomalies detected among CDC-referred and control group A children. Table 5.14 shows the distribution of anomalies among CDC-referred children by clinical category and among control group A children with and without NDD.

There was a significant excess of three or more anomalies among CDC-referred children as compared with control children who were within normal limits in behaviour and development (χ^2 = 6.457, p = <0.02). Similarly, control children with NDD were four times as likely to have three or more anomalies as normal control children, the proportions being 50 per cent of control children with NDD and 13 per cent of those without. This difference is also highly significant statistically (χ^2 = 21.028, p = <0.001). Control children with NDD had a significantly higher incidence of anomaly than had CDC-referred children (χ^2 = 9.832, p = <0.01). This is not easy to explain. It is possible that examiners became more alert to the detection of minor congenital anomalies as the study progressed: control children were examined between August 1977 and November 1979 when the study was well advanced.

Multiple minor congenital anomalies and severity of clinical condition

Multiple anomalies were more common among children with more severe NDD. This is shown in Table 5.15. The difference in distribution by severity between those

TABLE 5.15

CDC-referred children (N = 401), multiple congenital anomalies by severity of clinical condition

	Minor congenital anomalies						Total
	≤2		3-5		≥6		
	No.	%	No.	%	No.	%	No.
Overall severity grading							
Minor	47	89	5	9	1	2	53
Moderate	162	82	28	14	7	4	197
Moderately severe	71	66	29	27	7	7	107
Severe	20 }	52	6 }	18	9 }	30	35
Very severe	3 }		2 }		4 }		9
Total	303	76	70	17	28	7	401

TABLE 5.16

Neurological status of CDC-referred and control group A children with and without multiple minor congenital anomalies

	Neurological status						Total	
	Normal		Doubtful		Abnormal			
	No.	%	No.	%	No.	%	No.	%
CDC-referred children, MCA								
≤2	138	88	61	79	83	61	282	76
3-5	15	9	13	17	35	26	63	17
≥6	5	3	3	4	17	13	25	7
Total	158	100	77	100	135	100	370	100
Control group A, MCA								
≤2	75	86	17	68	10	62	102	80
3-5	11	13	8	32	4	25	23	18
≥6	1	1	—	—	2	13	3	2
Total	87	100	25	100	16	100	128	100

MCA = Minor congenital anomalies.

who exhibited up to two, and three or more anomalies was highly significant ($\chi^2 = 27.074$, 3df, p = <0.001).

Multiple minor congenital anomalies and neurological status

Table 5.16 details the neurological status of CDC-referred and control children with up to two, three to five, and six or more anomalies. CDC-referred children with cerebral palsy, deafness and postnatal brain damage were excluded from this analysis leaving a total of 370 children.

Among CDC-referred children there was a highly significant increase in anomaly score among children who were neurologically abnormal. The difference in distribution as compared with the neurologically normal children was significant at

TABLE 5.17

CDC-referred children with and without multiple minor congenital anomalies, by birthweight and intra-uterine growth distribution

	CDC-referred children, MCA score					
	≤2 (N = 302)		(3-5) (N = 70)		≥6 (N = 28)	
	No.	%	No.	%	No.	%
Birthweight (g)/intra-uterine growth						
≤2000	7	2	3	4	3	11
<2000 SFD	4	1	2	3	2	7
2001-2500	17	6	7	10	2	7
2001-2500 SFD	16	5	5	7	3	11
All LBW	44	15	17	24	10	36
>2500 SFD	10	3	1	1	3	11
All LBW/SFD	54	18	18	26	13	46

MCA = Minor congenital anomalies.

a p value of <0.001 (χ^2 = 29.141, 2df). In the control group, significantly more of the neurologically abnormal children had three or more anomalies than did those who were neurologically normal (χ^2 = 5.268, p = <0.05).

Multiple minor congenital anomalies and complications of pregnancy, delivery and the neonatal period

Table 5.17 gives the distribution by birthweight and intra-uterine growth of CDC-referred children with up to two, three to five and six or more anomalies. Obstetric history was not known for one child adequately examined for anomalies, leaving 400 CDC-referred children for this analysis. Of children with fewer than three anomalies, 15 per cent were of low birthweight. This compares with 28 per cent of those with three or more anomalies. This difference is statistically significant (χ^2 = 8.541, p = <0.01). More infants with three or more anomalies were small for date (16 per cent) than were those with up to two anomalies (10 per cent), but this difference is not statistically significant. Only six of the 128 control group A children had been LBW/SFD and no conclusions can be drawn about multiple anomalies in this small number.

Comparison with control group B

The perinatal histories of matched control group B children (p. 10) were compared with those of CDC-referred children with moderate or more severe NDD who did or did not have three or more minor congenital anomalies. The frequency of complications of pregnancy and delivery were little different in the three groups, but neonatal complications were more common among CDC-referred children, especially those with multiple anomalies. This applied to both LBW/SFD children and to those of normal birthweight and intra-uterine growth (Table 5.18). Among children of normal birthweight, the distribution by neonatal scores is significantly different for control children and CDC-referred children without multiple anomalies (χ^2 = 11.656, 2df, p = <0.01) and significantly higher for those with multiple

TABLE 5.18

Neonatal complications among CDC-referred and control group B who were not or were low birthweight/small for date

	MCA ⩾3		MCA ⩽2		All		Control group B	
	No.	%	No.	%	No.	%	No.	%
Neonatal score								
Normal birthweight/intra-uterine growth								
0	48	74	147	79	195	78	259	88
1	9	14	24	13	33	13	29	10
2	5	8	14	1	19	8	6	2
3	3	4	1	1	4	1	—	—
All	65	100	186	100	251	100	294	100
LBW/SFD								
0	10	37	26	57	36	49	18	64
1	12	44	11	24	23	32	6	21
2	4	15	5	11	9	12	3	11
3	1	4	4	8	5	7	1	4
All	27	100	46	100	73	100	28	100

MCA = Minor congenital anomalies; LBW = low birthweight; SFD = small for date.

anomalies. Differences in distribution were of the same order for LBW/SFD infants, but as the numbers involved were small, were not statistically significant.

Thus it appears that children who have suffered from early intra-uterine insult are more likely to be of low birthweight and, whatever the birthweight, are more likely to present with problems in the immediate postnatal period. In situations where an infant, subsequently found to have a handicapping condition, has a history of severe neonatal complications but also has evidence of early intra-uterine insult, it may be difficult to decide to what extent the neonatal complications caused the handicap or whether both complications and subsequent handicap were primarily due to pre-existing developmental abnormality. A case presenting this dilemma is described in Chapter 7 (p. 131). Postnatal growth of children with multiple minor congenital anomalies is discussed in Chapter 11 (pp. 204; 207).

COMPARISON WITH OTHER STUDIES

A number of authors have reported finding minor neurological abnormality among low-birthweight infants in the early years of life (*e.g.* Drillien 1972, Calâme *et al.* 1976) and among high-risk infants born at term (Amiel-Tison 1973, 1976). In one study (Drillien *et al.* 1980), low-birthweight children who exhibited transient abnormal neurological signs in the first year showed a highly significant excess of educational and behavioural impairments in school at six years eight months as compared with children of similar birthweight who had been neurologically normal in the first year of life.

Children included in the Collaborative Study on Cerebral Palsy, Mental Retardation and other Neurological and Sensory Disorders (United States: Department of Health, Education and Welfare 1966) all received three neurological examinations, administered by neurologists or paediatricians, in the first 48 hours of life, at four months and at 12 months. A sample of 1319 children born at the University of Minnesota hospitals, and included in this study, was followed up to age 12 years (Rubin and Balow 1980). 86 per cent were classified as neurologically normal throughout, 12 per cent as abnormal or suspect on one examination only and 2 per cent as abnormal or suspect on at least two examinations. Although the number of children in the third group was small (22), they were found to be at a significantly increased risk of later impairment of perceptuo-motor, cognitive and academic performance which was independent of socio-economic status and birthweight. Statistically significant differences were found between the three neurological groups on measures of school readiness and language development at five and six years and on all but two measures of academic achievement at seven, nine and 12 years. One-half of the third group were neurologically abnormal at seven years, as were 9 per cent of the second group and 1 per cent of the first group.

The extent to which neonatal risk factors are the cause of minor neurological disturbances later in life was examined in a group of Finnish children followed prospectively from birth (Michelsson *et al.* 1981). A neurodevelopmental examination, derived from Bax and Whitmore (1973), was carried out on 845 children aged four years ten months to five years three months who had had one or more of eight neonatal risk factors. These were: diabetic mother; birthweight <2000g; Apgar scores ≤6 at five minutes or later; hyperbilirubinaemia (at least two values ≥340mmol/l); hypoglycaemia (at least two values ≤1.67mmol/l for fullterm and ≤1.21mmol/l for preterm); respiratory difficulties needing continuous positive airway pressure or respirator care; neurological symptoms (including prolonged feeding difficulties); and septic infections. A control group of 70 children who had had no risk factors during pregnancy, delivery or the neonatal period was also examined. The mean neurodevelopmental scores for the high-risk groups were 21.3 for boys (who comprised 55 per cent of the total) and 19.7 for girls. Scores in the control group were significantly lower at 10.2 for boys and 7.5 for girls. The highest scores occurred for children who had had abnormal neurological signs, birthweight of ≤2000g or multiple neonatal risk factors.

Bax and Whitmore (1973), examining nine-year-old children, found that over half of those with a neurodevelopmental score of ≥28 had problems in school compared with less than 5 per cent of those with a score of ≤10. Michelsson and her colleagues (1981) predict that the proportion of children with school problems will be greater amongst those who were at risk in the neonatal period and anticipate failures in school because of clumsiness, perceptual disturbances, learning difficulties and behavioural disorders. These problems among CDC-referred children who were known to have exhibited minor neurological abnormality at younger ages are discussed in Chapter 13 (p. 260).

In the low birthweight study previously quoted (Drillien *et al.* 1980), multiple minor congenital anomalies, suggestive of adverse factors operating in early pregnancy, were significantly correlated with educational and behavioural difficulties in the second year of primary school. They were most commonly found among children with severe handicaps excluded from normal schools, of whom 44 per cent had a major or (more commonly) three or more minor anomalies. The possibility exists that some of these combinations of minor congenital anomalies with NDD could have been genetic in origin but none of the LBW children with handicap and multiple anomalies presented as any recognised syndrome. In another study three or more minor congenital anomalies were found in 21 of 50 children with idiopathic mental retardation (Smith and Bostian 1964) and in none of 100 control children.

Other authors, notably Waldrop and her co-workers, have recognised that the presence of several minor physical anomalies may be a non-specific indicator of neurodevelopmental disorder. In a 1971 study they demonstrated a significant relationship between high anomaly scores and deviations of behaviour in a group of normal two and a half year olds. On follow-up at age seven and a half years the anomaly scores remained stable and those with high scores still showed the same behavioural disturbances. In addition the high-scoring children tended to be clumsy, to have lower intelligence quotient (IQ) levels and to be below average in verbal abilities. Using the same anomaly and scoring system, Rosenberg and Weller (1973) found no significant correlation between anomaly scores and personality factors or performance IQ among first-year school children. However, verbal IQ was significantly lower among children with high scores and there was a very strong association between high scorers and the teacher's recommendation that the child should repeat the first year. Simmonds and Aston (1980) reported that there was a significant correlation (-0.35) between the number of minor physical anomalies and a measure of poor co-ordination in a sample of low birthweight and normal birthweight controls at age 10 to 11 years. The mean anomaly score was more than twice as high among children of birthweight ≤ 2000g than among normal birthweight controls.

Summary

Complications of pregnancy, delivery and the neonatal period
The perinatal histories of CDC-referred children with moderate or more severe NDD were compared with those of control group B children. There was a significant increase in the former of low birthweight, low weight for gestational age and neonatal complications. Within the whole group of CDC-referred children neonatal complications were related to complications of delivery.

Minor neurological abnormality
Different types of minor neurological abnormality among CDC-referred children are described.

CDC-referred children with NDD were much more likely to show minor neurological abnormality than were control group A children without NDD.

CDC-referred children who showed minor neurological abnormality were more likely to have been LBW and/or SFD and to have had neonatal complications than were children who showed no neurological abnormality.

Children with more severe degrees of NDD were more likely to be neurologically abnormal than were those with moderate or minor NDD. The frequency of neurological abnormality was not affected by social grade of home.

Multiple minor congenital anomalies

CDC-referred children with NDD were significantly more likely to exhibit multiple anomalies than were control group A children without NDD.

Multiple anomalies were more commonly found in children with the more severe NDD. The frequency was not affected by social grade of home.

Multiple anomalies were increased among CDC-referred and control children who showed minor neurological abnormality.

Children with multiple anomalies were more likely to be LBW and/or SFD and to have had neonatal complications.

APPENDIX V: **Some minor congenital anomalies (adapted from Drummond 1977)**

Hair
*Fine 'electric' hair
always 'standing up' and untidy
*Extra whorls on crown
one whorl is the normal finding
Low hairline
back or front

Ears
*Low set
i.e. when the anterior part of the helix joins
the skull below a horizontal line drawn
backwards from the outer angle of the eye
Slanting
i.e. when the ear slopes upwards and
backwards more than 10° to 15° from the
vertical
Simple
lack of normal convolutions
*Lack of lobule
the lobule normally extends below a
horizontal line drawn through its point of
contact to the skull
Prominent
'bat' ears
*Dissimilar (asymmetrical)
distinct difference in shape or size between
the two ears
Pre-auricular skin tags (accessory auricles),
pits or sinuses

Eyes and eyebrows
*Epicanthic folds
vertical skin folds covering the inner
canthi, usually bilateral, very common in
infancy, often disappearing later
*Hypertelorism
abnormally wide spacing of the eyes as
measured either by inner canthal and outer
orbital dimensions or inter-pupillary
distance
Slanting palpebral fissures
laterally and upwards (mongoloid) or
laterally and downwards (anti-mongoloid)
Brushfield spots
white speckles near the periphery of the
iris, found in 20 per cent of general
population
Small and/or deep-set eyes
may be familial
Coloboma
defect or notch in the upper or lower eyelid
(usually at junction of inner and middle
thirds) and/or in the iris

Eyes and eyebrows (cont.)
Bushy eyebrows
tendency to meet in the midline
Long straight eyelashes

Nose
Broad root
Beaked nose
Anteverted nares

Mouth and Lips
Macro/micro stomia
Long upper lip
increased distance between nose and upper
lip margin
Triangular or 'fish' shaped
down turning at corners, usually associated
with thin lips

Teeth
Enamel dysplasia
mild degrees show chalky spots of
hypoplasia; in severe forms the enamel is
aplastic
Abnormalities are most obvious on the
incisor teeth, canines and first molars;
may be present as pits, grooves or bands of
dysplasia.
Abnormal shape or spacing

Tongue
*Furrowing
one or more grooves other than the centre
groove; age-related and more frequent
among older than younger children
Macroglossia

Palate
*High arched
tented or smoothly arched
Low flat
Bifid uvula

Jaws
Malocclusion
associated with hypoplasia of
maxilla/mandible or protrusion of the
mandible with distortion of the usual
pattern of bite

Skin
Skin dimples
over bony prominences *e.g.* around the
elbow and shoulder
Multiple pigmented or vascular naevi

110

Hands
*Abnormal palmar creases
  simian, single complete transverse crease;
  Sydney, complete transverse with a partial
  ulnar transverse crease distally
*Incurving fifth finger
Single flexion crease fifth finger
Broad palms and short stubby fingers
Partial syndactyly (webbing)
  most commonly of third and fourth fingers
Polydactyly
  varying from a small nub of tissue (usually
  on ulnar side) to complete replication
Constriction bands of fingers
Hypoplasia of nails

Feet
*Wide separation of first and second toes
  gap more than half the width of the second
  toe
Prominent plantar crease
  between first and second toes
First toe longer than second
*Third toe equal to or longer than second
  age dependent, commoner in younger
  children

Feet (cont.)
*Partial syndactyly
  usually between second and third toes,
  minor degrees very common
Hypoplasia of nails

Neck
Short neck
Webbing

Spine
Midline anomaly
  lipoma, vascular naevus, hairy tuft, pit,
  sinus or deviation of natal cleft

External genitalia
Minor forms of hypospadias
Hypoplasia of scrotum and/or penis
Small soft testes
Undescended testes

Chest
Pectus excavatum
Shield shaped chest
Pigeon chest

*See Waldrop and Halverston (1971).

REFERENCES

Amiel-Tison, C. (1973) 'The follow-up of infants presenting neurological abnormalities in the first days of life.' *In:* Bossart, H., Cruz, J. M., Huber, A., Prod'hom, L. S., Sistek, J. (Eds.) *Perinatal Medicine.* Berne: Huber.

—— (1976) 'A method for neurologic examination within the first year of life.' *Current Problems in Pediatrics,* **7**, 1-50.

Bax, M., Whitmore, K. (1973) 'Neurodevelopmental screening in the school-entrant medical examination.' *Lancet,* **2**, 68-70.

Calâme, A., Raymond-Goni, I., Maherzi, M., Roulet, M., Marchand, C., Prod'hom, L. S. (1976) 'Psychological and neurodevelopmental outcome of high risk newborn infants.' *Helvetica Paediatrica Acta,* **31**, 287-297.

Drillien, C. M. (1972) 'Abnormal neurological signs in the first year of life in low-birthweight infants: possible prognostic significance.' *Developmental Medicine and Child Neurology,* **14**, 575-584.

—— Thomson, A. J. M., Burgoyne, K. (1980) 'Low-birthweight children at early school age: a longitudinal study.' *Developmental Medicine and Child Neurology,* **22**, 26-47.

Drummond, M. B. (1977) 'Physical and neurological examination.' *In:* Drillien, C. M., Drummond, M. B. (Eds.) *Neurodevelopmental Problems in Early Childhood.* Oxford: Blackwell Scientific Publications.

Michelsson, K., Ylinen, A., Donner, M. (1981) 'Neurodevelopmental screening at five years of children who were at risk neonatally.' *Developmental Medicine and Child Neurology,* **23**, 427-433.

Rosenberg, J. B., Weller, G. M. (1973) 'Minor physical anomalies and academic performance in young school-children.' *Developmental Medicine and Child Neurology,* **15**, 131-135.

Rubin, R. A., Balow, B. (1980) 'Infant neurological abnormalities as indicators of cognitive impairment.' *Developmental Medicine and Child Neurology,* **22**, 336-343.

Simmonds, J. F., Aston, L. (1980) Behavioural assessment of premature low-birthweight children a decade later.' *Developmental Medicine and Child Neurology,* **22**, 122-123 (Abstract).

Smith, D. W., Bostian, K. E. (1964) 'Congenital anomalies associated with idiopathic mental retardation.' *Journal of Pediatrics,* **65**, 189-196.

Thomson, A. M., Billewicz, W. Z., Hytten, F. E. (1968) 'The assessment of fetal growth.' *Journal of Obstetrics and Gynaecology of the British Commonwealth,* **75**, 903-916.

United States: Department of Health, Education and Welfare, Collaborative Study on Cerebral Palsy, Mental Retardation, and Other Neurological and Sensory Disorders of Infancy and Childhood (1966) *Part III-B Manuals: Pediatric Neurology.* Bethesda, Maryland: DHEW.

Waldrop, M. F., Halverston, C. F. (1971) 'Minor physical anomalies and hyperactive behaviour.' *In:* Hellmuth, J. (Ed.) *The Exceptional Infant Vol. 2.* New York: Brunner/Mazel.

CHAPTER 6

Global Delay and Mental Retardation

Frequency and severity of global delay

The frequencies of global delay not amounting to mental retardation as principal diagnosis (see definition, p. 47), identified preschool in the total population of 5334 children born 1974/75 and in the population of 3667 children who remained in Dundee from birth until after three years were 15 and 17 per 1000 (Table 4.3). 33 children referred to the Child Development Centre (CDC) in other clinical categories were also globally delayed, making a total of 110 children (27 per cent of all CDC-referred children) with developmental quotients (DQs) in the mid-80s or below that level. Two children with global delay were supervised elsewhere, one in the hospital infant clinic (he transferred out before referral to CDC was arranged) and one, who had transferred in after age three years with a known severe speech delay, in the hospital speech therapy department from where he was referred to the Child Guidance Service. Thus frequency of global delay, with or without other NDD, identified in the total population of 5334 children was 21 per 1000.

The severity of global delay among CDC- and hospital-referred children is detailed in Table 6.1. Globally delayed children graded as moderately severe had DQs in the upper 70s with or without additional problems, or in the low 80s with other problems (particularly behavioural) which were judged likely to affect school progress and behaviour. Children graded as moderate had DQs in the low 80s with or without less serious additional problems and the few children graded as minor had DQs around 85 without other problems.

No comparable UK data about frequency of global delay were found in the literature.

Frequency and severity of mental retardation

In the first three years of life, 33 CDC-referred children were classified as mentally retarded (see definition, p. 47) on the basis of developmental assessments. These children had DQs below 50 to 55 (severe) or between 55 and 75 (mild or borderline). One other child contracted meningo-encephalitis at age four years with resultant retardation. Many of the more severely delayed children were referred to the Child Guidance Service after age three years for formal testing of intellectual functioning (p. 116). Taking these results into account, 35 children could be considered borderline or overtly mentally retarded (Table 6.2). 12 children in other clinical categories and two with specific syndromes supervised elsewhere were also mentally retarded. Both children with specific syndromes died in the first year of life.

TABLE 6.1

CDC- and hospital-referred children, degrees of delay among children with mental retardation or global delay

	CDC	Hospital	Total	
			No.	%
Mental retardation				
Severe	6	—	6	5
Mild/borderline	27	—	27	24
Global delay				
Moderately severe	33	1	34	30
Moderate	41	1	42	38
Minor	3	—	3	3
Total	110	2	112	100

Because of the difficulty of applying an exact quotient to preschool children with moderately severe or severe retardation, particularly those with physical handicaps, three children with a 'best guess' intelligence quotient (IQ) in the low 50s are included here in the frequency figures for the severely retarded. All attend schools for the severely retarded.

Overall, 17 children were severely retarded with IQ levels below the mid-50s and 33 were mildly retarded, giving a frequency in the total population of 5334 children of 3.1 per 1000 severely and 6.1 per 1000 mildly retarded. These figures will underestimate the true frequency of mild retardation in this population as it would be expected that a few children amongst those who transferred out would be identified as mentally retarded between the time they moved and school-entry age. After excluding all retarded children who transferred in or out of Dundee and those who died before the age of three years, the frequency of retardation among the 3667 children who remained in the city from birth to three years was 3.0 per 1000 severely and 8.7 per 1000 mildly retarded. It is expected that other children with mild retardation will be identified after school entry (p. 265).

The frequency of severe retardation in this preschool population is rather lower than that given by the Home and Health and Education Departments for school-age children in Scotland (Great Britain: Mental Disorder Programme Planning Group 1979). On the basis of different surveys this was estimated to be between 3.4 and 4.0 per 1000. 50 years earlier, Lewis (1929) calculated the incidence to be 3.8 per 1000 school children in England and Wales.

Additional problems

Children considered to be globally delayed or mentally retarded were slow in all areas of development, apart from gross motor in a few cases. Some children were particularly delayed in one or another function and/or had significant problems of behaviour. Immature behaviour, reasonably appropriate for mental age, was not considered to constitute a problem, even if parents felt it to be so. Table 6.3 lists additional problems among mentally retarded and globally delayed children

TABLE 6.2

DQ and IQ assessments of CDC-referred children with mental retardation and moderately severe global delay

	CDC assessment		
	MR severe/ mod. severe	MR mild/ borderline	Global delay mod. severe
CGS assessment			
MR severe/mod. severe	9	—	—
MR mild/borderline	—	20	6
Well below average excess speech delay	—	2	—
Well below average	—	1	7
Low average excess speech delay	—	—	3
Low average	—	—	1
Average	—	—	1
Not referred	—	—	13
Transfer out	—	1	2
Total	9	24	33

CGS = Child Guidance Service; DQ = development quotient; IQ = intelligence quotient; MR = mental retardation.

referred to CDC. Behaviour disorders predominated, being present in 45 per cent of mentally retarded and 22 per cent of the globally delayed children. Behaviour problems of individual globally delayed children are discussed in Chapter 9 (Table 9.8).

Circumstances of referral

Circumstances of referral are detailed in Table 6.4. Of the six children with severe mental retardation, two were referred from screening clinics and four were already known. One of the 27 children with mild/borderline retardation transferred in with her handicap known and the other 26 were referred from screening clinics. 73 of the 77 children with global delay were referred from the screening clinics.

Referral was requested for 35 per cent of retarded and delayed children seen at CDC compared with 27 per cent requested referral for children in other categories of NDD (p. 00). This difference is not statistically significant but it does suggest that global delay may not be recognised as a problem as readily as are some other disorders, especially when the child comes from a poor home. Referral was requested for 46 per cent of the children with global delay who came from social grade 4 homes compared with 35 per cent of children from better homes.

Environmental factors

Table 6.5 compares some social indices among mentally retarded and globally delayed children and children attending CDC with other disorders. On all measures of disadvantage, *i.e.* social grade, specific social problems and considerable material deprivation, the differences between retarded and delayed children and those with

TABLE 6.3

Additional problems among CDC-referred children with mental retardation and global delay

	Mental retardation		Global delay	
	No.	%	No.	%
Additional problems				
Motor	3	9	8	10
Speech	2	6	10	13
Speech and behaviour	—	—	13	17
Behaviour	15	45	17	22
None	13	39	29	38
Total	33	100	77	100

TABLE 6.4

CDC-referred children with mental retardation and global delay, circumstances of referral

	Screening clinic		Other	Total
	Spontaneous	Requested		
Mental retardation				
Severe	2	—	4	6
Mild/borderline	18	8	1	27
Global delay				
Moderately severe	19	12	2	33
Moderate	22	17	2	41
Minor	2	1	—	3
Total (%)	63 (57)	38 (35)	9 (8)	110 (100)

other NDD were highly significant at p values of <0.001. The small numbers of severely retarded children did not fit this pattern, nor did those mentally retarded children in other clinical categories. 31 per cent of retarded and delayed children were considered to have suffered from emotional deprivation. This is not significantly different from the 22 per cent recorded for children with other NDD ($\chi^2 = 3.732$, p = >0.05).

Educational psychology assessments

Apart from one child who transferred out of the city, all children who were considered mentally retarded were referred to the Child Guidance Service for assessment and advice on school placement, as were 18 children with moderately severe global delay. Two children with moderately severe global delay transferred out before school entry as did six with moderate delay and two with minor delay.

Assessments were carried out between three and a half and five years, the majority of initial assessments around four years of age. Of the 50 children referred

TABLE 6.5

Some social indices for CDC-referred children with mental retardation, global delay and other categories of NDD

| | Mental retardation | | | | | | | | Mod. severe (N = 33) | | Global delay | | | | Other NDD (N = 304) | |
| | Severe (N = 6) | | Mild/ borderline (N = 27) | | All (N = 33) | | | | | | Mod./ minor (N = 44) | | All (N = 77) | | | |
	No.	%	No.	%	No.	%			No.	%	No.	%	No.	%	No.	%
Social grade																
1 and 2	3	50	3	11	6	18			—	—	5	11	5	6	85	28
3	1	17	6	22	7	21			12	36	19	43	31	40	160	53
4	2	33	18	67	20	61			21	64	20	46	41	54	159	19
Social problems																
0	3	50	5	19	8	24			19	58	18	40	37	48	211	69
1	1	17	9	33	10	30			7	21	13	30	20	26	59	20
≥2	2	33	13	48	15	46			7	21	13	30	20	26	34	11
Deprivation																
Emotional	2	33	12	44	14	42			7	21	13	30	20	26	66	22
Material	2	33	9	33	11	33			9	27	13	30	22	29	33	11

117

to the Child Guidance Service, 27 were assessed on two or more occasions before the age of school entry and 23 were assessed once. Initial assessments usually involved several testing sessions as well as interviews with parents.

Table 6.2 details the level of agreements between developmental assessments and initial IQ testing. There was total agreement in the cases of the six severely retarded children and three moderately severely retarded children who were functioning in the upper 50s. 20 of 23 children who functioned at a level of mild or borderline retardation on developmental tests performed at a similar level on IQ testing. Three performed better being categorised as well below average by educational psychologists; two of these children also had marked delay in language. Of the 18 children assessed as functioning in the upper 70s on developmental tests (moderately severe global delay), six who performed at a lower level on IQ testing were considered to be borderline retarded, four who performed at a higher level were rated as low average (three had more marked delay in language) and one child, subjected to considerable emotional deprivation, scored in the average range. There was agreement in seven cases.

POSSIBLE CAUSES OF DEVELOPMENTAL DELAY

An attempt was made to assess the relative importance of possible aetiological associations with mental retardation and moderately severe global delay. Three groups of children were considered: (1) severe or moderately severe retardation (including three children with IQs between 55 and 60); (2) mild or borderline retardation; and (3) moderately severe global delay. This last group includes one child supervised elsewhere. Eight mentally retarded children with specific conditions referred to CDC or supervised elsewhere, one child with hearing loss and five with cerebral palsy were added in, making a total of 81 children for this analysis. Educational psychologists' assessments of IQ were preferred to the results of developmental assessments for those referred to the Child Guidance Service.

Table 6.6 details what were considered to be the principal causative associations with developmental delay of differing severity.

Postnatal infection and injury, intra-uterine infections (one case each of rubella and varicella) and genetic conditions were clearly defined. Children having five or more minor congenital anomalies were considered to have suffered from some early intra-uterine insult. However, less confidence was felt in attributing this cause to children with three to four anomalies, since that number were found in 13 per cent of control group A children without any evidence of NDD (p. 103). In the cases of three children listed as '? prenatal', the only causative association found was the presence of three to four anomalies; possibly these children should be more properly included under 'cause not known'. The three children listed under '? pre- ? perinatal' factors all had five or more anomalies but also suffered moderate or severe perinatal complications.

No cause for moderately severe global delay other than low birthweight (<2000g) could be found for twins from an average working-class home who were

TABLE 6.6.

CDC and hospital-referred children, possible causative associations with mental retardation and moderately severe global delay (N = 81)

| | Mental retardation | | | | Global delay | |
| | Severe/ mod. severe | | Mild/ borderline | | Mod. severe | |
	No.	%	No.	%	No.	%
Aetiological factors						
Postnatal	2	10	1	3	1	3
Genetic	9	45	1	3	—	—
Intra-uterine infection	1	5	1	3	—	—
Prenatal						
MCA 5-7	1	5	5	17	3	10
≥8	6	30	3	10	2	6
? prenatal						
MCA 3-4	—	—	1	3	2	6
? pre- ? perinatal	1	5	2	7	—	—
Perinatal	—	—	—	—	2	6
Perinatal and social	—	—	6	20	4	13
Social	—	—	7	24	13	42
Not known	—	—	3	10	4	13
Total	20	100	30	100	31	100

MCA = Minor congenital anomalies.

noticeably slow as compared with their siblings. Neither had any complications in the neonatal period.

Social and perinatal factors were considered to be equally implicated in the mild or borderline retardation of six children from poor or very poor homes. Five children, including two twin pairs, were of very low birthweight (<2000g) without neonatal complications. Another retarded boy (2140g at 40 weeks) was born to a mother who had no neonatal care; minor problems ensued in the first three days of life. This boy showed some features suggesting the fetal alcohol syndrome.

Social and perinatal factors were probably involved in the cases of four boys with moderately severe global delay. They included a twin pair of birthweights 2260g and no neonatal complications and two singletons of birthweight 1980g and 2290g (SFD) whose mothers had no antenatal care. The only postnatal complications in these two cases were a moderate jaundice requiring phototherapy in the first and mild respiratory distress not requiring specific therapy in the second.

The home circumstances were poor or very poor without other possible obvious cause for mental retardation or global delay in 20 instances. In some of these cases parents or siblings had attended special school, thus genetic factors may have been implicated. No cause for retardation or delay was evident in seven cases.

Amongst those with the most severe degrees of handicap (20 children), postnatal infection, injury and intra-uterine infection were implicated in one case each, genetic or early intra-uterine influences in 16 cases (80 per cent), and in one cerebral-palsied child (further described on p. 131) both pre- and perinatal factors

TABLE 6.7
Preschool placements of mildly retarded and globally delayed CDC-referred children (N = 97)

Placement		Mental retardation		Global delay			
1st	2nd	Mild/ borderline		Mod. severe		Mod./minor	
		No.	%	No.	%	No.	%
Day nursery		3		2		5	
Day nursery	Nursery class	2 (2)* } 37		4 (1) } 83		7 (1) } 95	
Nursery class		6 (1)		18 (7)		24 (5)	
Special day nursery		—		1			
Special day nursery	Day nursery/nursery class	—		2			
Special day nursery	Assessment class	4 } 63		— } 17			
Assessment class		1		—			
Day nursery/nursery	Assessment class	14 (3)		2			
No placement		—		—		2	5
Total		30	100	29	100	38	100

*Figures in parentheses, placement refused or child was removed.

may have been involved. In no case were social factors considered to be the main cause, although one child's condition followed non-accidental injury in infancy.

In the mildly retarded/borderline group (30 children), genetic or early intra-uterine factors were probably or possibly involved in 43 per cent, perinatal factors in 27 per cent and adverse social factors in 43 per cent.

Adverse social circumstances predominated in the group with moderately severe global delay (31 children), being present in 55 per cent. In addition, the one child listed under 'postnatal' suffered from non-accidental injury in infancy.

Although adverse perinatal factors were seldom considered to be the main cause of global delay, low birthweight (LBW) and retarded intra-uterine growth (SFD) were significantly more common among globally delayed CDC-referred children than among control group B children of the same social who had not been suspected of showing NDD (p. 90).

After excluding delayed children with five or more multiple congenital anomalies (these tended to be poorly grown infants presumably due to some early intra-uterine influence), it was found that six (32 per cent) of 19 delayed children in social class III had been LBW/SFD infants compared with eight (5 per cent) of 154 control group B children; perinatal details were not known for one control child in social class III. In social classes IV and V, nine (25 per cent) of 36 delayed children and 12 (11 per cent) of 114 control children had been LBW/SFD; perinatal details were not known for one control child in social class IV. The number of delayed children in social classes I and II was too small to allow comparisons to be made. The differences in the other social class groups are statistically significant: $\chi^2 =$

TABLE 6.8

Final school placement of mildly retarded and globally delayed CDC-referred children

	Mental retardation Mild/ borderline		Global delay Mod. severe		Mod. minor	
	No.	%	No.	%	No.	%
Special education	3	10	—	—	—	—
Assessment class → special education	7	23	—	—	—	—
Assessment class → P.1 deferred	5	17	2	7	—	—
Assessment class → P.1	4	13	—	—	—	—
P.1 → special education	2	7	1	3	—	—
P.1 →? special education	1	3	1	3	—	—
P.1 deferred	3	10	5	17	2	4
P.1	4	13	17	60	35	78
Transferred out	1	3	3	10	8	18
Total	30	100	29	100	45	100

P.1 = Primary 1.

25.510, p = <0.001 for children in social class III; χ^2 = 4.761, p = <0.05 for children in social classes IV and V. Thus it seems that low birthweight and retarded intra-uterine growth contribute to delayed development even if unlikely to be the main cause in many cases.

MANAGEMENT

Preschool and school placements

With two exceptions one or more preschool day placements were arranged for all CDC-referred children with mental retardation and global delay apart from seven who transferred out of town before three years.

Table 6.7 details day placements for mildly retarded and delayed children. Figures in parentheses are the numbers of occasions on which the only placement or the second placement was not accepted by the parents, attendance was very poor or the child was removed after a short period of attendance. One or other of these circumstances occurred in 21 per cent of children offered placements. Table 6.8 details the final school placements of the children. Those listed as 'P.1'* entered their local primary schools at the usual age and those listed as 'P.1 deferred' delayed entry for 12 months.

*In Britain all children are required to be attending school by age five and a half years. Apart from those with special educational needs all children will enter a normal primary school at age four and a half to five and a half years. In the first class (Primary 1) they begin the formal study of reading, writing and number. This is the first year of school for most. Only about one-third of children attend preschool nursery classes.

The special day nursery at CDC is a National Health Service unit for handicapped preschool children. Long-term day places are available for 25 children and two additional places are reserved for short-term assessments (p. 216). The assessment class is an educational unit attached to a local primary school which can accommodate 24 children aged three and a half to six years who may require special education later, on account of mental retardation or severe behaviour disorder. Many children admitted to this class have multiple impairments both innate and environmental. The unit provides nursery class activities and Primary 1 teaching in two groups. Some children, who are expected to enter their local primary schools, may be placed part-time in an appropriate class in the main school.

Severe retardation

All children with severe mental retardation had a special preschool day placement apart from one child, in care of the local authority following non-accidental injury, who was admitted to a long-stay hospital from special day nursery. At school-entry age four others were placed in special schools and units locally and one child, with considerable behaviour problems and a severely disturbed mother/child relationship, was placed in residential school.

Mild/borderline retardation

Eleven of the 30 mildly retarded children were offered places in normal day nurseries or nursery classes. One child attended nursery class erratically and placement in the assessment class (where transport is provided) was recommended but no vacancy was obtainable. Two working mothers refused more suitable nursery class placements and their children stayed on in day nurseries. Three children from very poor homes were retained in day nurseries as it was thought unlikely that mothers would take them to nursery classes. Of these 11 children, three were admitted to special education at school-entry age and eight to normal school. The parents of one insisted (against advice) that their child should start in Primary 1 before her fifth birthday; she has made little progress in two years of primary education and special provision is being considered.

Sixteen children attended the assessment class. Placement was available for three more. This was refused in one case, the child remaining in normal nursery class for an additional 12 months; she is coping well in Primary 1 at an older age than most of her classmates. In one case the child was removed after a few months and enrolled in her local primary school against advice; she was transferred to special education at the end of Primary 1. The third child disappeared and could not be traced until he re-appeared in primary school in a different area of the city; he made no progress in his first year in school and has been transferred to special education. Of these 16, seven proceeded to special education and nine to normal school.

Global delay

Of the 29 children considered to be intellectually well below average three attended special day nursery and two the assessment class. Two others remained in normal day nurseries until school entrance and the remaining 22 children were

TABLE 6.9

CDC-referred children, referrals of retarded and globally delayed children to other agencies

	Retarded Mild/borderline (N = 30)		Delayed Mod. severe (N = 29)		Mod./minor (N = 45)	
	No.	%	No.	%	No.	%
Other referrals						
For treatment						
Speech therapy	25	83	16	55	9	20
Occupational therapy	2	7	3	10	1	2
Clinical psychology	4	13	1	3	3	7
Hospital referrals						
Eyes	12	40	4	14	8	18
ENT	4	13	7	24	2	4
Growth clinic	4	13	—	—	—	—
Social work	16	53	9	31	13	29
No other referral	5	17	12	41	22	49

ENT = Department of Otolaryngology

offered places in normal nursery classes. Eight of these attended erratically or were removed. All entered normal schools but one has been transferred to special education and this is being considered for another. The first child was discharged from CDC because of mother's failure to co-operate with any of the suggestions made.

The parents of two children with moderate or minor delay, eligible by date of birth to enter school before five years, chose to delay school entry. In one case the parents' judgement, that their son was too immature to start school proved correct. Even after an extra year in nursery class, he is having considerable problems in school. All other children entered school at the usual age.

Other referrals

Most retarded children and many with global delay had additional problems and were referred to other agencies. Details of some other referrals are given in Table 6.9. Squints were particularly common being confirmed in 22 per cent of mildly retarded and 12 per cent of delayed children. Squint was identified in 5 per cent of control group B children either preschool or following the school-entrance medical examination.

Summary

Frequency of global delay and mental retardation

Fifteen per 1000 of the total population and 17 per 1000 of those remaining in the city throughout the screening period were identified as having global delay as the principal problem.

Overall, the frequencies of severe and mild mental retardation in the total population were 3.1 and 6.1 per 1000. After excluding children who died before three years, the frequencies in the more stable population were 3.0 and 8.7 per 1000.

Severity of delay and additional problems

Classification of severity is detailed and additional problems listed. On all measures of social disadvantage the differences between retarded/delayed children and those with other NDD were highly significant.

Identification of retardation and delay

Apart from cases of severe retardation the majority of retarded and delayed children were referred from the screening programme. All children considered retarded on developmental assessment and over one-half of those with moderately severe global delay were further assessed by educational psychologists. Agreement was close in most cases.

Possible causes of retardation and moderately severe delay

Scrutiny of each individual case led to the following conclusions: in the group with severe or moderately severe retardation, genetic or early intra-uterine factors were involved in 80 per cent, perinatal factors possibly in 5 per cent and postnatal events in 10 per cent; in the mildly retarded group genetic or early intra-uterine factors were probably or possibly involved in 43 per cent, perinatal and postnatal factors in 19 and 3 per cent and social factors in 43 per cent; adverse social circumstances predominated amongst children with moderately severe global delay (53 per cent).

Management

Day placements and other referrals for retarded and delayed children are described.

REFERENCES

Great Britain: Scottish Home and Health Department and Scottish Education Department Mental Disorder Programme Planning Group (1979) *A Better Life: Report on Services for the Mentally Handicapped in Scotland* (Chairman: D. A Peters). Edinburgh: HMSO.
Lewis, E. O. (1929) 'An investigation into the incidence of mental deficiency.' *In: Report of the Mental Deficiency Committee Pt. IV.* London: HMSO.

CHAPTER 7

Motor Disorder, Cerebral Palsy and Minor Neurological Signs

MOTOR DISORDER

The frequency of motor disorder (see definition p. 47) as the only or final category of NDD identified preschool in the population of 3667 children who remained in Dundee throughout the screening period was 18 per 1000 (see Table 4.3, p. 57). A lower frequency of 14 per 1000 was recorded for the total population of 5334 children. This is due to the fact that the majority of motor disorders (80 per cent) were identified in the first two years of life and a lower frequency would be expected when children transferring in after that age are included. Children with motor disorder, resulting from specific neurological or physical defects are not included here.

Motor disorder was the only or final diagnosis for 59 CDC-referred children (14 per cent of the total referred to the Centre). 14 children (7 per cent) attending elsewhere had a motor disorder as their only disability. Eight of these children were noted to have significant motor delay during their attendance at the hospital infant clinic where their developmental progress was supervised by the authors.

Table 7.1 shows the distribution of different types of motor disorder and associated developmental problems among the 59 CDC-referred children. For 31

TABLE 7.1

CDC-referred children with motor disorder as principal problem (N = 59), types of motor disorder, associated problems and overall severity grading

| | Overall severity grading | | | Total |
	Minor	Moderate	Moderately severe	
Locomotor delay	15	16		31
+ speech disorder			2	3
+ speech and behaviour			1	
Gross and fine motor disorder		7	2	9
+ global delay (minor)		1	2	11
+ speech disorder			1	
+ speech and behaviour		1	2	
+ behaviour disorder		2	2	
Fine motor disorder				
+ speech disorder		1	1	5
+ speech and behaviour			1	
+ behaviour disorder		1	1	
Total (%)	15 (25)	29 (49)	15 (25)	59 (100)

TABLE 7.2

Later clinical categories of 22 CDC-referred children presenting initially with motor disorder

Locomotor delay	
→ global delay	4
→ mental retardation	2
→ speech disorder	2
→ speech and behaviour disorder	4
→ behaviour disorder	5
Gross and fine motor disorder	
→ mental retardation	2
→ speech and behaviour disorder	1
→ behaviour disorder	2

TABLE 7.3

Severity grading for all CDC-referred children with a motor disorder (N = 100)

	Overall severity grading				
	Minor	*Moderate*	*Moderately severe*	*Severe*	*Total*
Motor problem only	15	23	2	—	40
Motor problem + other	—	6	13	—	19
Motor problem → other	—	10	10	2	22
Global delay/retarded + motor problem	1	7	4	7	19
Total (%)	16 (16)	46 (46)	29 (29)	9 (9)	100 (100)

children (53 per cent), the only problem presenting during the period of attendance at the Centre was locomotor delay, defined as development quotient (DQ) on motor scale in the mid-80s or below. Nine children (15 per cent) exibited locomotor delay and delay or dysfunction in manipulative skills and 19 children (32 per cent) had other developmental problems in addition to motor disorder. Five of these 19 children had fine motor difficulties but unimpaired locomotor performance.

Fifty of the 59 CDC-referred children presented initially with motor disorder and the other nine children initially with other problems (see Table 4.4, p. 58). An additional 22 children presented initially with a motor problem (most usually locomotor delay) but later moved into another clinical category. This is shown in Table 7.2. The motor function of a further 12 children with moderate or more severe global delay and six children with mild mental retardation was disproportionately delayed. One other child from a severely deprived environment showed minor global delay and moderately severe motor delay; he made progress in all areas of development after being taken into care. Thus, overall, 100 children (24 per cent of the total referred) presented with motor disorder during their period of supervision at CDC.

126

TABLE 7.4
Neurological status of CDC-referred children with and without motor disorder

| | Neurological status | First examined | | | | All | |
| | | 1st year | | Later | | | |
		No.	%	No.	%	No.	%
Clinical category:							
Motor disorder*	Normal	1	3	4	18	5	8
	Doubtful	6	16	2	9	8	14
	Abnormal	30	81	16	73	46	78
	Total	37	100	22	100	59	100
Motor disorder	Normal	—	—	3	23	3	14
→ other	Doubtful	1	11	3	23	4	18
	Abnormal	8	89	7	54	15	68
	Total	9	100	13	100	22	100
Global delay/retardation	Normal	1	8	2	33	3	16
+ motor disorder	Doubtful	1	8	1	17	2	10
	Abnormal	11	84	3	50	14	74
	Total	13	100	6	100	19	100
Other NDD	Normal	8	15	139	62	147	53
no motor disorder	Doubtful	4	8	59	26	63	23
	Abnormal	39	75	21	9	60	22
	Not known	1	2	6	3	7	2
	Total	52	100	225	100	277	100

*Final diagnosis.

Severity grading of children with motor disorders

Table 7.1 also gives the overall severity grading for the 59 CDC-referred children with different types of motor disorder with and without other disabilities. 15 of the 31 children with locomotor delay only were graded as minor: five caught up in gross motor function and showed no abnormal neurological signs, seven had signs of doubtful significance and three had frankly abnormal signs of short duration which had disappeared by age nine months. These last three children presented in school with moderately severe problems (p. 256), indicating that our assessment of severity was unduly optimistic and early discharge from CDC had been unwise. The other 16 children with locomotor delay only were graded as moderate. These children were more obviously neurologically abnormal with signs persisting into the second year or first detected at that age or later. Of the remaining 28 children, 13 were graded as moderate and 15 as moderately severe.

Table 7.3 shows the severity grading for the total 100 children who presented with motor disorder at some stage. This figure includes the 19 children with a motor disorder in addition to global delay or mild retardation and the 22 who later changed category. Overall, 38 per cent of children with early motor problems were considered certain or very likely to have problems of education and behaviour in the

TABLE 7.5

CDC-referred children, other NDD associated with motor disorder

	Motor disorder* (N = 59)		Motor disorder → other category (N = 22)		Global/MR + motor (N = 19)		All (N = 100)
	No.	%	No.	%	No.	%	No.
Associated NDD							
Global delay	3	5	4	18	13	68	20
Mental retardation	—	—	4	18	6	32	10
Speech disorder	10	17	7	32	3	16	20
Behaviour disorder	11	19	14	64	4	21	29

*Final diagnosis; MR = Mental retardation.

early school years and 16 per cent unlikely to have any problems. In 46 per cent of cases the prognosis was less clear, mainly because the long-term significance of early neurological abnormality in this group could not be known until after school entrance (p. 258).

Neurological status

As would be expected, a higher proportion of motor-disordered children showed definite abnormal neurological signs than did those in any other category of NDD other than specific neurological conditions. This was due in part to the preponderance of motor-disordered children examined in the first year of life (Table 7.4).

Of the 59 CDC-referred children with motor disorder as a principal problem, five were neurologically normal. Of these, four children had a minor locomotor delay only. The fifth child, the sibling of the severely deprived child quoted above (p. 126), presented initially as globally delayed, particularly in gross motor function. He also caught up rapidly after placement in foster care and, when last seen, showed minor locomotor delay only. Eight children presented with neurological signs of doubtful significance. Seven had a minor locomotor delay only and one, examined for the first time at three and a half years, had associated fine motor dysfunction and behaviour disturbance. All other motor-disordered children were neurologically abnormal.

Patterns of neurological abnormality for 370 CDC-referred children are detailed in Table 5.4 (p. 94). 29 children (50 per cent of the 59 children with motor disorder as principal problem) presented with transient dystonia; in 22 of these cases other doubtful or abnormal signs appeared after dystonia resolved. Of the remaining 25 doubtful or abnormal children, 24 presented with different combinations of hypotonia, increased tendon jerks, clumsiness and hand tremor. One child was considered neurologically doubtful on the basis of asymmetries in posture and differences in tone and reflexes between right and left.

Of the 41 children in other clinical categories who had or retained sigificant motor problems at some stage, 15 per cent wre neurologically normal, 15 per cent were doubtful and 70 per cent were abnormal.

Of the total group of 100 children with a motor disorder as principal or related problem, 3 per cent of those examined in the first year of life were neurologically normal, 14 per cent were doubtful and 83 per cent were abnormal. This was not significantly different from the distribution among infants with no motor disorder examined for the first time in the first year of life (16 per cent normal, 8 per cent doubtful and 76 per cent abnormal). 22 per cent of children with motor disorder examined for the first time after the first birthday were neurologically normal, 15 per cent were doubtful and 63 per cent were abnormal. This showed a highly significant excess of neurological abnormality as compared with the other NDD children examined after the first birthday of whom 63 per cent were neurologically normal, 27 per cent were doubtful and only 10 per cent abnormal (χ^2 = 67.901, 2df, p = <0.001).

Associated problems

Other developmental problems among children with motor disorder are detailed in Tables 7.1 and 7.5. Of the 81 children whose main problem was a motor disorder initially or throughout, 10 per cent progressed to a moderate or more severe global delay or to mild mental retardation, 21 per cent had speech disorders and 31 per cent had behaviour disorders.

CEREBRAL PALSY

Incidence

Eighteen children in the total 1974/75-born population suffered from cerebral palsy (see Table 4.3, p. 57). The incidence was 3.3 per 1000 total population and 3.6 per 1000 of those remaining in the city throughout the screening period. The incidence was considerably higher than that reported in recent surveys and even higher than that reported in Scotland in the 1950s (p. 134).

Most surveys reporting incidence of cerebral palsy are based on hospital referrals and it is likely that varying numbers of mild cases remain unidentified. In this population study all children found on screening to have marked locomotor delay or obvious preference for one or other hand before the age of two years were assessed further. Of the 18 children identified as having cerebral palsy, seven were classified as mild according to a classification derived from Ingram (1964, Appendix VI). In contrast, only one of the 14 Dundee-resident children with cerebral palsy born 1972/73 was classified as mild. These 14 children had been referred to the authors at CDC for supervision and management. As far as is known, they comprised the total number of 1972/73-born children with identified cerebral palsy since no others were diagnosed between birth and six and a half to seven and a half years. It is possible that some other mild cases remained unidentified.

Circumstances of identification of cerebral palsy

Appendix VII details the different types of cerebral palsy, other disabilities, aetiology and educational placement of the 18 1974/75-born children with cerebral palsy. Table 7.6 details the circumstances of identification with special reference to the part played by the screening programme. In five cases the diagnosis was known from birth or was diagnosed in hospital during admission for the condition causing the cerebral palsy. One other child transferred into Dundee at age one year and was referred for a neurological opinion before his first screening examination had been carried out.

In 11 cases the condition was suspected on screening but in only four of these was the child referred in the first year of life. Three children were not diagnosed until their two-year screening examination or later. One child (No. 10) was being followed up in hospital on account of urinary tract infections following rupture of the bladder at birth. She was noted to be developmentally slow, particularly in locomotor function, but this was thought to be due to mental retardation. The mother was a poor attender at hospital and screening clinics, for which reason a request was made for the child's two-year screening examination to be carried out at CDC, where a diagnosis was made of ataxic diplegia in a child of normal intelligence. Another child (No. 9) was passed as normal in locomotor function at his 15-month screening examination which was carried out at a real age, allowing for prematurity, of 13 months. He was reported as 'upright and walking mainly'. It seems unlikely that locomotor function was observed as the child was not walking independently 12 months later. Following his two-year screening examination he was referred to an orthopaedic clinic where he was diagnosed as having a moderate diplegia. The third child (No. 17) was reported on his 39-week screening card to have signs highly suggestive of a hemiplegia. A request for referral did not elicit a positive response as the clinic doctor was 'quite happy about him'. This may have been due in part to the fact that he was the first child of an overanxious mother. He was finally referred after his two-year screening examination, by which age the parents were becoming concerned.

The child who was missed on screening (No. 8) was passed as normal in locomotor and all other areas of development at the 15-month and two-year developmental screenings. Two weeks after his two-year screening his family doctor (a partner of the screening doctor) referred the child to an orthopaedic clinic on account of abnormal gait. He was found to have a mild hemiplegia.

Probable or possible causes of cerebral palsy
There was no doubt about aetiology in two previously normal children (Nos. 13 and 14) who developed cerebral palsy following tuberculous meningitis in the one case and a frontal lobe abscess in the other. Genetic or familial factors were probably implicated in three cases (Nos. 1-3). One child suffered from the dysequilibrium syndrome (an autosomal recessive condition) and siblings of the other two children showed similar signs. The mother of one of these children had previously had one stillborn and two liveborn children, two late abortions and many early abortions. In four cases (Nos. 4-7) some adverse factor operating in early pregnancy seemed the most likely cause. All showed multiple minor congenital anomalies, had relatively uncomplicated pregnancy and delivery histories and were normal in the neonatal periods.

TABLE 7.6

Circumstances of identification of 18 CDC-referred children with cerebral palsy

Known	Case No.
From birth	11, 12
Transferred in, diagnosis known	16
Diagnosed in hospital	13, 14
Other	
Transferred in between screening ages	2
Identified on screening	
8 weeks	1
20 weeks	4, 6
39 weeks	7
15 months	3, 5, 15, 18
2 years	9, 10, 17
Missed on screening	
2 years	8

In one case (No. 12) it was difficult to disentangle the relative importance of pre- and perinatal factors. He was the second child of a tall healthy superior working-class (see p. 50) woman. Pregnancy was uncomplicated and she went into spontaneous labour at 41 weeks. After four hours the fetal heart rate dropped suddenly to less than 80 per minute and remained at this rate between contractions. Delivery was expedited by Ventouse extraction. The baby, who weighed 4000g, was severely asphyxiated at birth with bradycardia. External cardiac massage was carried out and intermittent positive pressure ventilation started. He gasped at 40 minutes and breathed spontaneously at one hour. From the beginning he was grossly abnormal neurologically, initially very floppy, becoming hypertonic during the following two weeks. He had repeated cyanotic and apnoeic attacks and repeated convulsions which were difficult to control. He presented later as a very severe spastic quadriplegic with microcephaly, profound mental retardation and epilepsy. In addition, on examination at four months, he was found to have inverted epicanthic folds, wideset eyes, a high-arched and narrow palate, abnormal palmar creases and large, long first toes which were medially deviated. It is possible that this was a developmentally abnormal baby unable to withstand the stress of a normal labour with severe brain damage superimposed as a result of anoxia.

Four cases (Nos. 8-11) were more obviously due to perinatal factors. Three were of low birthweight and delivered prematurely at 32 weeks or earlier. The fourth child suffered a cerebral haemorrhage at 27 hours, the cause of which was not known. Physical handicap among these children was mild or moderate and none were mentally retarded; all attend normal school.

In four cases (Nos. 15-18) the cause was unknown; one baby (birthweight 2501g at 40 weeks) was small for date, but he was entirely normal in the neonatal period.

Perinatal factors were clearly implicated for eight of the 14 cerebral-palsied children known to CDC who were born 1972/73 (Table 7.7). One child was a severely

TABLE 7.7

**1972/73 and 1974/75 births. Probable or possible
causes of cerebral palsy**

	1972/73	1974/75
Probable/possible cause		
Genetic/familial	—	3
Prenatal	3	4
Perinatal	8	4
? pre- ? perinatal	1	1
Postnatal	1	2
Unknown	1	4
Total	14	18

affected rhesus baby who required ventilator therapy for six weeks and sustained severe lung and brain damage. One child suffered a cerebral haemorrhage of unknown cause at three days and six presented with diplegia or ataxic diplegia associated with very low birthweight and premature delivery. Physical handicap was moderate in two, moderately severe in two and severe or very severe in four of these children. Four children were mentally retarded and only two attend normal school.

One further child was delivered by caesarian section at 42 weeks' gestation following a failed attempt at extraction with Kielland's forceps on account of deep transverse arrest. She required initial resuscitation, had repeated cyanotic attacks, was jittery and irritable and had one major convulsion. Her mild mental retardation and moderate diplegia were attributed to brain damage resulting from traumatic delivery. However, she was noted to have a small head at birth and obvious microcephaly when first seen at four months as well as marked brachycephaly and small podgy hands and feet. The paternal grandmother reported that her son had not walked until four years and his gait remained clumsy for some years thereafter. It is possible that a familial or other prenatal factor was also involved here.

Overall, it seems likely that there was a real reduction between 1972/73 and 1974/75 in the number of children with cerebral palsy attributable to perinatal factors (particularly to low birthweight) and also a reduction in the severity of the subsequent disabilities. From January 1975 all Dundee-born infants of very low birthweight were nursed in one centralised special care baby unit.

Management

The more severe motor disorders not amounting to cerebral palsy were assessed by a physiotherapist and an occupational therapist, and advice on management given to the parents. No formal physiotherapy was given after that, but some children with disordered hand function were given occupational therapy.

Children with mild or moderate cerebral palsy with no other problems were treated on an out-patient basis. They attended CDC (with transport provided) for regular physiotherapy and occupational therapy. All children with moderately severe or severe cerebral palsy attended CDC on a daily basis (again transport provided) for periods of between one and three years. These children with cerebral palsy were reviewed as soon as the diagnosis was made, and regularly thereafter by an orthopaedic surgeon at CDC.

MINOR ABNORMAL NEUROLOGICAL SIGNS ONLY

Six CDC-referred children presented initially with minor abnormal neurological signs only. Two of these children developed other problems later.

One female, birthweight 2200g at 39 weeks gestation, was followed up in the hospital infant clinic. She was transferred to CDC on account of the mother's anxiety. At six months of age she was developmentally up to age but exhibited fisting of hands and a persistent asymmetric tonic neck reflex to the right. Mother suffered from a severe personality disorder, was admitted to psychiatric hospital and the baby was taken into long-term foster care out of the city. She was next seen on her return to Dundee at three and a half years when she presented with mild mental retardation and disturbed behaviour. She remained neurologically abnormal with moderate hypotonia, bilateral hand tremor and clumsy gait.

The other child who developed other problems was also female (birthweight 2029g at 33 weeks) and followed up in the hospital infant clinic. At a real age (allowing for prematurity) of two months she was up to age developmentally but was jittery, with strong extensor thrust and an exaggerated Moro response. She was discharged from the clinic at ten months showing only hypotonia and some asymmetry in maturity of hand function. She did not attend local screening at 15 months and strenuous health visitor efforts to carry out home screening failed, for which reason CDC-referral was requested. At one year ten months the residual minor neurological signs persisted and by three years she presented with locomotor delay, difficulties in motor planning, clumsy hand function with tremor and speech delay.

Of the other four children who exhibited minor abnormal neurological signs only, one was a small-for-date, low birthweight male (2015g at 36 weeks), one male had suffered moderate birth asphyxia following a Kielland's forceps rotation and delivery and one female had a completely uncomplicated perinatal course. All exhibited definite abnormal neurological signs in the first six months of life without developmental disorder or delay and were neurologically normal at one year. The remaining child was referred to CDC at three and a half years because of mother's anxiety about her gait. On examination she had a generalised moderate hypotonia with increased tendon jerks. In all other respects she appeared entirely normal. The mother's exaggerated concern continued and no cause for this could be ascertained. This child has moderately severe problems of behaviour in school at age six and a half years. The other three children have no school problems.

COMPARISON WITH OTHER STUDIES

Motor disorder

Neligan and Prudham (1969) studied the relationship between delay in walking (based on near-contemporary history of ability to walk unsupported for at least 10 steps) and score on the Goodenough Draw-a-Man test among normal school children at five years. Early walkers were taken to be those who walked before 10 months (7 per cent of the total) and late walkers were those who walked after 17 months (also 7 per cent of the total). There was no sex difference for the walking 'milestone' but there was a significant difference (female advantage) in Draw-a-Man scores. A significant difference in test scores was found between boys who were early and late walkers, but none between girls. When delay in using sentences (defined as 'three or four different words for people or objects correctly used') was added in, it was found that test scores of those who both walked later than the 93rd centile and used sentences later than the 96th centile (1 per cent of the total school population) were significantly depressed, being some 20 points below the population mean. It is, of course, likely that late walking in some of these children was not an inappropriate index for their overall developmental level.

The significance of early delays in motor development was discussed by Silva (1979) reporting from the Dunedin Multidisciplinary Child Development Study. Over 1000 children were assessed at three years of age and their competence in gross co-ordination (Bayley 1961), fine co-ordination (Silva 1976), verbal comprehension and verbal expression (Reynell 1969) were compared with reported ages by which children could sit unaided and pivot without falling and walk at least six steps. Over two-thirds of mothers could refer to their 'Plunket books' (a developmental record) for confirmation. Children who were not sitting by 11 months and not walking by 19 months were four to 10 times as likely to be found among those with very low motor and language scores (≥ 2 SD below the total sample mean) at three years. However, one-half and one-third of children with early motor delay scored within the average or better range on later testing. Silva does not state how many (if any) of the children with early motor delay were at three years globally delayed or mentally retarded, with early motor performance and later motor and language abilities appropriate for level of intellectual functioning.

Cerebral palsy

Prevalence
In 1959 an attempt was made to ascertain all living cases of cerebral palsy under the age of 21 in the Eastern region of Scotland (Henderson 1961). The prevalence was calculated to be 1.5 per 1000 in those aged up to four years and 2.0 per 1000 in those aged five to 14 years. It was considered that ascertainment was incomplete in the preschool group and that the prevalence found at school age was likely to be the most accurate; no account was taken of cerebral-palsied children who died. A comparable figure of 2.3 per 1000 school-aged children was found by Ingram (1964) in a meticulous study of cerebral-palsied children living in Edinburgh in 1953.

The two most comprehensive surveys of recent years are those from one well-defined Swedish region (Hagberg *et al*, 1975) and from Western Australia (Stanley 1979). Hagberg and his colleagues studied the incidence of cerebral palsy over the years 1954 to 1970 and showed that the incidence per 1000 livebirths fell from 2.2 in 1954/59 to 1.3 in 1966/70. The main decrease was in spastic and ataxic diplegia,

TABLE 7.8
Distribution of different types of cerebral palsy in Sweden and Dundee

	W. Sweden 1966-70*	Dundee 1974/75	Dundee 1972/73
	%	%	%
Hemiplegia	41	39	7
Quadriplegia	5	11	14
Diplegia	26	4	43
Ataxic diplegia	4	28	21
Ataxia	12	6	—
Dyskinesia	3	6	14
Dystonic	8	6	—

*Figures from Hagberg *et al.* (1975).

especially in those cases associated with a birthweight of <2500g. Stanley reported that the total cerebral palsy rate in Western Australia rose steadily from 2.0 per 1000 in 1956 to 3.7 per 1000 in 1967 and thereafter fell to 1.2 per 1000 in 1975. The rates which particularly showed a rise and fall were those for the spastic syndromes, especially for spastic diplegia.

At a later date (1982) Stanley revised these figures. Re-analysis of the data, after a longer interval of time for ascertainment, suggested no significant fall in incidence rates between 1966/70 (2.6 per 1000) and 1971/75 (2.2 per 1000). Rates in those of birthweight ≤2500g were identical at 14.5 per 1000. A small decrease was recorded for those of birthweight >2500g (2.0 and 1.6 per 1000, respectively). Stanley suggests that one should wait at least five years before accepting incidence rates as reliable because of delay in diagnosis and change of diagnosis over time.

A relatively high incidence of cerebral palsy (2.6 per 1000) was reported for children born in 1977 in the Oxford area (Hardie and MacFarlane 1980). Children who were not walking ('taking five steps freely') by 18 months were referred by health visitors for neurological and developmental assessment by a paediatrician at home. The incidence of late walking in the 74 per cent of the total population screened by health visitors was 1.5 per cent. Among the first 160 late walkers examined, eight cases of cerebral palsy were newly diagnosed. The five cases of cerebral palsy diagnosed among 1977-born late walkers made a 31 per cent contribution towards the total of 16 cases for that year. Had these additional cases not been identified by screening, the incidence would have been 1.8 per 1000.

Types of cerebral palsy

Although the number of cerebral-palsied children in the Dundee research group is very small, the distribution by type of cerebral palsy is close to that reported by Hagberg for children born from 1966/70 in West Sweden (Table 7.8) except that the proportions of diplegic and ataxic diplegic children are reversed. In both populations hemiplegic children comprised the largest proportion. In contrast, only one child with hemiplegia (classified as mild) was known to CDC amongst children born 1972/73; the largest proportion were diplegic children of very low birthweight.

135

Summary

Motor disorders

The incidence of motor disorder as principal problem was 18 per 1000 in the total population and 14 per 1000 of the more stable population. A further 6 per cent in other principal clinical categories had a motor disorder initially or throughout.

Types of motor disorder are described and patterns of neurological abnormality found in motor-disordered children. Additional developmental and behavioural problems are listed.

Cerebral palsy

The incidence of cerebral palsy in the total population was 3.3 per 1000 and 3.6 per 1000 of the more stable population. Reasons for this high incidence are discussed. Age at diagnosis and circumstances of identification are detailed.

Of 18 cases of cerebral palsy, two were of postnatal origin, three were genetically determined, four were due to early intra-uterine factors, four to perinatal factors, one to early intra-uterine or perinatal factors and in four the cause was unknown.

APPENDIX VI

Classification of cerebral palsy by severity
(from Ingram 1964 and Drillien 1977)

Hemiplegia.
  Mild, the affected hand is used independently for everyday activities.

  Moderate, the affected hand is used only to assist the unaffected hand.

  Severe, the affected hand has no useful function except perhaps as a prop or support.

Bilateral hemiplegia.
  Mild, some use of the upper limbs is retained.

  Moderate, some use of the lower limbs is retained.

  Severe, there is no use of the limbs.

Diplegia and ataxic diplegia.
  Mild, gait is clumsy rather than disabled.

  Moderate, the child is unsteady when walking and cannot run.

  Severe, at best assisted walking only is possible.

Ataxic and dyskinetic syndromes, by four to five years.
  Mild, without significant functional loss in everyday activities though the child is abnormally clumsy, independent walking is achieved.

  Moderate, the child needs some assistance in everyday activities and may need some support for walking.

  Severe, the child needs total assistance in all but the simplest everyday activities and cannot walk even with support.

Children with different types of cerebral palsy,

No./ Sex	Probable/ possible cause	Type of CP, severity	Other disabilities	Educational placement
	Genetic			
1 M	Half-sib similarly affected	Dystonic quadriplegia, very severe	MR probably severe. Died 2 yrs. 7 mths.	Institution
2 M	Autosomal recessive	Disequilibrium syndrome, severe	MR moderate	NK, transferred out
3 M	Repeated abortions, sib mildly affected	Ataxic diplegia, mild	Arrested hydrocephalus	Primary school
	Prenatal			
4 F	Multiple MCA (6) v. small stature	Ataxic diplegia, mild	MR mild	Assessment class MH school
5 M	Multiple MCA (6) v. small stature	Ataxic diplegia, mild	Severe communiction disorder (familial)	Special day nursery Primary school def.
6 M	Multiple MCA (4)	Ataxic diplegia, moderate	Arrested hydrocephalus	Special day nursery Primary school
7 F	Multiple MCA (5)	R. hemiplegia, mild	—	Nursery class Primary school
	Perinatal			
8 M	LBW	R. hemiplegia, mild	—	Special day nursery Primary school
9 M	LBW	Diplegia, mild → moderate	—	Special day nursery Primary school
10 F	Severe respiratory difficulties	Ataxic diplegia, moderate	—	PH nursery class Primary school
11 F	Cerebral haemorrhage	Bil. hemiplegia, moderate	Severe dysarthria	PH nursery class Primary school
	? Pre- ? perinatal			
12 M	Severe fetal distress ? reason Multiple MCA (5)	Quadriplegia, very severe	MR severe epilepsy Died 6 yrs. 9 mths.	Day care unit

other disabilities, aetiology and educational placement

Social grade	Birthweight (g)	Gestation (wks.)	Pregnancy	Complications Delivery	Neonatal	MCA
3	3745	40	Pre-eclamptic toxaemia	Forceps	—	—
1	2835	40	Urinary tract infection	—	—	—
1	3200	41	—	Caesarian section, age/reproductive history	—	3
1	3190	39	—	Forceps	—	7
3	2440	38	—	Forceps	—	6
2	3530	40	Threatened abortion	—	—	4
1	2945	39	—	—	—	5
3	1800	32	Hypertension	—	—	—
4	1425	30	—	—	Repeated apnoea	—
3	2400	32	Appendix abscess 30 wks.	—	Urinary ascites, ruptured bladder, respiratory difficulties	—
1	3690	40	Hypertension	—	Cerebral bleed 27 hrs., convulsions	—
2	4000	41	—	Ventouse	Apnoeic (ventilator), gross neurological abnormality	5

Appendix VII-*cont.*

No./ Sex	Probable/ possible cause	Type of CP, severity	Other disabilities	Educational placement
	Postnatal			
13 M	TB Meningitis	L. hemiplegia, moderate	L. hemianopia hydrocephalus (VP shunt) precocious puberty MR mild	PH nursery class MH/PH school
14 M	Frontal lobe abscess	L. hemiplegia, moderate	—	PH nursery class Primary school def.
	Not known			
15 F		L. hemiplegia, mild	—	Nursery class Primary school
16 M		L. hemiplegia, moderate	—	PH nursery class Primary school def.
17 M		R. hemiplegia, mild	—	Primary school
18 M		Dyskinesia, moderately severe	Severe dysarthria	Special day nursery PH school

MCA = minor congenital anomalies; VP = ventriculo-peritoneal shunt; MH = mental handicap; deferred for 12 months.

140

Social grade	Birthweight (g)	Gestation (wks.)	Pregnancy	Complications Delivery	Neonatal	MCA
1	2976	38	—	—	—	—
3	3657	41	Hypertension	Forceps	—	—
2	3900	39	—	—	Jaundice, 2 days phototherapy	—
4	4394	43	—	—	—	—
2	2501	40	—	Forceps	—	—
4	3345	40	—	—	—	—

PH = physical handicap; MR = mental retardation; NK = not known; def = Primary 1 entrance

141

REFERENCES

Bayley, N. (1961) *Infant Scales of Development.* New York: Psychological Corporation.
Drillien, C. M. (1977) 'Cerebral palsy, classification'. *In:* Drillien, C. M., Drummond, M. B. (Eds.) *Neurodevelopmental Problems in Early Childhood.* Oxford: Blackwell Scientific Publications.
Hagberg, G., Hagberg, B., Olow, I. (1975) 'The changing panorama of cerebral palsy in Sweden 1954-1970. I: Analysis of the general changes; II: Analysis of the various syndromes.' *Acta Paediatrica Scandinavica,* **64,** 187-192; 193-200.
Hardie, J. de Z., Macfarlane, A. (1980) 'Late walking children: Oxford area: *Health Visitor,* **53,** 466-468.
Henderson, J. L. (Ed.) (1961) *Cerebral Palsy in Childhood and Adolescence.* Edinburgh: Livingstone.
Ingram, T. T. S. (1964) *Paediatric Aspects of Cerebral Palsy.* Edinburgh: Livingstone.
Neligan, G., Prudham, D. (1969) 'Potential value of four early developmental milestones in screening children for increased risk of later retardation.' *Developmental Medicine and Child Neurology,* **11,** 423-431.
Reynell, J. K. (1969) *Reynell Developmental Language Scales.* Windsor: National Foundation for Educational Research.
Silva, P. A. (1976) *A Thousand Dunedin Three-Year-Olds. Report to the Medical Research Council of New Zealand* (unpublished).
—— (1979) 'The significance of early delays in motor development.' *New Zealand Journal of Health, Physical Education and Recreation,* **12,** 78-83.
Stanley, F. (1979) 'An epidemiological study of cerebral palsy in Western Australia 1956-1975. 1. Changes in total cerebral palsy incidence and associated factors.' *Developmental Medicine and Child Neurology,* **21,** 701-713.
—— (1982) 'Using cerebral palsy data in the evaluation of neonatal intensive care: a warning.' *Developmental Medicine and Child Neurology,* **24,** 93-94.

142

CHAPTER 8

Speech Disorder and Severe Hearing Loss

Of all preschool neurodevelopmental disabilities (NDD) in this study, speech disorders comprised the largest group. The frequency of speech disorders in the total population of 5334 children was 45 per 1000; in 29 per 1000 the disorder was considered moderate or more severe (Table 4.3, p. 57). The frequency in the more stable population who remained in Dundee from birth until after three years was 57 per 1000 overall; in 42 per 1000 the disorder was moderate or more severe.

Speech and language was the main problem for 30 per cent of all children referred to the Child Development Centre (CDC) and 56 per cent of children referred to hospital clinics. After exclusion of NDD graded as of minor severity, 27 per cent of CDC children and 40 per cent of others had a speech problem as their main disability.

To some extent the identification and calculated frequency of speech and language disorders is determined by availability of facilities for assessment and treatment. In Dundee, speech therapy services are well developed and requests for assessments of preschool children are acepted from family practitioners, community child health doctors, paediatricians, other consultants dealing with children, dentists, clinical and educational psychologists, nursery class teachers, health visitors and occasionally directly from parents. In some parts of the city there are waiting lists for therapy but assessment appointments are offered with little delay.

Because what constitutes a speech problem in one area could remain unidentified or be considered acceptably normal in another, an attempt was made to specify as precisely as possible what was considered to be a speech disorder in this study. An attempt was made to assign a severity rating to each child's speech and language problem at three years or older based on (1) age levels in comprehension and expression derived from the Reynell Developmental Language Scales (1969) and (2) articulation age derived from the Edinburgh Articulation Test (Anthony *et al.* 1971), together with the speech therapist's comments on articulatory difficulties. It should be emphasised that these ratings can only constitute approximations to the severity of the children's speech problems.

Virtually all children with speech problems referred to the hospital speech therapy department (either directly or after prior referral to the Department of Otolaryngology or the Children's Hearing Assessment Clinic) received a formal speech and language assessment. In 10 cases, however, records of test results were not available (testing may not have been carried out in a few of these cases). 30 (24 per cent) of the 125 children referred to CDC were not formally assessed. Two children left the city before three years, *i.e.* before the age at which we considered an accurate and predictive assessment of speech and language could be obtained. Three children left town before their speech therapy appointment was made or did not

TABLE 8.1

Classification of speech disorders

Severity rating	Delay in comprehension/expression compared with CA	Delay in expression compared with comprehension
	%	%
Language delay		
WNL	⩾85	⩾80
Mild	80-84	75-79
Moderate	75-79	70-74
Moderately severe	70-74	65-69
Severe	⩽69	⩽64
Articulatory problems		
WNL	Articulatory level appropriate for age or some inappropriate developmental errors likely to resolve spontaneously	
Minor (A)	Many inappropriate developmental errors ± a few deviant	
Moderate (A+)	Many inappropriate developmental errors + more than a few deviant	
Severe (A++)	Unintelligible at 3½ to 4½ years	

WNL = Within normal limits; CA = chronological age.

attend for this. 24 children, all referred after the two-year screening examination, were considered to show mild expressive delays (21 children) or minor articulatory problems only (three children) and by three years demonstrated the improvements that had been anticipated. The remaining child had suffered from severe deprivation; language improved markedly after placement in foster care and speech assessment was no longer required.

In some instances formal assessment was difficult because of lack of co-operation or other behaviour disturbance and the therapist commented that test scores were probable under-estimates. In most of these cases repeat test results were obtained after a six-month interval but six children did not attend for re-assessment and the severity rating assigned was based on the therapist's stated opinion of spontaneous speech and not on test-score results. The overall severity grading (p. 48) could differ from the speech and language rating if the child had other problems of hearing, behaviour or motor clumsiness. Improvement over time and response to therapy were also taken into account in assigning the overall grading.

Table 8.1 details the criteria on which severity ratings were based. Language level was sub-divided into:
(1) expression and comprehension within normal limits;
(2) delay in both comprehension and expression as compared with chronological age with abilities in other areas of development within the normal range (general delay);
(3) delay in expression only, comprehension within normal limits;
(4) expressive level within normal limits but relative delay in expression as compared with comprehension.

144

Articulatory problems were categorised within each sub-division as detailed in the table. In functional terms, children whose articulation was considered to be within normal limits were, by age two and a half to three years, easily intelligible to family and reasonably so to strangers. Children with minor problems were usually intelligible to family although strangers had some difficulty in understanding them. The families of children with moderate problems had difficulty in understanding them and to strangers they were unintelligible. Articulatory problems were considered severe when children were equally unintelligible to families and strangers at three and a half to four years.

Children with speech and language problems in the following categories of NDD are not included in most of the analyses (numbers of children are given in parentheses):

(1) global delay and mental retardation with particular delay in speech and language (25);

(2) delay or disorder in gross and/or fine motor function with associated speech problems (10);

(3) behaviour disturbance and speech delay with the speech problems considered to be largely due to, or relatively minor as compared with the behaviour disturbance (15);

(4) speech disorder due to physical defect, *e.g.* neurological abnormality or hearing loss (10);

(5) initial speech disorder later changing to another main category (20).

Associated behaviour disturbance

Forty-three per cent of the group of children with speech disorders as principal problem referred to CDC also had significant behaviour disturbances. In the following discussions speech disorders among CDC-referred children have been detailed separately for those with and without behaviour disorder. In the group of hospital-referred children, only 11 (9 per cent) were reported to have associated behaviour disturbance and these have not been detailed separately. The two CDC-referred children with speech delay who left Dundee before the age of three years have been excluded from most analyses.

SPEECH DISORDERS

Distribution of speech disorders by type and severity

Appendix VIII details the distribution of speech disorders detected before school entry among CDC- and hospital-referred children. It was calculated that the number of 1974/75-born children in Dundee between two years and school entry (a diagnosis of primary speech disorder was not made before two years) was approximately 4245, giving an incidence of identified speech disorders, in that age period of 5.6 per cent. One-half of these children had relatively minor articulatory errors and/or mild expressive language delay only. This number does not include 86 children with speech problems who were included in other main clinical categories

TABLE 8.2

Children with speech disorder included in other main clinical categories (N = 86)

Global delay with more marked delay in speech	23
Mild mental retardation with severe communication problem	2
Speech disorder associated with motor disorder	10
hearing loss	4
specific neurological condition	6
Behaviour and speech disorder, behaviour predominant	15
Behaviour disorder with severe communication problem	6
Initial speech disorder, other major disorder later	20
Total	86

TABLE 8.3

Overall severity grading for CDC-referred children with a final diagnosis of speech disorder (N = 123)

	Speech		Speech and behaviour		All	
	No.	%	No.	%	No.	%
Overall severity grading						
Minor	25	36	2	4	27	22
Moderate	38	54	37	69	75	61
Moderately severe	5	7	13	25	18	15
Severe	2	3	1	2	3	2
Total	70	100	53	100	123	100

(Table 8.2). If these are included, the incidence of speech disorders is increased to 7.5 per cent with 42 per cent of the disorders rated as of minor severity. Moderately severe or severe speech disorder (*i.e.* highly likely or certain to pose difficulties at school-entry age) as principal problem was identified in 1 per cent of the population.

Of the 241 Dundee children with speech disorder as their major disability, the type and/or severity of the disorder was not known in 12 cases, two of whom transferred out before three years. Of the remaining 229 children, 87 (38 per cent) had articulatory disorders only with language development within normal limits, 119 (52 per cent) were delayed in expressive language (42 per cent of these also had articulatory problems) and 23 (10 per cent) were delayed in both comprehension and expression. Two of this last group had additional problems of articulation.

Overall severity grading.

Table 8.3 gives the distribution by severity grading for CDC-referred children with a final diagnosis of speech disorder. This grading takes account of total disabilities suffered by the child in predicting the probability of educational and behavioural problems in the early school years. For 27 children (22 per cent) the problems were considered minor and/or transitory; this number represented 36 per

TABLE 8.4

Children with speech disorders attending hospital speech therapy department (N = 116), circumstances of referral

	Speech therapy	ENT→ speech therapy	Referred to: Family doctor → speech therapy ± ENT	Outpatients* → speech therapy ± ENT	Total No.	%
Referred by:						
Screening programme	24	5	3	2	34	29
Family doctor	22	5	—	3	30	26
Community doctor	17	3	—	—	20	17
Nursery class/day nursery**	10	1	—	—	11	10
Health visitor	9	1	—	—	10	9
Parent	5	—	—	—	5	4
Hospital†	3	1	—	1	5	4
Teacher	1	—	—	—	1	1
Total (%)	91 (78)	16 (14)	3 (3)	6 (5)	116	(100)

*Children's Medical Outpatients Department; **child referred by community doctor attending nursery class/day nursery; †attending for unrelated condition; ENT = Department of Otolaryngology

cent of those with speech problems only and 4 per cent of children with additional behaviour disturbance. 21 children (17 per cent) were considered certain or very likely to have considerable problems in school and in 75 cases (61 per cent) the prognosis was less certain.

Circumstances of identification

Of the 125 CDC-referred children with a final main diagnosis of speech disorder, all but three were referred from the screening programme. The speech problems of one child were detected when attending hospital for an unrelated condition, one was referred by the family doctor and one by the hospital speech therapy department.

Of the 116 children attending the hospital speech therapy department, 34 (29 per cent) were referred from the screening programme and 82 (71 per cent) from other sources (Table 8.4). First attendance was at four years or older in nearly one-half of cases.

Sex distribution

The male:female ratio of all children identified as having a principal problem of speech disorder was 2.5:1. The male:female ratio of children with other principal problems was 1.5:1.

64 per cent of the total 414 CDC-referred children were boys as were 74 per cent of those referred to CDC with speech disorder as their main disability. 60 per cent of the remaining 281 children were boys. This difference is highly significant ($\chi^2 = 7.492$, p = <0.01). There were relatively more boys than girls among those with additional behaviour disturbance (79 per cent male) than among those with

TABLE 8.5
Preferred hand at three years for CDC-referred speech-disordered children and all children screened at three years

	Speech only		Speech and behaviour		Children screened at three years	
	No.	%	No.	%	No.	%
Preferred hand						
Right	38	54	27	51	2215	70
Left	7	10	3	6	282	9
Either	25	36	23	43	647	21
Total	70	100	53	100	3144	100

speech disorder only (69 per cent male). However, the difference is not statistically significant. 69 per cent of hospital-referred children with speech disorder were male.

Social class distribution

Children with speech disorders tended to be of lower social class than did children in the general population (see Tables 4.12, 4.13, pp. 65-66). The social class distribution of speech-disordered children was: I and II, 15 per cent; III, 51 per cent; IV and V, 34 per cent compared with 18, 48 and 29 per cent in the general population. Since mothers from higher social classes are more likely to seek advice about mild to moderate speech delays and articulatory problems, it could be that the real difference by social class is greater than appears here.

Hand preference

Hand preference was part of the routine examination at the three-year development screening. This information was recorded at the same age for all speech-disordered children referred to CDC before the age of three years and extracted from their three-year screening card if first attendance was after that age. Preferred hand was recorded for 92 per cent (3144) of all children born 1974/75 and screened at three years (3429).

Table 8.5 gives the preferred hand at three years for speech-disordered children and for the 3144 children screened at three years. 48 speech-disordered children (39 per cent) had not established a hand preference by age three years as compared with 21 per cent of the 3144 children. Children with speech and behaviour disorder were more likely to be ambidextrous (43 per cent) than were children with speech problems only (36 per cent). However, this difference is not statistically significant.

Other differences between speech-disordered children with and without behaviour disturbance
Distribution by severity of expressive delay

Children with behaviour disorders in addition to their speech problems were likely to have more severe degrees of expressive language delay than were children without behaviour disturbance. The difference in distribution by severity between

TABLE 8.6

Severity of expressive speech delays among 92 speech-disordered, CDC-referred children

	Speech only		Speech and behaviour	
	No.	%	No.	%
Severity of expressive speech delay				
Mild	31	62	12	29
Moderate	7	14	11	26
Moderately severe	7	14	6	14
Severe	5	10	13	31
Total	50	100	42	100

TABLE 8.7

Neurological status of CDC-referred speech-disordered children

	Speech only		Speech and behaviour	
	No.	%	No.	%
Neurological status				
Normal	45	65	23	43
Doubtful	16	23	16	30
Abnormal	8	12	14	26
Total	69	100	53	100

the 50 children with expressive delay and unexceptional behaviour and the 42 children with expressive delay and disturbed behaviour (Table 8.6) is significant at a p value of <0.01 ($\chi^2 = 12.313$, 3df).

Children with behaviour problems were also more likely to have articulatory disorders as well as their expressive speech delay. 36 per cent of the speech disorder only group had significant problems of articulation in addition to expressive delay compared with 62 per cent of the speech and behaviour group. This difference is statistically significant ($\chi^2 = 6.139$, p. = <0.02). However, the difference appears to be due largely to the increasing frequency of articulatory problems with increasing severity of expressive language delay, as shown in Appendix VIII.

Neurological abnormality

Table 8.7 details the neurological status of speech-disordered CDC-referred children with and without associated behaviour disturbance. One child with speech disorder who was not adequately examined at first attendance and did not re-attend is excluded. Children with behaviour disturbance were more likely to show doubtful or frankly abnormal minor neurological signs. The difference in distribution is statistically significant ($\chi^2 = 6.768$, 2df, p. = <0.05).

There was also a significant increase in the number of children who were clumsy in gait and/or hand function in the group with associated behaviour disturbance. 30

149

TABLE 8.8

Social grade distribution of speech-disordered CDC-referred children

	Speech only		Speech and behaviour	
	No.	%	No.	%
Social grade				
1 and 2	22	31	6	11
3	39	56	36	68
4	9	13	11	21
Total	70	100	53	100

per cent of this group were clumsy as compared with 12 per cent of those without behaviour disturbance. This difference is also statistically significant ($\chi^2 = 6.559$, $p = <0.02$).

Social grade

Children with behaviour problems as well as speech disorder were more likely to come from poorer homes than children with speech disorder only (Table 8.8). The difference in distribution by social grade is significant at a p value of <0.05 ($\chi^2 = 7.254$, 2df).

Types of behaviour disturbance associated with speech delay

The most common types of behaviour problems associated with speech delay were combinations of overactivity, poor concentration, attention seeking, tantrums, aggression, negative and disruptive behaviour (Table 9.8). These problems were reported for 45 (85 per cent) of the 53 CDC-referred children with speech and behaviour disorders; eight had additional problems. 13 children (25 per cent) presented with timidity, nervousness, excessive shyness, immaturity and clinging or withdrawn behaviour. Five of these were among the 45 in the other problem group.

MANAGEMENT OF CDC-REFERRED CHILDREN WITH SPEECH DISORDER

Referrals to the Department of Otolaryngology

Hearing testing of speech-disordered children was carried out at CDC by a senior community child health doctor.

Thirty-five children (28 per cent) were further referred to the Department of Otolaryngology mainly on account of suspected deafness or of secretory otitis with or without hearing loss. The hearing of eight children was found to be within normal limits and no diagnosis of secretory otitis was made. One child was found to have a mild degree of sensorineural hearing loss. 22 children (18 per cent) were found to have secretory otitis and intermittent hearing loss was confirmed or suspected. Myringotomy was carried out for all but three of these children, with the insertion of

150

TABLE 8.9
Nursery class placement for speech-disordered CDC-referred children

Nursery class recommended	
Normal nursery class	71
Assessment class	2
No vacancy available	6
Vacancy refused or child removed	12
Child in day nursery, nursery class vacancy refused	6
Nursery class not recommended	6
Removed, discharged, did not re-attend ≤3 years	22
Total	125

grommets in most cases. Two further children were found to have hearing loss associated with keratotis obturans. Two children were referred to the Department for investigation of palatal function. One other child received surgery for a severe degree of tongue-tie.

Nursery class and other day placement

Twenty-two children with speech disorders were discharged from CDC, did not re-attend or left Dundee at or before the age of three years, which is the youngest age for admission to nursery class. A nursery class placement was recommended for all but six of the remaining 103 children (Table 8.9). No suitable vacancy was available for six children. In 12 cases a vacancy was refused or the child was removed from the class after a short period of attendance and in six cases the child was attending day nursery and the mother refused a more suitable nursery class placement. 71 children attended normal nursery classes and two, with severe communication problems, attended the assessment class.

Referral to psychologists

Eleven of the 53 children with associated behaviour disturbance (21 per cent) were referred to the Department of Clinical Psychology for management. In three instances the appointment was not taken up or the mother did not attend subsequently.

Fifteen of the 19 children with moderately severe or severe speech disorder (excluding two who transferred out before four years) were referred to the Child Guidance Service as were six children with less serious speech problems. Overall, 20 per cent of children with speech disorders who remained in Dundee at school entry age were referred for advice about possible schooling difficulties in Primary 1. In 14 cases it was recommended that Primary 1 entrance should be deferred for 12 months and the child continue to attend nursery class or assessment class with speech therapy back-up. 10 of these children had additional behaviour disorder.

Speech therapy

Of the 95 children who had one or more speech and language assessments carried out at CDC, 59 (62 per cent) were offered speech therapy (Table 8.10). 47

TABLE 8.10

Speech therapy recommended or not for CDC-referred children with speech disorders

| | Therapy offered | | | |
	Therapy given	Refused/ removed	Therapy not offered	Total
Articulatory problems only	7	3	8	18
Severity of language disorder				
mild	7	2	16	25
moderate	11	3	7	21
moderately severe	6	3	4	13
severe	16	1	1	18
Total	47	12	36	95

children attended for regular speech therapy sessions extending over periods of six months to two years. A further 12 children were offered speech therapy but this was refused or the child attended only rarely. All but one of the children with severe language disorder were offered therapy; the one who was not had very overactive behaviour with limited concentration over an extended period and was considered unsuitable for therapy because of this. The same behaviour problems existed in the four children with moderately severe speech disorder who were not offered therapy.

SEVERE COMMUNICATION DISORDERS

Severe communication disorders were classified as primary or secondary. A primary disorder was defined as a language delay or disorder of such severity that the child would be unable to enter the Primary 1 class of a normal school at the usual age. Some would benefit from initial placement in a special educational unit for language-impaired children. Children with secondary disorders had other handicapping conditions with a resultant or superimposed severe disorder of communication which comprised the major disability. Children who failed to acquire speech on account of hearing defect or severe mental retardation, with language development consistent with that of other abilities, are not included. Nine children suffered from a primary disorder and 11 from secondary disorders (Appendix IX). All but one child with a primary disorder were referred to CDC.

Primary disorder

All but one of the nine children in this category were male of whom four had a history of slow speech development in a family member. Nos. 1 and 2 were brothers. Their father was admitted to special education at five years having only recently started to speak. He was returned to the normal school system after a few weeks when it became evident that he was not mentally retarded. The mother (the daughter of a teacher) was reported to have said her first words at four years. The older brother of No. 3 has similar language difficulties and received educational provision in a special language unit. The father of No. 4 was also very slow to speak preschool.

152

Five of the eight boys with a primary severe communication disorder exhibited multiple minor congenital anomalies. Two were also of very small stature and had been small for date at birth. One boy was found to have a chromosome abnormality (8/14 translocation) and another had a cleft lip. Although the number of cases is very small, the high proportion of major or multiple minor anomalies in this group of children (67 per cent) is significantly higher than that found among other speech-disordered children, of whom only 12 per cent showed multiple anomalies (χ^2 = 4.573, applying Yates correction, p. = <0.05).

Five children were described as definitely clumsy in gait and/or hand function and one boy had a mild ataxic diplegia. Thus the majority had evidence of neurological dysfunction. Only 18 per cent of other speech-disordered children were clumsy. This difference is also highly significant (χ^2 = 11.370, p. = <0.001).

In five cases Primary 1 placement was deferred for 12 months, the children remaining in normal nursery classes with language stimulation programmes. All proceeded therafter to normal school. Three are keeping up with class work and have no problems of behaviour (Nos. 1, 4, 5). Two have severe educational and behavioural problems (Nos. 2, 9). All but one (No. 5) had limited ability in expressive language at six and a half to seven and a half years and all are still difficult to understand because of poor speech.

Four were offered places in the assessment class in the hope that normal school entrance would be possible at a later age. This was achieved in only one case (No. 7) who is a non-reader at age seven and a half years. One boy (No. 6) from a disturbed and disorganised home background with considerable behaviour problems (anti-social and immature) and continuing expressive speech delay was admitted to a small group in a special school for maladjusted children. One other (No. 8) with behaviour disturbance and co-ordination problems was transferred to the Language Unit and in the last case (No. 3) the parents refused both speech therapy and special placement. They enrolled their child in the local primary school, where he has made little educational progress in the first two years; it is likely that he will join his brother in the Language Unit. Overall, six of nine children classified as having severe primary communication disorders were experiencing severe educational problems at age seven years.

Secondary disorders

Six children, five of them male, suffered from severe behaviour disorders with failure to communicate and social isolation as outstanding handicapping features (p. 173). Two children had suffered severe emotional deprivation; one (No. 11) came from a disorganised and disruptive home and the other (No. 12) had been exposed to the practices of a psychiatrically disturbed father who had an obsession with the macabre. She attained near normal levels in language development on testing but remained largely non-communicating in the social situation.

All these children were offered places in the assessment class; the parents of one (No. 13) refused. One boy of good intelligence (No. 14) made striking progress in speech and entered normal school, though he remained somewhat withdrawn. All others required special educational provision.

153

Two girls with mental retardation, considered mild on non-verbal intelligence testing, were non-communicating. Both exhibited multiple minor congenital anomalies and were of very small stature. One (No. 16) had experienced a period of deafness (p. 155) but language did not develop when this resolved. The second child (No. 17) is being trained in the use of the Bliss symbolic language system as a means of communication.

Two of the 18 children with cerebral palsy had severe dysarthrias (Appendix 7). Language development of one (No. 18) was above her chronological age but speech remained very difficult to understand because of involvement of the articulatory musculature. The other (No. 19) was virtually unintelligible even to familiars and Bliss symbolics are being used to assist communications. The Amerind system of gestures is being taught to a severely retarded boy (No. 20) with myotonic dystrophy. Weakness of facial muscles, lips and tongue precludes even the most elementary development of spoken language.

SEVERE HEARING LOSS

Severe hearing loss is defined here as one necessitating attendance at nursery school or primary school for the hearing impaired and/or the use of a hearing aid. This definition was preferred to one involving degree of hearing (decibel, dB) loss since there was considerable variation in audiometric results over the period of preschool supervision.

Ten 1974/75-born children came into this category (Table 8.11). Three other children with specific syndromes also had severe hearing loss: one suffering from congenital rubella had a profound sensorineural deafness with other disabilities (p. 000), one who died later was deaf, blind and severely retarded as a result of osteopetrosis and the third suffered from Down's syndrome. The frequency of severe hearing loss was 2.4 per 1000 in the total population of 5334 1974/75 births although only six of the 12 surviving children required special educational provision on account of hearing loss.

Four children with severe sensorineural hearing loss were identified or suspected in the first year of life. The parents of one child, referred to CDC at eight months because of doubts expressed by the health visitor following hearing screening, were both profoundly deaf. This had been attributed to congenital rubella in the case of the father and to measles at 13 months in the mother. Initially the baby's inconsistent responses to sound were attributed by the otolaryngologist to her being reared in a non-hearing environment. Admission to day nursery did not result in any improvement and a hearing aid was provided at one year nine months. Severe hearing loss was confirmed at two years three months. This child is of normal intelligence and attends deaf school. A younger brother has normal hearing. In spite of the parents' medical histories it seems likely that a genetic element was operating here. A second child with severe sensorineural loss was suspected at the 20-week development screening examination and the loss was confirmed shortly afterwards. He attends deaf school. No cause for his deafness was found nor for the severe

TABLE 8.11
Types of severe hearing defect among 10 children excluding those with specific syndromes

	Probable/possible cause	*No. cases*
Type of hearing defect		
Sensorineural loss	Familial	2
	Other prenatal	1
	Unknown	3
Sensorineural + conductive loss	Prenatal + secretory otitis	1
	Unknown	1
Conductive loss	Secretory otitis	1
	Purulent otitis	1

sensorineural loss in another boy who transferred into Dundee from Canada at age one year nine months with hearing loss already confirmed. He attended deaf nursery class before his return to Canada; special educational provision was anticipated. Hearing loss was suspected on health visitor screening at eight months and global delay with deafness on 39-week development screening in the daughter of a mentally retarded mother who refused further referral until her child was 16 months old. This child was found to have a chromosomal abnormality with one chromosome in the D group having very long short arms (46, xx, Dp +). Attempts to carry out chromosome analyses on parents were unsuccessful; this might have been interesting academically but of limited practical significance as the mother had already been sterilised. This child is profoundly deaf, probably mildly mentally retarded with very withdrawn behaviour and failure to communicate by non-verbal means.

Two children were considered to have a conductive loss superimposed on a moderate or more severe sensorineural loss. One was missed on hearing screening at eight months and suspected but not identified on development screening at 39 weeks. Screening at 15 months was missed and the child did not attend the clinic at two years. Referral was requested on the basis of a home screen at two and a half years, when the child was reported as only having five words. Neither mother nor health visitor agreed to this request, choosing to wait until the child was three years old. Once more he did not attend for screening but was referred by the family doctor to the Children's Medical Outpatient Department and thence to the Department of Otolaryngology. He was found to have a conductive loss due to secretory otitis superimposed on a moderately severe sensorineural loss of unknown cause. He was considered to have been significantly deaf 'for some time'. This child attended deaf nursery class until age five years and thereafter attended an educational unit for partially hearing children. Deafness was suspected in the other child at 15-months screening. She was a very odd-looking child with 13 minor congenital anomalies and global delay, especially in locomotor function. In the first year she had exhibited dystonic signs and at 15 months showed marked hypotonia with increased tendon jerks. She appeared to have a marked degree of nasal obstruction with constant nasal discharge. Choanal atresia was not confirmed but she underwent tonsillectomy, adenoidectomy and choanal bougienage at one year eight months. At two years six months electrocochleography confirmed a sensorineural loss of 60 dB or more and hearing aids were supplied. She developed bilateral secretory otitis and at three and a half years electrocochleography suggested a loss of 90dB on the left and 80dB on the right with a conductive loss superimposed. On two occasions bilateral myringotomy with insertion of grommets was carried out. At age four years ten months electrocochleography confirmed that hearing had improved and a trial without aiding was instituted. The child is mildly retarded but has developed virtually no speech, although her hearing has been considered adequate for the acquisition of speech for 12 months. She attended deaf nursery class and the assessment class before admission to special education.

Three children with hearing aids entered normal school at the usual age without prior attendance at deaf nursery class. Two had been missed previously on hearing screening and on development screening. One child was referred to the Department of Otolaryngology by the family doctor at three years 10 months on account of suspected secretory otitis which was not confirmed. She was re-referred at four years five months with suspected deafness, mother having become concerned, and was found to have a moderately severe sensorineural loss. At two-year screening she was doubtful in speech, not joining words, not vocalising all needs and her intelligibility was rated as fair. At three-year screening all speech items were passed and intelligibility said to be good. That the screening doctor might not have been mistaken in her conclusion is supported by the opinion of the otolaryngologist who commented, at four and a half years, 'speech is remarkably good for this degree of deafness'. The fact that the father and a sister both suffered from a degree of sensorineural hearing loss was not recorded at any screening examination. The child attends normal school and is said to have no problems. A second girl was referred to the Speech and Hearing Clinic at three years 11 months by the clinical medical officer of her nursery class on account of poor speech and possible hearing loss. This was not confirmed. At four years 11 months electrocochleography demonstrated a moderately severe sensorineural loss. At two-year screening she was not joining words; intelligibility was not recorded. She did not attend for three-year screening but at home screen five months later the health visitor wrote 'speech has greatly improved since being in nursery class'. However, this was as reported by mother who has throughout been aggressive towards professionals and unaccepting of the degree of her child's difficulties. Aetiology was unknown in this case.

The third child attended CDC after two-year screening on account of poor speech and overactive behaviour. He was referred to the Speech and Hearing Clinic with suspected deafness at three years. This was not confirmed and poor speech was attributed to immaturity and behaviour disturbance. He was re-referred at four years with secretory otitis; by this age mother had become concerned about hearing. He was found to have a moderately severe conductive loss and a hearing aid was prescribed after myringotomy. He attends a school for the partially hearing.

One other child suffered from a moderately severe conductive loss following longstanding bilateral purulent otitis media with large perforations in the tympanic membranes. She was referred to CDC on account of suspected mental retardation at 15-month screening. The first appointment was not kept and thereafter the family disappeared. The child was first seen at two years and admitted to the special day nursery for a period of assessment. It was considered that she was within the normal range of intelligence but severely deprived and that speech delay was further exacerbated by hearing defect. She had had untreated discharging ears for 12 months. Social conditions were appalling with the family constantly on the move, intermittently housed in a tent even in severe winter conditions. Admission to hospital for treatment of the ear condition was achieved with difficulty. Thereafter the child was re-admitted to special day nursery and made rapid strides in all areas of development other than speech. Hearing improved to a level considered adequate for the acquisition of speech. On language assessment auditory comprehension progressed to within the normal range but expressive language did not, the child continuing to use non-verbal methods of communication no doubt developed during the age period one and a half to two and a half years when hearing loss was probably severe. It was considered that she would benefit from teaching methods appropriate for deaf children and she was admitted to deaf nursery class at age three years 10 months. Expressive language gradually improved and she should have been admitted to the Primary 1 class of the local school at five years eight months. However, the family again disappeared and, although she is known to have had a few weeks in school in another part of Scotland, the family remains untraced. The mother seldom attended school and is illiterate; it appears likely that her three children will follow that pattern.

COMPARISON WITH OTHER STUDIES

Incidence of speech disorders

In the Dundee study 7.5 per cent of two to five year olds were identified as having speech disorders either as principal or secondary problems. 42 per cent of the disorders were minor problems of articulation or mild expressive delays. The incidence of disorders considered certain or highly likely to pose considerable problems at school-entry age was 1 per cent. These figures are similar to those found in other preschool surveys, although those quoted below are not strictly comparable with the present study as they refer to numbers of children with speech disorders detected at specified ages rather than numbers with disorders detected over a period of years. The Dundee figures are based on referrals for assessment and it is likely that some other children with mild or moderate disorder would not have been identified.

In the Newcastle Child Development Study (Fundudis et al. 1979), 133 (4 per cent) of 3300 1962-born children were identified as having moderate or more severe speech retardation. This was defined as 'failure to use three or more words strung together to make some sort of sense' at three years (Neligan and Prudham 1969) and based on health visitor reports. The earlier 'one thousand families' Newcastle study (Spence et al. 1954) reported a 6 per cent incidence of speech retardation at age three years using broadly similar criteria. Of the 102 speech-retarded children remaining in the city at five years, 18 were 'pathologically deviant', suffering from marked intellectual handicap, cerebral palsy and specific syndromes. The remaining 84 children were categorised as the 'residual speech-retarded group'.

A 1:4 random sample (705 children) of a total population of non-immigrant three year olds living in an outer-London borough was studied by Stevenson and Richman (1976). Following a simple language screening procedure, a full psycho-developmental assessment was carried out with children having suspected language delay. Two criteria of language delay were used: (1) expressive language age less than or equal to two-thirds of chronological age, which would be equivalent to the Dundee category of severe disorder and (2) expressive language age less than or equal to 30 months (*i.e.* six months behind chronological age), equivalent to the Dundee categories of mild to moderately severe disorder. The prevalence rate of expressive language delay was 3.1 per cent but one-half of these children also showed non-verbal delay. Non-verbal mental age was based on hand-eye co-ordination and performance items from the Griffiths Mental Development Scale (Griffiths 1970). Non-verbal delay was taken as performance no better than two-thirds of that expected for chronological age. The rate of severe expressive delay was 2.3 per cent with over one-third of children being delayed in non-verbal abilities. The rate of specific language delay not associated with general retardation was 0.6 per cent which is much lower than that reported in most other surveys.

In the Dunedin Multidisciplinary Child Developmental Study (Silva 1980), the Reynell Developmental Language Scales were applied to 937 children at age three years. Children were considered to be delayed in verbal comprehension or expressive language if they had scores ≥ 2SD below the mean, which would be comparable to the Dundee categories of moderately severe/severe disorder. 79 children (8.4 per cent) were delayed in one or both aspects. They were divided into three groups: (1) 28 children with delayed comprehension only, of whom 7 per cent of those tested were generally retarded (Stanford-Binet IQ scores of <77); (2) 23 children with delayed expression only, of whom 11 per cent were generally retarded; and (3) 28 children with delay in both aspects, of whom 84 per cent were generally retarded. After excluding children whose delayed language development could have been appropriate for their abilities in other areas, 5.5 per cent of the population had marked speech delay, a higher rate than that reported in any other study. That over one-half had delay in comprehension only is surprising. In the Dundee sample no children showed this pattern apart from those with pathological conditions affecting speech production and those whose delayed expressive language was attributed to behavioural causes.

In a survey of four-year-old children attending preschools in Adelaide, 4.6 per cent had articulation problems and language delays which were described as minor in one-third (Johnston 1980). In the study of all children aged three years nine months to four years three months in two counties of England and Wales (Chazan *et al.* 1980), 4.4 per cent were said to have problems of speech and language development other than mild.

Curtis Jenkins (1977) reported that 8.8 per cent of children attending for developmental surveillance at three years had speech delay of sufficient severity to merit speech therapy referral, as did 4.6 per cent of those attending at four and a half years. This total of 13.4 per cent referred for speech therapy at three to four and a half years indicates a high incidence of speech disorder, but it is not stated how many children (if any) were considered to be within normal limits by speech therapists. In another group of children seen for developmental assessment at three and four and a half years (Bax and Hart 1976), speech and language problems were detected in 15 per cent of the three year olds and 5 per cent of those aged four and a half years. These children were independently assessed later using the Reynell Developmental Language Scales and good correlations found with developmental measures. This study also demonstrated a high incidence of speech and language delay, identified on developmental tests at three years but also that two-thirds of the delayed children appeared to have caught up by age four and half years.

Sex and social class

All the studies quoted reported a preponderance of males amongst children with speech disorder. In the Dundee study the male:female ratio was 2.5:1.

In the Newcastle 'pathologically deviant' speech-retarded group (Fundudis *et al.* 1979) there were equal numbers of boys and girls. In the residual speech-retarded group the male:female ratio was 2:1, as it was in the Dunedin (Silva 1980) and London (Stevenson and Richman 1976) studies. In the Adelaide group of children with speech and language delay the male:female ratio was 2.6:1.

In the Newcastle study (Fundudis *et al.* 1979) social class of the families of children in the residual group was rather lower than that of a random sample of children, but not significantly so. However, speech-retarded children were found to be at a significant disadvantage on other measures of social-economic status. In the Adelaide study (Johnston 1980) the incidence of speech disorder was increased among children of manual workers as compared with those in higher social classes but the differences by occupation of father were not statistically significant. Social factors are not mentioned in the other studies quoted.

Social class differences were not very striking in the Dundee study, but it seemed possible that children with speech problems from the lower social classes were less likely to be referred and identified (p. 148).

Behaviour problems among speech-retarded children

Only in the London study (Stevenson and Richman 1976) was reference made to coincident problems of behaviour at preschool ages. Of 18 children with language delay at three years, eight were also included in a group of 99 children identified as having behaviour problems at the same age. In our study, 43 per cent of 123 speech-disordered children attending CDC at three years or older had significant problems of behaviour.

Incidence of hearing loss

Sheridan (1972) reported on the incidence of hearing loss at seven years in the National Child Development Study cohort of 1958 births. Over 90 per cent of the 16,750 infants who survived the neonatal period were traced at seven years and full audiograms were obtained for 11,276 children. Serious hearing impairment was defined as unilateral or bilateral hearing loss of 54 to 74dB and severe impairment as loss of $\geq$75dB. 55 children were found to have serious loss and 20 to have severe loss (6.6 per 1000). Adding together the results of audiometer selection and clinical sifting it was considered that 40 children (2.5 per 1000) would probably require special educational treatment in a unit for the partially hearing or school for the deaf because of serious/severe loss in one ear and moderate or more severe loss in the other. 46 children had unilateral loss only and could probably attend ordinary school.

Summary

Speech disorder

Frequency. The frequency of speech disorders in the total population was 42 per 1000 and 57 per 1000 in the more stable population. After excluding disorders of minor severity, frequencies were 29 and 42 per 1000. These numbers do not include children with speech problems included in other clinical categories. When these are included the frequency of speech disorder among children aged two to five years was 75 per 1000, with 58 per cent of the disorders considered moderate or more severe.

Circumstances of identification. Of 125 speech-disordered children attending CDC all but three were referred following screening. Of 116 children attending hospital clinics only 34 were referred from the screening programme. Nearly one-half attended first at four years or older.

Sex distribution. Male:female ratio was 2.5:1 as compared with 1.5:1 in children in other categories of NDD.

Hand preference. 39 per cent of speech-disordered children had not established hand preference at three years compared with 21 per cent in the general population.

Speech disorder with and without behaviour disturbance
As compared with behaviourally normal speech-disordered children, those with additional behaviour disturbance were more likely to suffer from more severe degrees of expressive delay, to show doubtful or abnormal neurological signs, to be clumsy in gait and/or hand function and to come from poorer homes. Types of behaviour disturbance are described.

Management. Management of speech-disordered children is described.

Severe communication disorders
These were defined as (1) a primary disorder of such severity that the child was unable to enter a Primary 1 class at the usual age (nine children) and (2) a disorder secondary to other handicapping conditions with the communication disorder comprising the major disability (11 children). These cases are described.

Severe hearing loss

Because of the variability of audiometric results over the period of preschool supervision, severe hearing loss was defined as one necessitating attendance at nursery or primary school for the hearing-impaired and/or the use of a hearing aid. Frequency was 2.4 per 1000. Types of hearing loss and circumstances of identification are described.

	CDC Speech	CDC Speech and behaviour	All		Hospital		Total	
	No.	No.	No.	%	No.	%	No.	%
WNL*								
A	13	3	16		52		68	
A + / + +	3	2	5		15		20	
Articulation only	16	5	21	17	67	57	88	37
Expressive delay								
Mild	26	7	33		9		42	
A	4	2	6		3		9	
A + / + +	1	3	4		2		6	
All mild expressive	31	12	43	35	14	12	57	24
Moderate	3	3	6		7		13	
A	2	6	8		—		8	
A + / + +	2	2	4		1		5	
All moderate expressive	7	11	18	15	8	7	26	11
Moderately severe	2	4	6		1		7	
A	2	1	3		—		3	
A + / + +	3	1	4		—		4	
All moderately severe expressive	7	6	13	10	1	1	14	6
Severe	1	2	3		2		5	
A	—	3	3		1		4	
A + / + +	4	8	12		—		12	
All severe expressive	5	13	18	15	3	3	21	9
General delay								
Mild	—	3	3		—		3	
A	—	1	1		1		2	
A + / + +	—		—		1		1	
All mild general	—	4	4	3	2	2	6	2
Moderate	1	—	1		3		4	
A	1	1	2		—		2	
A + / + +	1	—	1		—		1	
All moderate general	3	1	4	3	3	3	7	3
Moderately severe	1	—	1		1		2	
A	—	—	—		1		1	
A + / + +	—	—	—		2		2	
All moderately severe general	1	—	1	1	4	3	5	2
Severe	—	1	1		3		3	
A	—	—	—		—		1	
A + / + +	—	—	—		1		1	
All severe general	—	1	1	1	4	3	5	2
Not known	—	—	—		10	9	10	4
Total	70	53	123	100	116	100	239	100

*See Table 8.1 for explanation of articulatory problems; WNL = within normal limits.

APPENDIX IX: Details of children with severe communication disorders

No.	Sex	Family history	Social grade	Neuro. status	MCA	IQ	Reynell age	Comprehension/ expression ages	Articulation	Educational provision
Primary										
1.	M	Fa.Mo.	3	Normal	—	Low average	3.05 5.02	2.06 1.11 5.04 4.06	A+ +* A+	Nursery class with speech therapy P.1 deferred
2.	M	Bro.	3	Ataxic diplegia mild	4 v. small	Low average	3.03 5.01	2.03 2.05 4.05 4.04	A+ WNL	Nursery class with speech therapy P.1 deferred
3.	M	Bro.	4	Doubtful clumsy	4 v. small	Low average	3.03 6.06	2.07 2.06 5.10 4.04	A+ + A+ +	Assessment class refused P.1 → Language Unit
4.	M	Fa.	2	Normal	—	Average	3.02 5.00	3.04 2.05 4.10 3.03	A+ + A+ +	Nursery class with speech therapy P.1 deferred
5.	M	—	3	Normal	4	Good average	3.06 5.08	4.06 2.07 6.09 6.02	A+ + WNL	Nursery class with speech therapy P.1 deferred
6.	M	—	4	Doubtful clumsy	3	Average	4.03 6.00	4.01 3.07 5.01 3.11	WNL WNL	Assessment class with speech therapy Special school (maladjusted)
7.	M	—	4	Abnormal clumsy	8 Chrom. abn.	Low average	3.05 5.09	3.00 2.05 5.04 5.02	A+ + + A+	Assessment class with speech therapy P.1 deferred
8.	M	—	4	Doubtful clumsy	Cleft lip	Average	3.06 4.11	3.00 2.20 3.00 2.10	A+ A+	Assessment class with speech therapy Language Unit
9.	F	—	3	Doubtful clumsy	—	Low average	3.07 5.00	2.90 2.40 3.90 2.10	A+ + A+	Nursery class with speech therapy P.1 deferred
Secondary severe behaviour disturbance										
10.	M	—	1	Doubtful clumsy	—	Average	4.07	2.00 2.04	WNL	Assessment class with speech therapy Residential school (autistic)
11.	M	—	3	Normal	—	Well below average	3.06 4.09	1.08 2.02 1.08 2.02	A+	Assessment class with speech therapy Residential school (severely disturbed)
12.	F	—	3	Normal	—	Average	4.05	2.10 3.40	WNL	Assessment class with speech therapy Special school (maladjusted)
13.	M	—	4	Normal	6	Average	5.05 3.05	4.05 4.08 2.05 2.02	WNL	Assessment class refused P.1 (no progress)
14.	M	—	3	Doubtful	—	Above average	3.11 4.00	3.01 2.06 4.00 2.03	WNL	Assessment class with speech therapy P.1 deferred
15.	M	—	3	Normal	2	Average	5.04 3.04	5.04 5.01 2.03 1.06	WNL	Assessment class with speech therapy Language Unit

cont.

Appendix IX—cont.

No.	Sex	Family history	Social grade	Neuro. status	MCA	IQ	Reynell age	Comprehension/ expression age		Articulation	Educational provision
Mild mental retardation											
16.	F	—	4	Abnormal	13	?	4.11	2.08	2.00	A++	Assessment class with speech therapy
					v. small	60s	5.10	3.04	2.07	A++	Special school (MH)
17.	F	—	4	Abnormal	12	?	4.04	2.08	none	A++	Assessment class Bliss symbolics
					v. small	60s	5.10	3.04	2.07	A++	Special school (MH)
Neurological impairment											
18.	F	—	1	Bil. hemip. moderate	—	Average	3.06	3.08	2.09	A+++	PH nursery class with speech therapy
							4.06	5.00	4.11	A++++	P.1
19.	M	—	4	Dyskinesia mod. sev.	—	Low average	3.02	3.04	2.05	A+++	PH nursery class Bliss symbolics
							4.05	4.01	3.02	A+++	Special school (PH)
20.	M	—	4	Myotonic dystrophy	—	? 45-55	5.00	None	None		Special day nursery Amerind
											Special school (MH/PH)

*See Table 8.1 for explanation of auticulatory problems; MCA = minor congenital anomalies; WNL = within normal units; P1 = Primary 1; PH = physically handicapped; MH = mentally handicapped.

REFERENCES

Anthony, A., Bogle, D., Ingram, T. T. S., MacIsaac, M. W. (1961) *The Edinburgh Articulation Test.* Edinburgh: Churchill-Livingstone.

Bax, M., Hart, H. (1976) 'Health needs of preschool children.' *Archives of Disease in Childhood,* **51,** 852-858.

Chazan, M., Laing, A. F., Bailey, M. S., Jones, G. (1980) *Some of our Children: The Early Education of Children with Special Needs.* London: Open Books.

Curtis Jenkins, G. H. (1977) 'Surveillance of pre-school children in general practice.' *In:* Drillien, C. M., Drummond, M. B. (Eds.) *Neurodevelopmental Problems in Early Childhood.* Oxford: Blackwell Scientific Publications.

Fundudis, T., Kolvin, I., Garside, R. F. (1979) *Speech Retarded and Deaf Children: Their Psychological Development.* London: Academic Press.

Griffiths, R. (1970) *The Abilities of Young Children.* London: Child Development Research Centre.

Johnston, O. (1980) 'Ill health and developmental delays in Adelaide four-year-old children.' *Australian Paediatric Journal,* **16,** 248-254.

Neligan, G., Prudham, D. (1969) 'Norms for four standard developmental milestones by sex, social class and place in the family.' *Developmental Medicine and Child Neurology,* **11,** 413-422.

Reynell, J. K. (1969) *Reynell Developmental Language Scales.* Windsor: National Foundation for Educational Research.

Sheridan, M. D. (1972) 'Reported incidence of hearing loss in children at 7 years.' *Developmental Medicine and Child Neurology,* **14,** 296-303.

Silva, P. A. (1980) 'The prevalence, stability and significance of developmental language delay in preschool children.' *Developmental Medicine and Child Neurology,* **22,** 768-777.

Spence, J. C., Walton, W. S., Miller, F. J. W., Court, S. D. M. (1954) A Thousand Families in Newcastle-upon-Tyne. Oxford: Oxford University Press.

Stevenson, J., Richman, N. (1976) 'The prevalence of language delay in a population of three-year-old children and its association with general retardation.' *Developmental Medicine and Child Neurology,* **18,** 431-441.

CHAPTER 9

Behaviour Disorder

The frequency of preschool behaviour disorder of sufficient concern to parents or medical personnel to merit referral was 22 per 1000 in the total population of 5334 1974/75-born children. In 20 per 1000 the problems were considered to be moderate or more severe. In the more stable population of 3667 children who remained in Dundee throughout the screening period, the frequencies were 26 and 25 per 1000 (Table 4.3, p. 57).

Eighty-three (20 per cent) of the 414 children with neurodevelopmental disabilities (NDD) referred to the Child Development Centre (CDC) had a behaviour disorder as principal problem. 36 (17 per cent) of the 206 children with NDD seen in hospital clinics were referred on account of behaviour disorder. Significant behavioural problems were also present in 121 (37 per cent) of the 331 CDC-referred children in other clinical categories (Table 9.1). Overall, 49 per cent of CDC-referred children had behaviour problems other than what would be considered acceptable aberrations of behaviour in young children. When children with behaviour disorder (moderate or more severe) in other clinical categories are added in, the frequency of disorder in the more stable population rises to 54 per 1000.

Our attempts to categorise behaviour disorders posed considerable difficulties. The classification described below was based on age of presentation, functional impairment and the most common combinations of problems. All

TABLE 9.1

Behaviour problems among CDC-referred children

	No.	%
Behaviour as main problem	83	20
Behaviour problem with:		
global delay	30	7
mental retardation	15	3
motor disorder	11	3
cerebral palsy	7	2
speech disorder	53	13
hearing loss	1	<1
specific conditions	4	1
No behaviour problem	210	51
Total	414	100

166

TABLE 9.2
Classification of CDC-and hospital-referred children with behaviour disorder as principal problem

	CDC		Hospital		Total	
	No.	*%*	*No.*	*%*	*No.*	*%*
Behaviour disorder*						
First-year problems	7	9	3	8	10	8
'Handicapping'	13	16	4	11	17	14
Behaviour and speech	13	16	1	3	14	12
Other	50	60	28	78	78	66
Total	83	100	36	100	119	100

*Final diagnosis.

children with behaviour disorder as a principal or subsidiary problem could be accommodated in one of four subdivisons.

(1) Problems of behaviour and management in the first year of life only.

(2) 'Handicapping' behaviour disturbance. These children suffered from behaviour problems of such severity that they were not acceptable in normal school at the usual school-entry age.

(3) Behaviour disturbance with speech disorder. These children had significant speech delay or disorder as previously defined (p. 145) but this was either minor as compared with the behaviour problem or was more severe but considered to be behavioural in origin.

(4) Other problems of behaviour not included above. These are further divided into four subgroups (p. 177).

Table 9.2 shows the distribution of behaviour problems among CDC- and hospital-referred children in these subdivisions.

Distribution by severity and sex

Table 9.3 gives the severity gradings allotted to these categories of behaviour disorder for CDC- and hospital-referred children by sex.

Although the 10 children with disturbed behaviour in the first year only were all, as far as is known, problem-free after that age, severity was graded as moderate because most presented with minor abnormal neurological signs which are associated with other problems at later ages.

Eight children with 'handicapping' behaviour disorders were graded moderately severe as it was expected that they would be acceptable in normal school after 12 months delay. One was enrolled in normal school against advice at four years 10 months. Nine children with 'handicapping' behaviour disorders graded as severe were expected to need special educational provision. In the event, two of them were able to enter normal school after one to two years in the assessment class.

Fifty-one (61 per cent) of those referred to CDC with behaviour disorders were male as were 26 (72 per cent) of those referred to hospital. Behaviour problems were both more common and more severe among males. Severity gradings of behaviour were compared for males and females and found to be significantly different, with

167

TABLE 9.3

Distribution of CDC- and hospital-referred children with behaviour disorder as principal problem by overall severity grading and sex

Sex	First-year problems			'Handicapping' disturbance			Behaviour and speech			Other			Total			
	CDC	Hosp.	All	CDC	Hosp.	All	CDC	Hosp.	All	CDC	Hosp.	All	CDC	Hosp.	All No.	(% M)
Overall severity grading																
Minor																
M	2	2	4							3	1	4	3	1	4	(31)
F	5	1	6							5	4	9	5	4	9	
All	7	3	10							8	5	13	8	5	13	
Moderate																
M				5	1	6	3	3	3	23	16	39	28	18	46	(64)
F				2	—	2	2	2	2	15	2	17	22	3	25	
All				7	1	8	5	5	5	38	18	56	50	21	71	
Moderately severe																
M				5	3	8	7	1	8	3	2	5	15	4	19	(73)
F				1	—	1	1	—	1	1	3	4	4	3	7	
All				6	3	9	8	1	9	4	5	9	19	7	26	
Severe																
M				5	3	8							5	3	8	(89)
F				1	—	1							1	—	1	
All				6	3	9							6	3	9	
Total																
M	2	2	4	10	4	14	10	1	11	29	19	48	51	26	77	(65)
F	5	1	6	3	—	3	3	—	3	21	9	30	32	10	42	
All	7	3	10	13	4	17	13	1	14	50	28	78	83	36	119	
(% M)			(40)			(82)			(79)			(62)				

the proportion of males increasing steadily from 31 per cent of those with minor problems to 89 per cent of those with severe problems. The difference in severity distribution between males and females was statistically significant ($\chi^2 = 9.660$, 3df, p = <0.05).

BEHAVIOUR PROBLEMS IN THE FIRST YEAR

Advice was sought about problems of behaviour and management in the first year of life for 16 infants, 10 referred to CDC and six to hospital clinics. All infants were very irritable with constant crying, wakefulness and problems of feeding and/or handling. The 10 infants referred to CDC all exhibited dystonic signs (p. 93) in the first six to 18 months of life. All were difficult to handle with a characteristic dislike of the bath, the infant described as arching his back or throwing himself backwards in extension and 'going stiff' when mother attempted to place him in the water. Similar postures were exhibited in the care-taking activities of undressing, dressing and nappy changing. Most mothers, especially those who had had other normal infants, commented that this one felt 'different', was 'stiff' or 'tense' and did not 'cuddle' in a normal way. Feeding problems such as slow sucking, excessive wind, frequent small vomits and not settling after feeds were common. Neurological status and handling problems were not recorded for hospital-referred infants but most were reported as having feeding difficulties.

These problems had resolved by 12 months for seven CDC-referred and three hospital-referred children. Problem behaviours persisted beyond the first year for three each of those referred to CDC and hospital.

Irritable baby syndrome in all categories of NDD

'Irritable baby syndrome' was the description given to the combination of minor abnormal neurological signs and severe problems of behaviour and management in the early months. It is an early manifestation of the dystonic syndrome in which problems of behaviour and management predominate.

All CDC children referred in the first year came into this category. In addition, 30 children in other clinical categories were known to have suffered from the syndrome in the first year or the history of marked irritability and handling problems typical of dystonia was highly suggestive. Irritable babies without these handling problems were not included as having suffered from the syndrome.

Infants who exhibited irritable baby syndrome, with or without other NDD later, were more likely to have complicated perinatal histories than were children with NDD who had not shown this behaviour in infancy. Table 9.4 shows the infant behaviour and perinatal histories of the 324 CDC-referred and 322 control group B children for whom information was available.

The proportions of LBW/SFD infants were identical for CDC-referred children with and without the syndrome and significantly higher than that found in the control group. Complications of pregnancy were significantly more common

169

TABLE 9.4

Perinatal complications and infant behaviour of CDC-referred children
(N = 324) and matched control group B children (N = 322)

| | CDC-referred | | Control group B |
	IBS (N = 40)	No IBS (N = 284)	(N = 322)
Complications	%	%	%
Pregnancy and delivery			
None	35	48	52
Pregnancy	23	15	14
Delivery	20	23	20
Both	23	14	15
Neonatal			
0	55	74	86
1	30	15	11
2	10	4	3
3	5	2	<1
LBW/SFD	23	23	9
No complications	23	32	44

IBS = irritable baby syndrome; LBW = low birthweight; SFD = small for date.

in association with the syndrome than they were in association with NDD but no history of the syndrome (χ^2 = 3.866, p = <0.05), and also as compared with the control group (χ^2 = 4.738, p = <0.05). There was no significant difference in the frequencies of delivery complications for these three groups. Neonatal complications were also more common among those who had suffered from irritable baby syndrome compared with those with NDD but no history of the syndrome (χ^2 = 8.917, 3df, p = <0.05) and as compared with the control group (χ^2 = 12.290, 3df, p = <0.01).

Sixteen of the 30 additional children in other clinical categories had been examined in the first year of life; two were cases of cerebral palsy, 13 others showed dystonic signs and one showed other minor neurological signs of doubtful significance. Of the 14 children examined after the age of one year, one was dystonic, three showed other abnormal neurological signs, five had signs of doubtful significance and five (all seen first after two years) were neurologically normal.

Table 9.5 details the behavioural and other problems of the 40 CDC-referred infants and young children who exhibited irritable baby syndrome in the first year of life. All but seven (17 per cent) developed other problems. 60 per cent had disturbed behaviour later with or without other NDD.

Overall, 10 per cent of CDC-referred children exhibited the syndrome. In control group A, three of 102 children without NDD and two of 26 children with NDD appeared to have suffered from the same condition. The excess of the syndrome among CDC-referred children as compared with normal control children is statistically significant (χ^2 = 4.839, p = <0.05).

TABLE 9.5

**Neurodevelopmental problems among
CDC-referred children who had exhibited the
irritable baby syndrome (N = 40)**

	No.
Clinical category at referral:	
First year behaviour problem	7
→ later behaviour problem	3
Later behaviour problem	9
Global delay	1
+ behaviour problem	3
Mental retardation	
+ behaviour problem	2
Motor disorder	5
+ behaviour problem	1
Cerebral palsy	1
+ behaviour problem	1
Speech disorder	2
+ behaviour problem	5
Total	40

'HANDICAPPING' BEHAVIOUR DISORDERS

Seventeen of the total population of 5334 1974/75-born children (13 of the 3667 who remained in the city from birth to three years) presented with behaviour disorders of sufficient severity to preclude admission to normal school at the usual entry age. This represents frequencies of 3.1 and 3.5 per 1000 in these groups. 13 were referred to CDC and four to hospital clinics.

Types of disorder

Severe behaviour disorders can be subdivided into those resulting mainly from abnormal environmental situations (reactive disorders) and those arising mainly from 'within the child' (Graham 1977). In this group of 17 children, six were considered to suffer from reactive disorders, 10 from disorders 'within the child' and in one case classification was less clear. Some details are given in Appendix X.

Reactive disorders

All six children in this category suffered from severe emotional deprivation and came from poor working-class homes; in four cases, material deprivation was also severe. Three children referred to CDC were physically and neurologically normal. This information was not available for the three children supervised elsewhere.

Four boys presented with combinations of immature, withdrawn and uncontrollable behaviour with restlessness, overactivity and aggression. Three required special educational provision after a period in the assessment class and one was able to enter a Primary 1 class at six years.

The problems of two girls were different. One (No. 5), the eldest of three children, came from a highly disorganised and unstable home in which aggression and violence were a routine part of frequent parental quarrels and of child-rearing practices. With her younger siblings the girl attended day nursery where her behaviour was described as being subject to extreme mood changes, at times pleasant and reasonably co-operative (though always mistrustful of adults while usually 'maternal' with younger children), at others vicious and uncontrollable, with kicking, biting and swearing. On one occasion she strangled the nursery canary and on another stabbed a child with a knife. She was admitted to the assessment class and with patient and consistent management, together with a relatively high amount of adult attention, gradually evidenced some adaptation to the routine demands of a small group. After six months' attendance the child was taken into care (following non-accidental injury to a sibling) and placed with experienced foster parents. Within a few weeks she began to show a marked change from being a severely impaired child in terms of her social-emotional development to a happy, pleasant little girl establishing good relationships with her teachers, peers and foster family. The child has entered normal school out of Dundee and will continue to remain in care.

Another girl (No. 6) was first referred to CDC after 15-month development screening as possibly mentally retarded. The mother was severely depressed and admitted to psychiatric hospital after the first attendance. The child also appeared to be depressed and was passive, apathetic and withdrawn. Arrangements were set in motion for admission to day nursery but further appointments at CDC were not kept and the family could not be traced. The child reappeared following a hospital admission at age two years. Mother had discharged herself from the psychiatric hospital and deserted. The child was still depressed and apathetic and had developed no speech although, in other areas of development, she appeared to be only moderately delayed. She was admitted to day nursery and within six months had changed to a happy child joining in with and enjoying nursery activities. However, she did not develop any speech although she communicated by facial expression, gesture and mime. She was admitted to special day nursery for language stimulation and a programme of behaviour modification. Progress was minimal for six months when quite suddenly the child started to speak and with familiars quickly became quite chatty. It was considered that this child's failure to acquire more than a few words of speech until near three years of age resulted from a period of depression from the ages of 15 to 24 months, the age when she should have been acquiring useful speech. Thereafter she developed non-verbal means of communication. The fact that she progressed from being almost mute to communicating freely by speech within a few days suggests a diagnosis of elective mutism. The child retained other evidence of anxiety (grimacing and mannerisms) and of immaturity and was recommended for placement in the assessment class. While waiting for a vacancy she was placed in a normal nursery class where she made sufficient progress to warrant admission to a normal Primary 1 class at age six years. Unfortunately she has made no educational progress in her first year in school and has multiple problems of behaviour.

172

Hyperkinetic behaviour

Three boys were hyperactive to a degree that precluded admission to normal school at five years. One (No. 7) from a superior working-class home was described as extremely active from his first birthday. He was admitted to a normal nursery class at three and a half years but had to be removed because of disruption caused to the rest of the class. At three years nine months he was observed in class to spend most of his time running from one room to another, engaging in various tasks for no longer than 30 seconds at a time, showing no interest in group activities or the individual activities of other children and ignoring direct instructions from his teacher. He was admitted to the nursery group of the assessment class at four years eight months and made significant progress in his ability to regulate his own behaviour. He was moved to the formal teaching group and was finally placed for a trial period in a normal Primary 1 class of the school to which the assessment class is attached. Thereafter he moved on to his local primary school.

Another boy (No. 8) from a poor, but caring, working-class home was also described as increasingly overactive from early in the second year of life. In addition he had marked language delay with virtually no speech at three years. After a period in day nursery he was admitted to the assement class at school-entry age and made sufficient progress in learning style, behaviour and speech to warrant transfer to a normal Primary 1 class after 12 months. Both these boys are making slow progress in reading and number work with poor attention, concentration and persistence. They are described as restless and clumsy. Both were neurologically abnormal preschool.

In the third case (No. 17), overactivity was of shorter duration and behaviour was unremarkable in the first two years of life. He was referred to CDC at three years three months with marked hyperactivity and severe language delay with echolalia. On the Reynell Developmental Language Scales he scored at age two years three months on comprehension and two years one month in expression. The father was said to be a heavy drinker and violent and the parents separated before the child's first birthday. Mother was apathetic, depressed and lethargic and looked very anaemic. She was extremely resistant to the suggestion that she should consult her family doctor about her own health, maintaining that in no circumstances would she 'take pills, I don't believe in them'. Later severe anaemia was confirmed and medication accepted. The child was admitted to a normal nursery class but was found to be very difficult to contain. He was referred to the Child Guidance Service as a possible candidate for the assessment class. Four months later he sustained severe head injuries (an extensive fracture in the left parietal region) in a road traffic accident and was noticeably subdued on discharge from hospital. He was retained in the normal nursery class and was able to enter his local primary school after 12 months' delay. This boy was neurologically normal. He is having the same problems in school as the two boys described above.

Autistic-type behaviour

Seven boys and one girl (Nos. 9 to 16) exhibited behaviour showing some features of autism: six were non-communicating by speech or other means as well as showing bizarre behaviour patterns and one did speak but avoided social contacts and displayed odd ritualisms. One boy came from a poor working-class home, one from a middle-class background and all others from average working-class homes.

Three children, who were all physically and neurologically normal had suffered degrees of emotional deprivation which might have exacerbated their problems. The father of No. 11 died in Canada when the child was two and a half years old. During the six months of his terminal illness mother was frequently separated from the child as she had to travel long distances from home to hospital to visit her husband. She experienced considerable stress and grief and her health deteriorated. The child clearly suffered double separations and intense turmoil in his home situation related to his mother's grief. However, after the father's death, mother and child returned to the maternal grandparents' home in Dundee and subsequently mother remarried. The second husband accepted this problem child well.

The mother of No. 13, separated from her husband, was an odd, socially isolated woman who admitted that her son's behaviour somewhat resembled her own. It was felt that a degree of emotional deprivation existed here on account of personality disorder in the mother.

The one girl (No. 12) with autistic type behaviour had been subjected to a very abnormal early environment on account of psychiatric disturbance in the father. Six weeks after the birth of the child this man became unable to swallow. No organic cause was found and it was thought that this was a hysterical reversion to the feeding patterns of infancy following loss of his mother-figure with the arrival of the first baby. Because of weight loss and deteriorating health he was obliged to give up his job as a bus conductor. He seldom left the house and developed an obsession with the macabre. An alcove of the living-room was turned into a gruesome shrine to vampires. The child's development was relatively normal in the first two years although she acquired no speech and was referred to CDC on this account after two-year development screening. Thereafter she became increasingly withdrawn, prey to irrational fears with panic reactions and many bizarre behaviour patterns. Soon after the first referral the father's behaviour improved. He began to take some solids, regained employment, demolished his 'magic corner' and switched his interests to astronomy and verse-writing. Four years later, and after 18 months in the assessment class, the child is still a very odd little girl with retarded expressive language, making little social contact and still showing bizarre patterns of behaviour.

Three other children had physical and/or neurological abnormalities. Nos. 14 and 16 both had four minor congenital anomalies and were neurologically abnormal. No. 15 had seven minor congenital anomalies but was neurologically normal. These findings suggest that organic factors may be involved for some children with bizarre or autistic-like behaviour disturbances.

All the children with autistic-type behaviour were offered places in the assessment class. The parents of one boy (No. 15) refused and enrolled him in the Primary 1 class of the local school against advice; he is making little progress. Three children were able to enter normal school after 12 months' delay and three required continued special education. One boy (No. 9) attends a residential school for autistic children.

TABLE 9.6

**Actions taken on behalf of 17 children with
'handicapping' behaviour disorders**

	No.
Day placements	
Assessment class	15 (1)*
Nursery class	11
Day nursery	2
Special day nursery	1
Therapy	
Speech	11 (1)
Occupational	3
Psychology	
Educational	17
Clinical	12
Hospital referrals	
Squint	4
Hearing	6 (1)
EEG	6
Child psychiatry	2
Social agencies	
Educational social work	14
Other social work	7
RSSPCC	3

*Figures in parentheses refused or did not
attend; RSSPCC = Royal Scottish Society for
Prevent of Cruelty to Children.

Management of children with 'handicapping' behaviour disorders

Apart from the special educational provisions described above and the Child Guidance Service, which was involved with all cases, the other agencies concerned in the management of children with 'handicapping' behaviour disorders are outlined in Table 9.6. Clinical psychologists were involved with 12 children. 11 children who were non-communicating or had marked speech delay received regular therapy, as did three children with problems of hand function and perceptual-motor disorders. Seven non-communicating children were referred to hospital for hearing assessment (one did not attend); a mild sensorineural loss was detected in one and one other might have had some impairment due to glue ears. Four children had squints.

Non-specific abnormalities were reported in the electroencephalograms of two of the six children referred for this investigation. Both these children (Nos. 10 and 12) were treated empirically with the anticonvulsant drug carbamazepine. The effect on No. 10 was striking, with parents and teachers reporting a decrease in more bizarre behaviour patterns and improvement in communication. On three occasions attempts were made to wean the child off the drug with obvious deterioration in behaviour at home and in school during the first two attempts. The drug was finally discontinued without adverse effect after two and a half years. The drug was not considered to have any effect on behaviour by the parents of No. 12 who, although loving, expressed little concern about the child's development and behaviour. The

175

school thought otherwise, and on one occasion of obvious deterioration in behaviour in school it was discovered that mother had not renewed the prescription. Medication was intermittent in this case and probably ceased before 12 months.

BEHAVIOUR AND SPEECH DISORDERS

Thirteen children were referred to CDC and one to hospital with a principal problem of behaviour and associated speech delay or disorder. Types of problems were as described below for 'other problems'. 10 of the 14 children had problems in subgroup A. The problems of five children were considered to be moderate in severity and nine to be moderately severe, although all were expected to enter normal school at the usual age.

Severity grading moderate
Of the five children (three boys and two girls) whose problems were graded as of moderate severity, four had mild expressive speech delay or problems of articulation only. One appeared to have a moderately severe expressive delay but testing was difficult because of overactivity and poor concentration. Behaviour problems were sufficiently severe to warrant clinical psychology referral in four cases. The uncontrollable overactive behaviour of the fifth child appeared to be a reaction to the six months' terminal illness of his father and resolved with day-nursery admission and gradual adjustment of the mother.

One child with severe preschool problems was graded as moderate because he was not expected to have problems in school. He was the first child of prosperous middle-class parents with unrealistic conceptions of normal young child behaviour, resentment of any alterations in social life or previous routines and with very rigid and punitive methods of discipline. The mother-child relationship was seriously disturbed and the child reacted by being extremely 'naughty', using considerable initiative in devising ways of annoying his mother. Clinical psychology assistance was refused and further attendance at CDC discontinued. The child is doing well in school and presents no problems to his teacher although mother requested referral to Child Guidance Service soon after school entry, maintaining that he was still completely out of control at home. It is unlikely that the advice given will be followed.

Severity grading moderately severe
All but one of these nine children were male. One boy's speech could not be asssssed because of extreme timidity and shyness and one boy was found to be within normal limits but speech was very limited in the social situation. The rest had moderately severe or severe expressive delays. Six were referred to clinical psychology and seven to the Child Guidance Service. All were referred either to clinical or educational psychology or to both. One transferred out before Child Guidance Service referral could be made and transferred in again just before school entry; he is having problems in Primary 1. All other children referred to the Child

176

Guidance Service were considered capable of entering Primary 1 classes at the usual age but problems were anticipated and the children's progress will be monitored closely in school.

OTHER PROBLEMS OF BEHAVIOUR

The combinations of different problems of behaviour in this and the preceding subdivision were multiple, although all could be included in one or more of four subgroups.

(A) 1. Overactive ± poor concentration
2. Combinations of attention-seeking, temper tantrums, negative and disruptive behaviour
3. Aggression
4. Uncontrollable, usually with overactivity.

(B) 1. Combinations of timidity, nervousness, clinging and shy behaviour
2. Immature behaviour for mental age
3. Withdrawn.

(C) 1. Sleeping problems
2. Feeding problems
3. Encopresis ± enuresis
4. Nocturnal eneuresis at four years or older, diurnal eneuresis at three years or older.

(D) 1. Other including pica, excessive eating, tics, mannerisms
2. Referred on account of suspected minor fits, manifestations considered to be behavioural.

The problems of individual CDC- and hospital-referred children with problems of behaviour and speech and other behavioural problems are detailed in Table 9.7.

Thirty of 63 CDC-referred children had problems in more than one subgroup compared with only one of the 29 hospital-referred children. It could be that multiple problems were more common among the hospital-referred children than was apparent but that these were unreported in hospital records.

Of the 29 hospital-referred children, the largest number (15) had problems of management only (subgroup C); five had sleeping or feeding problems, five were encopretic and five eneuretic. Eight children, one of whom was also encopretic, had problems in subgroup A, four were suspected of having minor fits but this was not confirmed, one had a facial tic and one was referred to paediatric outpatients from an orthopaedic clinic with pains in the legs considered to be behavioural in origin.

In the CDC-referred group, the largest number (49 cases) presented with combinations of the problems listed under subgroup A, with problems from another subgroup in over one-half. 12 children were included in subgroup B, all but one having other problems. Problems of management (subgroup C) were reported for 31 children, only four of whom (all encopretic) were without other problems.

TABLE 9.7

Distribution of behaviour problems among CDC- and hospital-referred children with disorders of behaviour and speech and other behavioural problems

	CDC (N = 63)	Hospital (N = 29)
Behaviour problems		
Problems in subgroup A only	24	7
+ other	25	1
All subgroup A	49	8
Problems in subgroup B only	1	—
+ other	11	—
All subgroup B	12	—
Problems in subgroup C only	4	15
+ other	27	1
All subgroup C	31	16
Problems in subgroup D only	1	6
+ other	3	—
All subgroup D	4	6

TABLE 9.8

Distribution of behaviour problems among CDC-referred children in other main categories of NDD (N = 94)

	Main category		
	Global delay (N = 30)	Motor disorder (N = 11)	Speech disorder (N = 53)
Behaviour problems			
Problems in subgroup A only	15	4	37
+ other	9	5	9
All subgroup A	24	9	46
Problems in subgroup B only	3	—	4
+ other	3	2	8
All subgroup B	6	2	12
Problems in subgroup C only	1	1	—
+ other	8	2	7
All subgroup C	9	3	7
Problems in subgroup D only	—	—	—
+ other	2	2	—
All subgroup D	2	2	—

TABLE 9.9

Combinations of problems among all CDC-referred children with behaviour disorder with and without other NDD (N = 157)*

	Subgroup A					Subgroup B					C	D	
Subgroup	1	2	4	1+2	2+3	1	2	3	1+3	2+3	3	1	Total
A 1	17												17
2		14											14
4			5										5
1+2				37									37
2+3					7								7
B 1	2	2			1	5							10
2	1	1											2
3		3		1				2					6
1+3													—
2+3										1			1
C 1		9		5			1						15
2		3	1	1		2		1					8
3		2		3		2	2	1	1		6		17
4	1							1	1				3
1+2		2		2	2								6
3+D1				1									1
D 1		1		3	1			2				1	8
Total	21	37	6	53	11	9	3	7	2	1	6	1	157

*Excluding those with 'handicapping' and first-year-only disorders, mental retardation and other specified conditions.

Children with behaviour problems in other main clinical categories

The combinations of behaviour problems among children with principal problems of global delay, motor disorder and speech disorder are detailed in Table 9.8. Problems in subgroup A predominated, being reported for 84 per cent of children.

Distribution of problems among all CDC-referred children with behaviour disorder

Table 9.9 details the combinations of problems among all children referred to CDC who had behaviour disorder ± other NDD, after excluding behaviourally disturbed children with mental retardation, cerebral palsy, specific conditions and deafness and those with 'handicapping' behaviour disturbance and behaviour problems in the first year of life only. Table 9.10 gives the distribution of problems in the four subgroups detailed above from the ages of one to five years.

The majority of problems presented between the ages of two and five years. During this age-period the most common problems causing concern to parents (and presenting in over four-fifths of cases) were those of overactivity, attention seeking, negativism, aggression and disruptive behaviour. Problems of management,

179

TABLE 9.10

Distribution of problems among all CDC-referred children with behaviour disorder with and without other NDD (N = 157)*

	CDC (N = 157)	
	No.	%
Behaviour problems		
Problems in subgroup A only	80	51
+ other	48	31
All subgroup A	128	82
Problems in subgroup B only	8	5
+ other	14	9
All subgroup B	22	14
Problems in subgroup C only	6	4
+ other	44	28
All subgroup C	50	32
Problems in subgroup D only	1	1
+ other	8	5
All subgroup D	9	6

*Excluding those with 'handicapping' and first-year only disorders, mental retardation and other specified conditions.

sleeping, feeding and toiletting were present in one-third of children. With the exception of encopresis, no child was referred to CDC solely on account of a management problem, although over one-half of children referred to hospital clinics had a problem of management only, enuresis and encopresis being the most common. After excluding those with mental and physical handicaps, 18 CDC- and six hospital-referred children were persistent soilers after the age of three and a half years.

MANAGEMENT

Table 9.11 details some recommendations on management of CDC-referred children with principal problems of behaviour disorder (other than first-year problems only) and those with behaviour problems allied to global delay, motor disorder and speech disorder. Those with mental retardation and specific syndromes and conditions have been excluded, as have five children who left the city soon after three years or younger. After these exclusions 165 children remained.

The table also shows whether or not the recommendations were accepted. Non-acceptance of clinical psychology referral includes refusals, failures to attend the first and subsequent appointments, failures to re-attend after one or more sessions and erratic attendance. Non-acceptance of preschool day placements includes refusal to accept a vacancy, removal of the child after a short period of attendance and frequent absences.

180

TABLE 9.11

Psychology referrals, preschool and primary school placements recommended for CDC-referred children with behaviour disorder aged three to five years excluding those with mental retardation, other specified conditions and children who transferred out at three years or younger (N = 165)

	Behaviour			Global delay + Behaviour (N = 28)	Motor disorder + Behaviour (N = 11)	Speech disorder + Behaviour (N = 53)	Total			
	Handicapping (N = 13)	+ Speech (N = 13)	Other (N = 47)				Accepted Yes	No	All (N = 165)	
	No.	No.	No.	No.	No.	No.	No.	No.	No.	%
Psychology										
Educational	13	7	3	12	8	14	57	—	57	35
Clinical	12	9 (5)	28 (11)	5	5 (1)	11 (3)	50	20	70	42
Both	12	3	3	3	3	4	28	—	28	17
Day placement										
Nursery class	2	8	31 (8)	23 (7)	6 (1)	45 (11)	88	27	115	70
Assessment class	11 (1)*	1 (1)	—	4	1	4	19	2	21	13
Day Nursery	—	2	9 (2)	1	2	3 (2)	13	4	17	10
None	—	2	7	—	2	1	—	—	12	7
Primary School										
P.1	—	12	45	22	8	45	—	—	132	80
P.1 deferred	9 (1)	1 (1)	2	6	3	8	27	2	29	18
Spec. Ed.	4	—	—	—	—	—	4	—	4	2

*Figures in parentheses = recommendation not accepted; P1 = Primary 1.

181

Educational psychology referral

Fifty-seven children with behaviour disorders (35 per cent) were referred to the Child Guidance Service for advice about primary school placement and assistance with problems of behaviour. These referrals were accepted in all cases. 23 children had a principal problem of behaviour and 34 had other NDD. Four children with 'handicapping' behaviour disorders were recommended for special education and Primary 1 deferment was recommended for 29 (51 per cent) of other children referred to the Child Guidance Service. This recommendation was not accepted by the parents of two children.

Apart from children with 'handicapping' behaviour disturbance, the highest proportion of children referred to the Child Guidance Service, because of concern about their ability to cope in Primary 1, was in the group with motor disorder and behaviour problems. Serious concern was felt for eight of the 11 children in this category.

Clinical psychology referral

Referral to clinical psychology was recommended to the parents of 70 children (42 per cent). Referral was refused by four and 16 accepted the recommendation but did not attend on the first or subsequent occasions or were erratic in their attendances. In 11 other cases co-operation was obtained on second referral after failure to attend previously. It was explained to parents that acceptance of a clinical psychology referral would involve rather frequent attendances of child, mother and sometimes father over three to six months or longer and that parents would need to put a lot of effort and hard work into the programmes of behaviour modification devised by psychologists and parents working together. Nevertheless, over one-quarter of parents who agreed to a clinical psychology referral either thought better of it before the first attendance (three cases) or were unable to co-operate with the demands made (13 cases). In other instances, clinical psychology referral was not suggested because it was judged that mother would be unable or unwilling to co-operate. Some were unable to accept any advice or to expend the necessary effort to maintain the child in a preschool day placement.

Preschool day placements

Preschool day placements were offered to 64 (88 per cent) of children with a principal problem of behaviour and 89 (97 per cent) of behaviourally disturbed children in other clinical categories.

Twenty-one children (11 with 'handicapping' behaviour disturbance and 10 others) were offered placed in the assessment class. The parents of two children would not accept this or other placement.

Places were found in normal nursery classes for 41 children with a principal problem of behaviour and 74 with additional NDD, comprising 70 per cent of the total. Regular attendance was achieved for 88 (77 per cent) but vacancies were refused by the parents of 18 children and in nine instances the child was removed from class or attendance was erratic.

In 11 cases with a principal problem of behaviour and six with other NDD, day nursery was recommended as it seemed unlikely that mothers would accept nursery-class placements which were usually part-time initially and not available during school holidays. All places were accepted but in four cases the children were removed after a short period of attendance.

CIRCUMSTANCES OF IDENTIFICATION

CDC-referred children

Of the 83 children with a principal problem of behaviour referred to CDC, 72 (87 per cent) were referred from the screening programme and 11 (13 per cent) from other sources. Family doctors referred the children in two cases, nursery class medical officers referred four children, two with siblings attending CDC were seen following requests from mothers, and in one case each referral was requested by the hospital speech therapy department and the local authority social work department.

In one more case, professional parents, whose middle child (the second of three) had never attended for development screening, visited their local clinic when he was aged two years 10 months to demand psychiatric referral because of what was described as the child's anti-social behaviour. In the event they accepted a CDC referral. At first interview, without the child being present, father gave a dramatic history of the child having been completely withdrawn and passive in the first year of life and from the age of two years having episodes of 'collapsing in a heap on the floor and moaning' many times a day and whenever he was asked a question. The child presented as an entirely normal little boy and it was difficult to account for the father's bizarre story. Parents did not re-attend the Centre as they reported an unaccountable and 'miraculous' improvement in behaviour after the initial visit. However, 10 months later the child was referred by the family doctor to a children's medical outpatient clinic and he was taken there by his father. The consultant reported on the 'graphic and detailed description' given of periods when the child 'falls down and has difficulty with walking'. No abnormality could be detected though the comment was made 'the father's expectation and responses to his son were very inappropriate'. Following this referral there was again said to be a marked improvement. In Primary 2 the child is progressing well educationally and his behaviour was reported as unexceptional apart from being somewhat unforthcoming and shy and over-dependent on adults. The falling fits reported by father were never observed outside the family.

Hospital-referred children

Of the 36 children referred to hospital clinics with a primary problem of behaviour, four (11 per cent) were referred from the screening programme, 24 (67 per cent) by family doctors and seven (19 per cent) by clinical medical officers (five from day nurseries or nursery classes). The remaining child was referred by the clinic doctor to CDC but a request was made by the psychiatrist treating his mother that he should be seen by a colleague in child psychiatry; this was agreed.

Of behaviourally disturbed children attending hospital clinics, 25 (69 per cent) were referred to children's medical outpatient clinics, five to child psychiatry, three to clinical psychology and three to the Child Guidance Service.

COMPARISON WITH OTHER STUDIES

Few studies of the prevalence and types of behaviour problems among preschool children have been carried out with the exception of two notable epidemiological studies. The first (Richman *et al.* 1975) examined a one-in-four sample of non-immigrant three year olds resident in a London borough (comprising 705 families) using a behaviour screening questionnaire. Overall, 7 per cent of children were considered to have moderate or severe behaviour problems and 15 per cent to have mild problems. Surprisingly there was no significant sex difference, although boys were significantly more often described as overactive, eneuretic or encopretic and girls as fearful. The social class distribution was not significantly different for children with and without behaviour problems.

In another group of 418 preschool children, comprising all those living in a geographically defined area of North London (Jenkins *et al.* 1980), a history of behaviour problems was elicited at each of seven developmental examinations between six weeks and four and a half years. Again, standard questionnaires were used (one for children aged six weeks to 23 months and another for two to five year olds) to elicit information about specific areas of behaviour. The percentage of mothers worried about their child's behaviour was highest at three years (23 per cent) and fell off by four and a half years to 15 per cent worried. The opinion of doctors was that 10 per cent of three year olds had mild behaviour problems, 10 per cent moderate and 1 per cent severe. At four and a half years the proportion of mild problems was considered to remain at 10 per cent while 5 per cent had more severe problems. In the behaviour problem group as a whole (children under and above the age of two years) the sex ratio boys: girls was 1.8:1. Social data were not included.

In the Dundee study, between 5 and 6 per cent of children were identified as having preschool behaviour problems of sufficient severity to merit referral for assessment and advice. This is not strictly comparable with the total population studies quoted but the prevalences are not dissimilar. The ratio of boys: girls was 1.8:1, identical to that found in the second study quoted. In Dundee more children from social classes IV and V presented with behaviour problems (Tables 4.13, 4.14) though the excess was not large. It is expected that problems of behaviour at early school age will be more obviously associated with social deprivation (p. 227).

Summary

Frequency of behaviour disorders

Frequency of behaviour disorders in the total population was 22 per 1000. In 20 per 1000 problems were moderate or more severe. The frequencies in the more stable population were 26 and 25 per 1000. When children with moderate or more severe behaviour disorders in other clinical categories were added in, frequency in the more stable population rose to 54 per 1000.

Types of disorder

Disorders were subdivided into: (1) problems of behaviour and management in the first year of life only; (2) 'handicapping' disorders of such severity that the children were not acceptable in normal school at the usual entry age; (3) behaviour and speech disorders, with behaviour problems predominating; and (4) other problems not included above.

Distribution by severity and sex

Behaviour problems were both more frequent among boys (65 per cent male) and more severe (ranging from minor disorders, 31 per cent male to severe disorders, 89 per cent male).

Behaviour problems in first year and irritable baby syndrome

All CDC-referred infants with irritability and constant crying were neurologically abnormal. Overall, 10 per cent of CDC-referred children exhibited the irritable baby syndrome in the first year of life compared with 3 per cent of matched controls. Children with NDD and the syndrome were more likely to have had complications of pregnancy and in the neonatal period than children with NDD and no history of the syndrome.

'Handicapping' behaviour disorder

Frequency was 3.1 per 1000 of the total population and 3.5 per 1000 of the more stable population. Of the 17 children, six suffered from reactive disorders, three from hyperactivity and eight from autistic-type behaviour.

Behaviour and speech disorders

Fourteen children were included in this category; problems were moderately severe in nine.

Other problems of behaviour

These were further subdivided into: combinations of (A) overactivity, attention seeking, tantrums, aggression, negative and disruptive behaviour; (B) immaturity, timidity, nervousness and withdrawn behaviour; (C) problems of feeding, sleeping and excretion; and (D) other.

Over two-thirds of all behaviour disorders were included in this category. The most common problems causing concern to parents were those in subgroup A (82 per cent); two-thirds of these children had additional problems in other groups.

Management

Management of children with behaviour disorders is detailed. Day placements were not accepted by parents of 22 per cent and clinical psychology assistance by 29 per cent.

Circumstances of identification

The majority (87 per cent) of children attending CDC were referred from the screening programme. Of those attending hospital clinics, 67 per cent were referred by family doctors and most often to a children's medical outpatient clinic.

APPENDIX X: Some details about 17 children with 'handicapping' behaviour disorders

Type of disturbance	Severity	Sex	Social class	Social grade	Deprivation Material	Deprivation Emotional	Educational provision At 5 years	Educational provision Later
Reactive								
1. Unhappy, withdrawn, restless	Severe	M	III	4	+	+ + +	Assessment class	Spec. Ed. (residential)
2. Uncontrollable, overactive, demanding	Severe	M	V	4 Single pt.	+ + +	+ + + NAI	Assessment class	Spec. Ed.
3. Immature, restless, demanding	Severe	M	IV	4	+ + +	+ + +	Assessment class	Spec. Ed.
4. Withdrawn, aggressive, constant soiling	Mod. severe	M	V	4 Separated	+ + +	+ + +	Assessment class	P.1 deferred
5. Uncontrollable, very aggressive	Mod. severe	F	V	4	+ + +	+ + + NAI to sib; in care	Assessment class	P.1 deferred
6. Depression, elective mutism	Mod. severe	F	IV	4 Separated	+	+ + +	Spec. day nursery Nursery class	P.1 deferred
'Within the child'								
7. Hyperactive	Mod. severe	M	III	2	–	–	Assessment class	P.1 deferred
8. Hyperactive, marked speech delay	Mod. severe	M	IV	4	+	–	Assessment class	P.1 deferred
9. Autistic	Severe	M	II	1	–	–	Assessment class	Spec. Ed. (residential)
10. Autistic traits, non-communicating	Severe	M	III	3	–	–	Assessment class	Language unit
11. Autistic traits, non-communicating	Severe	M	III	3 Fa. died	–	+ +	Assessment class	Spec. Ed.

		Sex		Age				Spec. Ed.
non-communicating			IV	3	—	+ + +	Assessment class	
13. Autistic traits, non-communicating	Severe	M	III	3 Separated	—	+ +	Assessment class	P.1 deferred
14. Autistic traits, poor social contacts	Severe	M	III	3	—	+	Assessment class	P.1 deferred
15. Autistic traits, non-communicating	Mod. severe	M	V	4	+	—	Assessment class (refused)	P.1 against advice
16. Bizarre, unpredictable, marked temper	Mod. Severe	M	III	3	—	—	Assessment class Nursery class	P.1 deferred
Type uncertain								
17. Hyperactive, marked speech delay	Mod. severe	M	V	3 Separated	—	+ +	Nursery class	P.1 deferred

P.1 = Primary 1; Spec. Ed. = special education.

REFERENCES

Graham, P. J. (1977) 'Behaviour disorders: a child psychiatric approach.' *In*: Drillien, C. M., Drummond, M. B. (Eds.) *Neurodevelopmental Problems in Early Childhood.* Oxford: Blackwell Scientific Publications.

Jenkins, S., Bax, M., Hart, H. (1980) 'Behaviour problems in pre-school children.' *Journal of Child Psychology and Psychiatry,* **21,** 5-17.

Richman, N., Stevenson, J. E., Graham, P. J. (1975) 'Prevalence of behaviour problems in 3-year-old children: an epidemiological study in a London borough.' *Journal of Child Psychology and Psychiatry,* **16,** 277-287.

CHAPTER 10

Specific Conditions and Visual Defects

SPECIFIC CONDITIONS

The category of specific conditions included all those syndromes and specific physical conditions which are invariably, or likely to be, associated with neuro-developmental delay or disorder (NDD) in all or in certain areas of development. Overall, 50 children came into this category. The frequency of specific conditions with associated NDD or disorder was seven per 1000 of the total population of 5334 1974/75-born children and nine per 1000 of the more stable population of 3667 children. Specific conditions with moderate or more severe NDD were found in five and seven per 1000 of the two populations (Table 4.3, p. 57).

The conditions in this category are listed in Table 10.1. Figures in parentheses refer to the numbers of children with specific conditions who are included in other main clinical categories. The table also details which children were supervised at the Child Development Centre (CDC) (3 per cent of all children with NDD) and which at hospital clinics (14 per cent).

One infant with congenital dislocation of hip (CDH) progressed to marked delay in both gross motor function and speech. She is included here as having CDH as an additional disability. The dislocation was detected in the neonatal period in only seven of the total 13 cases. In two cases CDH was suspected at the 20-week screening examination and in one at the 39-week examination. Two other infants, both attending local clinics for reasons other than screening, were referred on account of suspected CDH, one at three months and the other at 12 months. The last child transferred into town before two years but did not attend that screening. She was referred to an orthopaedic clinic ('not walking properly') at two years eight months and found to have a left hip dislocation.

Children with talipes were all those who required prolonged treatment with splintage, serial plasters or surgery. Talipes is included as an additional disability in one boy of borderline intelligence attending CDC on that account. One boy, who required multiple surgery, transferred out after three years and his overall developmental status at that age is not known. Another boy appeared to be globally delayed at two-year screening. Referral to CDC was not requested as he was still attending orthopaedic clinic and a medical outpatient clinic following an episode of melaena. At three-year screening he was said to be performing appropriately in all areas other than motor, but he is having considerable problems of education and behaviour in school. A very similar pattern of school failure was apparent at seven years in the fourth boy. The educational psychologist to whom he was referred commented on his awareness of his physical handicap (he was required to wear surgical boots) and

TABLE 10.1
Children suffering from specific conditions (N = 50)

	CDC	Hospital	All
Congenital dislocation hip	—	12 (1)	12 (1)
Talipes	— (1)*	3	3 (1)
Dyschondroplasia	1	—	1
Rickets	—	1	1
Hemimelia	1	—	1
Erb's palsy	—	1	1
Cleft lip and/or palate	—	4 (1)	4 (1)
Osteopetrosis	1	—	1
Hydrocephalus	— (3)	2	2 (3)
Subdural hygroma	— (1)	1	1 (1)
Cerebral atrophy	— (1)	—	— (1)
Cerebral tumour	—	1	1
Spina bifida	—	1	1
Neuromuscular disorder	2 (1)	1	3 (1)
Neurodegenerative disorder	—	1	1
Down's syndrome	3	1	4
? Fetal alcohol syndrome	— (1)	—	— (1)
Congenital rubella	2	—	2
Incontinentia pigmenti	1	—	1
Total	11 (8)	29 (2)	40 (10)

*In parentheses, children with specific conditions in other clinical categories.

very low self-image, which were considered to be significantly undermining his confidence and lowering his self-expectations. Thus, three out of four boys with severe talipes presented later with other developmental and behavioural problems.

One girl, referred to CDC on account of slow motor development and unsteady gait, was found to have a dyschondroplasia. An Asian boy, found to have rickets, was also referred to a hospital clinic on account of slow motor development.

One boy was born with a partial absence of the right ulnar, marked bowing of the radius and absence of fourth and fifth digits. The mother had been well throughout her pregnancy, no drugs had been taken and the cause of the deformity remained unknown. Although of reasonable birthweight (2778g at 40 weeks) the boy remained very small, being well below the 3rd centile in height and weight at five years. He showed dystonic signs in the first year and later presented as globally delayed (particularly in gross motor function) and markedly overactive. Primary 1 entrance was delayed by 12 months.

A boy with Erb's palsy, resulting from birth injury, was included in the category of specific conditions as he continued to show restriction in use of the right hand and arm at three to four years. At three-year development screening he achieved few successes on tests of hand function, but needed to use his left hand which might not have accorded with natural dominance.

Cleft lip is included as an additional disability in a boy (p. 153) with a severe communication disorder, disturbed behaviour and clumsiness. Two other children with cleft lip and palate, one with cleft palate and Pierre-Robin syndrome and one with cleft palate alone were not reported as having any neurodevelopmental problems other than moderately severe articulatory difficulties.

The three children with hydrocephalus as an additional disability are included in the main category of cerebral palsy. Two boys had ataxic diplegia with moderate degrees of hydrocephalus demonstrated by computerised axial tomography (CAT). The hydrocephalus arrested in both cases and shunt procedures were not carried out. A third boy (p. 201), who developed hydrocephalus following tuberculous meningitis in infancy which necessitated shunt procedure, is also included in the category of cerebral palsy.

One low birthweight baby (1600g) developed E. coli meningitis at 48 hours of life. He was described as 'an extremely ill baby who recovered well'. The family transferred into Dundee when the child was aged two years one month, too late for two-year screening. At two years 10 months he was referred to a hospital clinic on account of large head size (occipitofrontal circumference was above the 90th centile for age) and on CAT scan was demonstrated to have a moderate generalised ventricular enlargement. He was kept under review and it appeared that the hydrocephalus had arrested. He showed some motor delay and clumsiness but in other respects was performing up to age by four and a half years.

Hydrocephalus (with an occipitofrontal circumference of 46.5cm) was suspected at 20-week screening in a boy whose recorded occipitofrontal circumference at eight weeks was 40cm. The infant exhibited sunsetting, a bulging fontanelle, fisting of hands, brisk phasic reflexes and was irritable and vomiting. Intelligent parents had noticed no abnormality in this, their first-born child. A ventriculogram following immediate hospital admission demonstrated gross symmetrical dilatation of the ventricular system without any evidence of tumour to account for this. The condition was treated as a communicating hydrocephalus with a ventriculo-atrial shunt. Subsequent development has been satisfactory.

Two children suffered from subdural hygromata, the one (p. 205) following a second hospital admission with a decorticate neurological presentation, dehydration and metabolic disturbance and the other following head injury considered to be non-accidental. He required a temporary subdural-peritoneal shunt. The first child appeared to have moderately severe global delay before she transferred out of town to long-term foster-care at two years eight months and is included in that clinical category. The second child also appeared globally delayed at two- and three-year screening but requested referral to CDC was not achieved because of temporary transfer-out. The child returned before school entry and appears to be coping reasonably well in Primary 2.

One boy (p. 201) with cerebral atrophy following a viral meningo-encephalitis at four years is included in the category of severe mental retardation. A posterior fossa astrocytoma was diagnosed in a girl aged three years one month. A part of the tumour was removed and later a ventriculo-peritoneal shunt inserted. She entered Primary 1 at five years and at that age was neurologically and developmentally normal.

One boy with a neuromuscular disorder is included in the category of severe mental retardation. He had bilateral rigid club feet requiring multiple surgery.

TABLE 10.2

	Male	Female	All
Congenital dislocation hip	1	11 (1)	12 (1)
Talipes	3 (1)*	—	3 (1)
Dyschondroplasia	—	1	1
Rickets	1	—	1
Hemimelia	1	—	1
Erb's palsy	1	—	1
Cleft lip and/or palate	1 (1)	3	4 (1)
Osteopetrosis	1	—	1
Hydrocephalus	2 (3)	—	2 (3)
Subdural hygroma	1	— (1)	1 (1)
Cerebral atrophy	— (1)	—	— (1)
Cerebral tumour	—	1	1
Spina bifida	1	—	1
Neuromuscular disorder	3 (1)	—	3 (1)
Neurodegenerative disorder	—	1	1
Down's syndrome	3	1	4
? Fetal alcohol syndrome	— (1)	—	— (1)
Congenital rubella	2	—	2
Incontinentia pigmenti	—	1	1
Total	21 (8)	19 (2)	40 (10)

*In parentheses, children with specific conditions in other clinical categories.

Electromyography was suggestive of a neuropathic process. Of two other boys with neuromuscular disorder supervised at CDC, one suffered from myotonic dystrophy and the other from a non-progressive myopathy. A third boy was referred to a hospital clinic at two years on account of marked hypotonia and motor delay. He was found to be floppy and weak with a raised serum creatine phosphokinase, but the family left town before investigations were completed.

A baby girl suffered from fits from birth (grand mal and myoclonic jerks). Initally she showed signs of increasing developmental maturity, then development ceased and finally regressed. Fits were poorly controlled. She died at age 11 months and autopsy findings suggested a neurodegenerative brain disorder.

One boy with osteopetrosis died at four years nine months. The only child with spina bifida attends a school for physically handicapped children.

The four children with Down's syndrome and two with congenital rubella are described elsewhere (pp. 201; 202). One boy in the category of moderately severe global delay showed some features of the fetal alcohol syndrome. One baby girl, who appeared to be developmentally normal, was referred to CDC because her profoundly retarded older sister suffered from incontinentia pigmenti. The baby was found to show minor skin lesions characteristic of the condition and was kept under review. Her subsequent development was satisfactory.

Table 10.2 gives the distribution by sex of the conditions described. In most conditions there was a preponderance of boys, but 12 of the 13 children with CDH were female.

VISUAL DEFECTS

Visual handicap

Only two children, both boys, had a principal problem of visual handicap. Both suffered from congenital cataract.

The first boy transferred into Dundee before age two years. A family history of congenital cataract was known but the child had not been referred for ophthalmological opinion. This was arranged at one year 10 months by the local community child health doctor who noted right convergent squint and nystagmus. He was found to have a right-sided cataract with peripheral retinal degeneration and high myopia. Right lens aspiration was carried out at two and a half years. At four years three months he was found to have a left funnel detachment of retina with marked anterior vitreous fibrosis. This eye was considered untreatable but prophylactic cryotherapy was carried out on the left eye, with a remaining visual acuity of 6/36. At five years, severe secondary glaucoma in the blind eye necessitated enucleation. The boy has started his education in normal primary school but is expected to require transfer to partially sighted school later.

The second boy came from a family well known to the eye department because of the many members with congenital cataract, including the boy's mother and sister. Nothing abnormal was noted at birth but by eight months dense central cataracts had developed. A right optical iridectomy was carried out at age 14 months and repeated on the left eye at two years. At four and a half years visual acuity without glasses was less than 6/60 and he was registered as partially sighted. Binocular vision with glasses was 6/36. This boy has started at special school for the partially sighted.

Visual defects in other clinical categories

Nine children in other clinical categories had visual defects other than squints and refractive errors. They are detailed below by presumed cause.

Defects due to intra-uterine infection

Two boys suffered from congenital rubella. In one child, rubella keratopathy was noted at birth with a dense white corneal opacity on the right and a faint greyish opacity on the left. There was a right coloboma of iris. By 15 months there was obvious right microphthalmos but the opacity in the left cornea was resolving and some vision apparent in that eye. By three years useful, though limited, vision was apparent on the left and no vision on the right.

In the second boy a right corneal opacity was noted at four weeks and right ptosis at four months. By seven months there was obvious right microphthalmos, conic protrusion of the cornea (keratoconus) and nuclear cataract. Visual acuity in the left eye was normal.

One girl, whose mother contracted varicella at 20 weeks gestation, was noted at birth to have a left microphthalmos with cataract. She also had a vesicular eruption due to varicella. Although an infection at 20 weeks' gestation might be considered rather late to cause these ocular defects, no other explanation was found. The left eye is amblyopic but visual acuity in the other eye is normal.

Defects due to postnatal causes

One boy suffered an extensive parietal fracture at age six weeks. At that time pupils were equal and reacting to light but the baby was not seen to focus or smile. At five months he was referred for ophthalmological examination because he had developed a roving nystagmus and did not seem to be responding to visual cues. He was found to have bilateral optic atrophy. He is thought to have some vision but this is difficult to assess because of profound mental retardation.

Two boys developed left hemianopias following infection: tuberculous meningitis at six months resulted in hydrocephalus in one and viral encephalitis in the other at four years. In the first case there appeared to be marked visual impairment with binocular vision at two years in the region of 6/60. However, by four years binocular vision was acceptably normal. In the second case considerable visual impairment remains; the boy is thought to have islets of clear vision but is difficult to assess on account of severe mental retardation.

Defects associated with specific syndromes

One boy suffered from osteopetrosis with optic nerve compression. At age six weeks he was fixating, following and smiling. By three months, mother reported that he had 'stopped paying attention' and by 10 months he had no detectable vision.

One girl was considered to demonstrate bilateral Duane's syndrome (congenital fibrosis of the external rectus muscles). She showed other minor congenital anomalies having hypertelorism, a big mouth, 'pixie' ears, a single palmar crease on the right and medial deviation of the second and third toes on the left. She is of low average intelligence but is having considerable schooling difficulties. No treatment has been recommended and visual acuity appears acceptable but the educational psychologist, to whom she was referred, questions the extent to which the eye condition may be affecting the child's attainments in visual tasks in the primary school curriculum.

Defect with no obvious cause or association

One girl was first noted by mother and health visitor to have roving eye movements at age 13 weeks. She was admitted to hospital at 16 weeks for ophthalmological examination under anaesthetic and no peripheral abnormality was detected. Pupils reacted to light but there was no spontaneous response to this or other visual cues. A diagnosis of cortical blindness was made. By eight months the baby was beginning to follow a light, watch moving fingers and respond to mother's smiling face by smiling back. By two years it was possible to test visual acuity which was considered to be 6/18, 6/18. Fixation nystagmus remained. The child shows moderate global delay which may be due in part to very poor social circumstances. She was discharged from further follow-up at the eye department at four years because of repeated non-attendance. The cause of her visual defect has not been elucidated.

SQUINTS AND REFRACTIVE ERRORS

After excluding squints occurring in some of the children detailed above and those in children with severe mental retardation, cerebral palsy and specific conditions, squint was confirmed in 31 CDC-referred children (8 per cent) in other clinical categories of NDD.

Squint was most commonly found among children with mild mental retardation, global delay and motor disorder. The incidence in children with speech disorders and behaviour disturbance was rather lower than that found in control group B children (5 per cent). Squint was also found to be significantly increased among those with definite minor neurological abnormality.

Table 10.3 details the numbers of children with squints by type of NDD and neurological status. Neurological status was not known for two globally delayed children and one with speech disorder. Two other globally delayed children are excluded because of other coincident visual defect. The difference in incidence of squint by neurological status is highly significant ($\chi^2 = 17.863$, 2df, p = <0.001).

Refractive errors, other than minor, were present in 24 of these 31 children. The types of squints and refractive errors found are set out in Table 10.4.

Four of the 31 children with squint ± refractive error, but no other visual defect, became amblyopic in the squinting eye with a visual acuity no better than 6/60.

One girl was referred to the eye department at two years with a mild right ptosis. The eyelid was not obstructing the pupil and at that age no squint was evident. In spite of repeated appointments and the efforts of the health visitor, the child was never seen. At five years seven months she did attend on account of right convergent squint and was found to be amblyopic in that eye. At that age there was little hope of restoring vision.

A second girl attended the eye department at age one year eight months with a left convergent squint and severe amblyopia. She was to return for atropine refraction, occlusion and squint surgery but did not re-attend for 15 months, by which time the mother was concerned about the child's appearance. Following surgery and prescription of glasses the child was not seen again until four years four months, when hopes of restoring vision in the amblyopic eye were fading. She was finally discharged one year later because of failure to attend. This was a disturbed home. The mother suffered severe postnatal depression and was under psychiatric care. The child was referred to CDC at four and a half years with global delay (more particularly in speech development) and behaviour disturbance.

One hyperactive boy was referred to CDC at three years four months and found to have a left convergent squint. This had not been noticed at any previous screening examination. Attendance at the eye department was achieved with difficulty. The mother had severe anaemia, was lethargic and apathetic and the child's behaviour in public places caused her great embarrassment. He did attend at four years when visual acuity in the left eye was barely 6/60. Treatment of the mother's anaemia facilitated further treatment of the child and visual acuity in the squinting eye has improved to 6/18.

195

TABLE 10.3

Distribution of squints among CDC-referred children by clinical category and neurological status

| | Squint | Category of NDD | | | | | Total | |
		Global delay	Mild MR	Motor disorder	Speech disorder	Behaviour disorder	No.	%
Neurological status								
Normal	No	33	7	5	65	42	152	97
	Yes	—	—	—	3	2	5	3
Doubtful	No	15	6	8	31	14	74	96
	Yes	2	—	—	1	—	3	4
Abnormal	No	17	8	37	23	24	109	83
	Yes	6	6	9	1	1	23	17
Total	No	65	21	50	119	80	335	
	Yes	8	6	9	5	3	31	
(% squint)		(12)	(22)	(15)	(4)	(4)		(8)

MR = Mental retardation.

TABLE 10.4

Types of squints and refractive errors found among CDC-referred children

| | Refractive error | | | | | Total | |
	None	Hypermetropia	Hypermetropia + astigmatism	Astigmatism	Myopia	No.	%
Type of squint							
R. convergent	2	7	1			10	32
L. convergent	3	4	1			8	26
Alternating convergent	1	6	1	1		9	29
R. divergent					1	1	3
L. divergent					1	1	3
Alternating divergent					2	2	7
Total (%)	6 (19)	17 (55)	3 (10)	1 (3)	4 (13)	31	(100)

A second hyperactive boy with right convergent squint was referred to the eye department by the family doctor at two years. No squint had been noticed at 15-month screening. He was found to be amblyopic in the squinting eye and considerable difficulties ensued in attempted left occlusion as the child would not tolerate this. He was eventually admitted to hospital for a period of occlusion. Resultant acuity has risen to 6/18.

In addition to these 31 children, squint was present in five children with other visual defects, two of the 13 cerebral-palsied children without mental retardation and two of the five who were mentally retarded and in two children with specific conditions, the one having Down's syndrome and high myopia and the other a congenital myopathy. Overall, squint was confirmed in 42 (10 per cent) of the 414 children with NDD referred to CDC.

COMPARISON WITH OTHER STUDIES

In the National Child Development Study, 492 (3.5 per cent) of 14,110 seven year olds who underwent medical examination were reported to exhibit manifest squint (Alberman *et al.* 1971). In a further 551 children, mothers reported a squint or suspected squint in the past. It is not stated in how many of these cases squint was confirmed and treated before the age of seven years. The incidence of squint (including latent forms) is given as between 4 and 6 per cent by Harcourt (1977) at the age of five to six years. These figures are comparable with the 5 per cent of children with confirmed squint in the Dundee control group B.

A lower incidence of squint detected preschool is reported from the British Births Survey cohort of children born in the week beginning 5 April 1970 (Chamberlain 1979). A 10 per cent randomly selected sample was examined at 22 months and three and a half years, largely by clinic medical officers. Of this group, 948 children were examined at both ages. After excluding children with visual handicaps and mental retardation, squint was confirmed in 1.8 per cent. 1.2 per cent were described as probably squinting although this had not been confirmed.

In the National Child Development Study, squinting children were twice as likely (at 24 per cent) to be described by teachers as clumsy or somewhat clumsy than were children in a control group with no evidence or history of squint (12 per cent). On other assessments (reading ability, copying design and Draw-a-man test), squinting children scored significantly worse than controls. The authors suggest that even after the exclusion of known cases of cerebral palsy and mental subnormality some of the remaining squinting children had evidence of mild cerebral dysfunction and recommend that the presence of squint should alert the physician to the possibility of other neurological signs.

Summary

Specific conditions

The frequency of specific conditions with associated NDD was seven per 1000 of the total population and nine per 1000 of the more stable population. In five and seven per 1000 specific conditions were associated with moderate or more severe NDD.

Children with different specific conditions are described. 12 of 13 children with congenital dislocation of hip were female. 71 per cent of children with other conditions were male.

Visual defects

Only two children had a principal problem of visual handicap; both suffered from congenital cataract. Nine children in other clinical categories had visual defects other than squints and refractive errors: three due to intra-uterine infection, three to postnatal infection and injury, two to association with specific syndromes, and the cause of one was unknown.

Squint was associated with refractive error in 24 of 31 cases. Four children became amblyopic in the squinting in the squinting eye.
mental retardation, cerebral palsy and specific syndrome. Squint was most commonly found with mild mental retardation, global delay and motor disorder. Incidence of squint was increased four-fold in those with minor neurological abnormality.

Squint was associated with refractive error in 24 of 31 cases. Four children became amblyopic in the squinting eye.

REFERENCES

Alberman, E. D., Butler, N. R., Gardiner, P. A. (1971) 'Children with squints. A handicapped group?' *Practitioner,* **206,** 501-506.
Chamberlain, R. N. (1979) 'Sensory defects and screening for handicapping conditions.' *In:* Chamberlain, R. N., Simpson, R. N. (Eds.) *Prevalence of Illness in Childhood.* Tunbridge Wells: Pitman Medical.
Harcourt, B. (1977) 'Visual disability and visual handicap.' *In:* Drillien, C. M., Drummond, M. B. (Eds.) *Neurodevelopmental Problems in Early Childhood.* Oxford: Blackwell Scientific Publications.

CHAPTER 11

Causes of Handicap and Moderately Severe Disability

Some aetiological associations with the whole group and subgroups of neuro-developmental disability (NDD) have been discussed in previous chapters. In this chapter an attempt is made to ascertain as precisely as possible, from scrutiny of each individual case, what were the probable or possible main causes of all handicapping conditions and moderately severe NDD identified preschool in the total population of 5334 1974/75-born Dundee children.

'HANDICAPPING' CONDITIONS

The term 'handicap' is applied here to the following categories of NDD:
(1) Mental retardation not associated with cerebral palsy or other specific conditions. In all cases mental retardation was confirmed by educational psychologists of the Child Guidance Service.
(2) Cerebral palsy subdivided into those with and without associated mental retardation.
(3) Specific conditions and syndromes with mental retardation ($\pm$ physical handicap) or with physical handicap of such severity that special education or delay in entry to normal school was required.
(4) Visual defects necessitating special education.
(5) Hearing defects necessitating special education and/or the use of hearing aids.
(6) Global delay and disorders of motor function, speech and behaviour of such severity that special education was required or primary school entrance was delayed by 12 months for children who had attained their fifth birthdays by the beginning of the school session. All these children were assessed by the Child Guidance Service and decisions about educational provision taken by that service.

Nine other children with moderately severe NDD, eligible by date of birth to enter primary school before the age of five years, were kept out of school until the following year. These are not included here nor are a few children with less severe disabilities kept out of school before five years because of parents' wishes.

Overall, 104 children were considered handicapped on these criteria. This is 1.9 per cent of the total population of 5334 1974/75-born children. Of the more stable population of 3667 children, 2.2 per cent could be considered handicapped. 93 children attended CDC and 11 were supervised elsewhere. Two CDC-referred children suffered from dual handicaps. One boy with a mild ataxic diplegia also had a severe communication disorder; he is included here as cerebral-palsied. One mentally retarded girl had severe hearing loss; she is included here as mentally retarded.

TABLE 11.1

CDC- and hospital-referred children, probable and possible causative factors in the aetiology of 'handicapping' conditions (N = 104)

Probable/possible causes	Mental retardation	Global delay & behaviour	Cerebral palsy MR	Cerebral palsy not MR	Motor and behaviour	Speech	Behaviour	Specific conditions MR	Specific conditions not MR	Vision and hearing	Total No.	Total %
Postnatal	2		1	1						2	6	6
Genetic/familial	1		2	1		4		7	1	4	20	19
Intra-uterine infection	1							1			2	2
Prenatal MCA 5-7	4	1	1	2	1		1				10	10
Prenatal MCA ≥8	9	1							1		11	10
major anomaly						1					1	1
? Prenatal MCA 3-4	1		1		1	2	2				7	7
? Pre- ? perinatal	2			1							3	3
Perinatal				4							4	4
Perinatal + social	6										6	6
Social	7	1					6				14	13
? Emotional deprivation							4				4	4
Not known	3			4		1	4			4	16	15
Total (%)	36 (34)	3 (3)	5 (5)	13 (12)	2 (2)	8 (8)	17 (16)	8 (8)	2 (2)	10 (10)	104	(100)

MCA = Minor congenital anomalies; MR = mental retardation.

Table 11.1 details the clinical categories of these 104 children and what were considered to be the probable or possible principal causes of handicaps.

Probable or possible causes

Postnatal infection and injury

Of the six children with handicaps of postnatal origin, five resulted from infection. One previously normal boy contracted a Coxsackie B meningo-encephalitis at age four years leaving him with cerebral atrophy, progressive ventricular enlargement requiring a shunt procedure, severe mental retardation, a left hemianopia and severely disturbed behaviour. One cerebral-palsied boy (left hemiplegia) contracted tuberculous meningitis at age six months. Six weeks later he developed a hydrocephalus and a shunt procedure was carried out. He remains mildly mentally retarded with a left hemianopia, epilepsy and precocious puberty. Another boy developed a rapidly progressive left hemiplegia at age 15 months. He was found to have a large loculated frontal lobe abscess. He is of low average intelligence, attends normal school but has considerable problems of behaviour. The severe conductive hearing loss of two children was attributed to postnatal infection, secretory otitis in one case and longstanding purulent otitis in the other.

One boy sustained a severe fracture of the right parietal area at age six weeks. The circumstances surrounding his 'fall' were never clearly elucidated but non-accidental injury was strongly suspected. He is profoundly mentally retarded, epileptic, visually impaired with bilateral optic atrophy and is thought to have hearing loss of central origin. He was admitted to long-term institutional care at age 13 months because of the risks imposed by low intelligence of mother, non-acceptance by father and instability of the home.

Genetic/familial

Twenty children (19 per cent) suffered from familial or genetic conditions including chromosomal abnormalities.

Four children had Down's syndrome. Only two of these children were born in Dundee, giving an incidence of one in 2200 births compared with one in 600 to 800 reported in the general population. One boy with a large ventricular septal defect (or possibly a single ventricle) died at age six weeks with cardiac failure.

Two other children were found to have chromosomal abnormalities. The abnormality in the mentally retarded deaf girl was described as 46, xx, Dp + . One boy with a severe communication disorder had an 8/14 translocation and exhibited multiple (nine) minor congenital anomalies.

Four other children suffered from specific conditions which were considered to be genetically determined, including one case each of neurodegenerative disorder (this girl died at 11 months), osteopetrosis (this boy died at four years nine months), myotonic dystrophy with severe mental retardation and a form of non-progressive autosomal recessive congenital muscular dystrophy. The last-named child has considerable physical disability but is within the normal range of intelligence.

One mildly retarded cerebral-palsied boy suffered from the dysequilibrium syndrome which is an autosomal recessive condition. Following the death (at two and a half years) of a severely retarded boy with a dystonic quadriplegia, a second boy was born into the family with a similar condition. An older brother of another cerebral-palsied boy of normal intelligence (mild ataxic diplegia with hydrocephalus) suffers from a mild spastic diplegia.

The parents and/or siblings of two girls, with severe and moderately severe sensorineural hearing loss, were similarly affected and a family history of the condition was obtained for two boys with congenital cataracts. A history of similar problems in parents and/or siblings was obtained for three children with severe communication disorders and for another boy who is also cerebral-palsied.

Intra-uterine infections

The mother of one boy with rubella embryopathy had contact with rubella at about four weeks gestation and later developed a rash with occipital node enlargement. Subsequently paired specimens were sent for haemagglutination inhibition (HAI) tests and both gave HAI levels of 1/256. The failure to demonstrate rising HAI titres, indicative of recent rubella infection, may have been due to the interval of 18 days between the appearance of the rash and the first estimation. The boy has microcephaly, mental retardation, mild spastic diplegia, right microphthalmos, cataract and coloboma, a ventricular septal defect (a patent ductus arteriosus was corrected surgically) and profound deafness with no response to aiding. An added complication in this case has been intermittent severe depression in the mother necessitating admissions to psychiatric hospital. Another research-group child suffered from congenital rubella (p. 193), but at last attendance at three years 10 months (achieved with difficulty) his disabilities were considered to be only moderate in severity and he is not included here. This boy entered school at the usual age and is having severe difficulties in both education and behaviour, suggesting that preschool prognosis was unduly optimistic. His 18-year-old unmarried mother was thought to have had rubella at four and a half months gestation but HAI tests failed to confirm this.

The mother of a borderline retarded girl suffered from a generalised varicella infection at 20 weeks gestation. She lost a previous infant at seven days on account of a disseminated herpes simplex infection. The child with congenital varicella has a left microphthalmos with cataract and degeneration in the cornea. A cosmetic contact lens greatly enhanced the child's appearance and decreased maternal anxieties about this.

Prenatal

The presence of five or more minor congenital anomalies was considered highly suggestive of some adverse influence operating in early pregnancy. It is possible that some of these children were suffering from a genetic disorder (p. 108). When no cause for handicap was apparent but the child did exhibit three to four anomalies, a prenatal causative factor was considered possible, though not probable. One boy with a severe communication disorder, disturbed behaviour and clumsiness had a cleft lip. He was supervised elsewhere and it is not known if he showed any other anomalies. Including this boy, 21 per cent of handicapped children were considered to have suffered some early intra-uterine insult other than recognised intra-uterine infection. In a further 7 per cent the possibility existed of some adverse early prenatal influence. Three more children with five or more anomalies had perinatal complications. Two were of low birthweight with moderate postnatal complications and one was a large baby with severe complications in the four weeks following birth.

Perinatal and social

The handicaps of four children, all with cerebral palsy and of normal intelligence, were attributed to low birthweight and/or postnatal complications. Five mildly mentally retarded children from poor or very poor homes were of very low birthweight (<2000g); none caused any anxiety in the postnatal period. One more was 2140g at 40 weeks and had minor problems postnatally. In these cases it seemed reasonable to attribute the cause of handicap in part to perinatal factors. Handicap may have been caused by LBW or traumatic delivery in three children who also had evidence of early intra-uterine insult. Adding all these together it appears that perinatal factors were involved in no more than 13 per cent of the handicaps identified preschool in this total population of 5334 children.

Adverse social factors alone were held responsible for 13 per cent of handicaps and the severe behaviour disorders of four children may have been due in part to emotional deprivation. Overall, social and environmental factors were implicated in 23 per cent of handicapping conditions. It is expected that adverse social factors will predominate in the cases of children identified as requiring special educational provision after school entry (p. 265).

Not known

In 16 cases (15 per cent) no obvious cause for handicap was apparent. The children came from adequate homes with caring parents. Parents and siblings were of normal intelligence and no significant family history of similar disorders could be obtained. The children were or normal birthweight, appropriate weight for gestational age and entirely normal neonatally. None exhibited more than one or two minor congenital anomalies.

All 'handicapping' conditions

Overall, 43 per cent of all handicaps identified preschool were attributed to genetic or early intra-uterine factors. In a further 10 per cent, adverse early intra-uterine influences may have been involved. Perinatal factors were considered to be certainly causative in 4 per cent and possibly in a further 9 per cent. Adverse social circumstances were considered to be the primary cause of handicap in 13 per cent and a possible or contributory factor in a further 10 per cent. Postnatal factors were clearly causative in 6 per cent and no obvious causes for handicap was found in 15 per cent of cases.

TABLE 11.2

Distribution of height among CDC-referred children with 'handicapping' conditions by numbers of minor congential anomalies (N = 72)

	≤3rd		>3rd -≤10th		>10th		Total	
	No.	%	No.	%	No.	%	No.	%
Minor congenital anomalies								
0-2	5	14	2	5	30	81	37	100
3-4	2	18	1	9	8	73	11	100
≥5	9	37	4	17	11	46	24	100
Total	16	22	7	10	49	68	72	100

Height at 3-5 yrs. (centile) (column header spanning ≤3rd, >3rd-≤10th, >10th)

TABLE 11.3

CDC-referred children, probable and possible causative factors in the aetiology of moderately severe NDD (N = 68)

	Global delay	Motor disorder	Speech disorder	Behaviour disorder	Total	
					No.	%
Probable/possible causes						
Postnatal	1	—	—	—	1	1
Prenatal MCA 5-7	3	1	1	2	7	10
Prenatal MCA ≥8	1	2	—	1	4	6
? Prenatal MCA 4	2	3	1	1	7	10
Perinatal	2	2	1	—	5	7
Perinatal + social	4	—	—	—	4	6
Social	11	3	3	3	20	29
Emotional deprivation	—	—	—	4	4	6
Not known	3	4	8	1	16	24
Total (%)	27 (40)	15 (22)	14 (20)	12 (18)	68	(100)

MCA = Minor congenital anomalies.

Stature of handicapped children

Children categorised as handicapped tended to be of small stature. Table 11.2 gives the centile distribution for height at three to five years using the Tanner and Whitehouse (1959) scales of 72 CDC-referred children. 19 children with handicaps due to genetic conditions, intra-uterine infection or postnatal causes are excluded as are two others whose height was not recorded at or after three years. 22 per cent were at or below the 3rd centile in height and 32 per cent at or below the 10th centile.

In addition, handicapped children with multiple minor congenital anomalies tended to be of smaller stature than those without. The number of children with three to four anomalies in Table 11.2 is greater than that given in Table 11.1 which details possible causes of handicap. Children were classified as '? prenatal' (three to four anomalies) only if no other aetiological association was found. Four children with three to four anomalies are classified under 'social' or 'perinatal + social' in Table 11.1. 19 per cent of children with up to two anomalies were at or below the

10th centile in height compared with 27 per cent of those with three to four anomalies and 54 per cent of those with five or more anomalies. The increasing proportion of small or very small children with increasing number of minor anomalies is statistically significant (χ^2 = 7.450, 2df, p = <0.02).

Neurological status

After excluding 33 children with specific neurological conditions and handicap due to postnatal and genetic conditions and intra-uterine infection, 29 (48 per cent) of the remaining 60 CDC-referred children showed definite though minor neurological abnormality, 15 (25 per cent) were neurologically doubtful and 16 (27 per cent) were normal.

OTHER MODERATELY SEVERE NEURODEVELOPMENTAL DISABILITIES

Sixty-eight CDC-referred children, not included in the 'handicapped' group, had moderately severe disabilities, as did 28 children supervised elsewhere. Causes of disability were less clearly defined than in those categorised as handicapped but a similar breakdown of probable or possible causes has been attempted for CDC-referred children (Table 11.3). Children referred elsewhere are not included because of the paucity of background information in many cases.

Global delay

The one girl in the postnatal category was born to highly unstable and violent parents, both of whom were of low intelligence and had served prison sentences for assault. The child spent most of her first year in care together with two older brothers. She was returned to her parents, under social work supervision, at age 13 months and appeared to develop normally until age 17 months, when she was admitted to the Neurosurgical Unit unconscious, convulsing, showing decorticate posturing and in a condition suggesting longstanding malnutrition and more recent dehydration and metabolic disturbance. Carotid angiography was normal and X-ray screen revealed no bony injuries. She responded to resuscitative measures and after a prolonged period of medical care was discharged home. She was re-admitted a few months later with convulsions and a decorticate neurological presentation. On this occasion bilaterial subdural hygromata were found and drained; neurological recovery appeared complete. Thereafter the child returned to foster-care. When first examined at CDC at age two years three months, locomotor performance was appropriate for 13 months, expressive language was virtually absent but comprehension of speech, adaptive behaviour, play behaviour and self-help skills were appropriate for near 18 months. She was admitted to special day nursery and gradually improved in all areas and when last seen presented as well below average rather than mentally retarded. She moved to foster parents outside the city before referral to the Child Guidance Service could be arranged.

Four globally delayed children had five or more minor congenital anomalies and two others each showed four anomalies. Six children were of low birthweight, of whom four came from very poor homes. 11 other children came from poor or very poor homes. No obvious cause for moderately severe global delay could be found in three cases. All of these children were noticeably clumsy suggesting the possibility of some neurological dysfunction.

Motor disorder

Fifteen children with a principal problem of motor disorder were considered to have moderately severe NDD. All showed minor neurological abnormality and all but two had additional developmental and/or behavioural problems.

Three children had five or more minor congenital anomalies and three had four anomalies each. The two children with motor problems only had complicated perinatal histories. One of them was 2020g at 34 weeks, caused no anxiety in the postnatal period but was found to be neurologically abnormal in the first year of life at follow-up in the hospital infant clinic. The other was of normal birthweight (3200g), delivered spontaneously by the vertex after a normal pregnancy. She did not breathe spontaneously at birth and required intermittent positive pressure respiration from three to eight minutes. Thereafter she was described as wide-eyed and irritable with repeated short-lived cyanotic attacks during the first 36 hours of life. Three children came from very poor homes which may have accounted for their additional problems of speech and behaviour. In four cases no cause for motor disorder could be found.

Speech disorder

All but three of the children with moderately severe speech disorder included here had additional problems of behaviour. In no case was there a history of slow speech development in parents or siblings.

One child had six minor congenital anomalies and another had four. One adopted child had suffered severe meconium aspiration at delivery and had repeated and prolonged cyanotic attacks over the next 17 days. He was noted to be jittery, jumpy and overactive in the first six months and later presented as a clumsy child. Three children with speech and behaviour disorder came from poor or very poor homes. In the majority (57 per cent) no cause for speech disorder was apparent, but in five of the eight children there was definite, though minor, neurological abnormality and/or marked clumsiness.

Behaviour disorder

Of the 12 children with moderately severe behaviour disorder four, from adequate homes with caring (though often anxious) parents, showed four to eight minor congenital anomalies. One of these, with eight anomalies was LBW (1580g at 31 weeks), delivered by caesarian section on account of maternal toxaemia. The infant was initially somewhat hypotonic and had mild respiratory distress but caused little anxiety. Later she presented as a very small odd-looking child with height and weight well below the 3rd centile at three to five years. Her subsequent problems were attributed to early intra-uterine insult rather than to low birthweight and

TABLE 11.4

Distribution of height among CDC-referred children with moderately severe NDD by numbers of minor congenital anomalies

| | Height at 3-5 yrs. (centile) | | | | | | | |
	≤3rd		>3rd -≤10th		>10th		Total	
	No.	%	No.	%	No.	%	No.	%
Minor congenital anomalies								
0-2	2	4	5	11	38	85	45	100
3-4	1	11	1	11	7	78	9	100
≥5	5	45	—	—	6	55	11	100
Total	8	12	6	9	51	79	65	100

premature delivery. Three children came from very poor homes and four from more adequate homes had suffered considerable emotional deprivation. No obvious cause for behaviour disorder could be found in one child who was neurologically abnormal.

All moderately severe NDD

Overall disabilities were associated with probable early intra-uterine insult in 16 per cent of cases and in a further 10 per cent, four minor anomalies were the only suggestive aetiological associations found. Adverse perinatal situations had occurred in 13 per cent of cases and adverse social or environmental circumstances existed in 35 per cent. No obvious cause could be found in 24 per cent.

Neurological status and stature

After excluding the one child with NDD of postnatal origin, 54 per cent (36 children) were neurologically abnormal, 21 per cent (14 children) were doubtful and 25 per cent (17 children) were normal. The neurological status of these children is very similar to that of CDC-referred children without specific physical or neurological conditions classified as handicapped.

Fewer children in this group with moderately severe NDD were of small or very small stature than were those classified as handicapped (Table 11.4). The height of three children was not recorded. However, the increase in the proportion of children with height ≤10th centile at three to five years with increasing numbers of minor congenital anomalies is again statistically significant ($\chi^2 = 11.683$, 2df, p = <0.01).

PROBABLE/POSSIBLE CAUSES OF ALL CASES OF VERY SEVERE, SEVERE AND MODERATELY SEVERE NEURODEVELOPMENTAL DISABILITY

Table 11.5 combines the figures given separately for handicapping conditions and other moderately severe NDD.

Overall, genetic and early intra-uterine influences predominated being certainly or very likely implicated in 32 per cent of cases and possibly implicated in a further 10 per cent. If those with cause unknown are excluded, the proportions of dis-

TABLE 11.5

Probable and possible causes of all cases of very severe, severe and moderately severe NDD (N = 172)

	Total	
	No.	%
Probable/possible causes		
Postnatal	7	4
Genetic/familial	20	12
Intra-uterine infection	2	1
Prenatal MCA 5-7	17	10
Prenatal MCA ≥8/major anomaly	16	9
? Prenatal MCA 3-4	14	8
? Pre- ? perinatal	3	2
Perinatal	9	5
Perinatal + social	10	6
Social and emotional deprivation	42	24
Not known	32	19
Total	172	100

NK = Not known; MCA = minor congenital anomalies.

abilities due to these causes rise to 39 per cent probable and 12 per cent possible.

Perinatal factors were considered to be the main cause of disability in only 5 per cent of cases and a possible or contributory factor in a further 8 per cent. Excluding cause unknown the proportions rise to 6 per cent probable and 9 per cent possible.

Adverse social circumstances were considered causative in 24 per cent and contributory in a further 6 per cent, the proportions rising to 30 per cent and 7 per cent after exclusion of those with cause not known. It is to be expected that adverse social factors will predominate in the aetiology of school failure among children who were not identified as having NDD preschool (see Appendices XII and XIII, pp. 253-4).

COMPARISON WITH OTHER STUDIES

The Court report (Great Britain: DHHS 1976) accepted the definition of handicap given in the report of the National Children's Bureau working party on children with special needs (Younghusband *et al.* 1970): 'A disability which for a substantial period, or permanently, retards, distorts or otherwise adversely affects normal growth, development or adjustment to life'. The Court committee estimated that 6.5 per cent of children from birth to four years will be moderately or severely handicapped by either physical (somatic), motor, visual, hearing and communication, or learning disorders which require special health care. Even allowing for the exclusion of chronic illness (*e.g.* asthma, epilepsy), the proportion of children designated as handicapped is much greater than the number considered handicapped in the Dundee study and probably includes those categorised here as having moderately severe NDD not amounting to 'handicap'.

The relatively minor contribution of perinatal complications to the incidence of severe or moderately severe NDD in this cohort of Dundee children is at variance with suggestions made to the Short committee (Great Britain, Parliament: House of

Commons Social Services Committee 1980) that 20 to 50 per cent of 'handicaps' (stated to affect 6 to 10 per cent of all children at age five years) could be prevented by improved perinatal care and an expansion of regional intensive care centres for high-risk newborns. Most of the Dundee children with NDD attributed to perinatal factors caused little anxiety in the immediate postnatal period and highly specialised intensive care facilities wre not required, although these were available. It could be that improvements in pre- and intrapartum care of mothers are enabling the obstetrician to present healthier low birthweight babies to the neonatologist, hence the relatively uncomplicated postnatal progress of most.

Our findings are comparable to those reported by Jones and Radford (1981) who carried out a survey of all infants born in Southampton and south-west Hampshire in 1975 to assess the incidence and causes of handicapping conditions at age two to three years. Of 4998 surviving children, 24 (0.5 per cent) were said to have major handicap (defined as likely to prevent the child from attending a normal school) and 202 (4 per cent) to have minor handicap, *i.e.* a definite problem but unlikely to prevent the child from attending normal school. A prenatal cause was identified in 15 children (63 per cent) with major handicaps. Perinatal factors were implicated for five children (21 per cent), three of whom had cerebral palsy, with severe perinatal problems in two cases and mild irritability with feeding problems in one case. Postnatal head injury was the cause of handicap in two cases (8 per cent). Of 536 children with identified perinatal problems, 4.5 per cent had minor handicap as did 4 per cent of the 4544 children without perinatal problems. The authors conclude that by far the greater part of childhood handicap has its origin in the prenatal period. Social factors and mild mental retardation are not mentioned in this study, presumably because of the young age of the children involved.

In a population-based study of all births to residents in the City of Exeter between 1967 and 1971, comprising 6876 infants who survived beyond 27 days of life, 1.1 per cent were considered to suffer from severe handicap and 3.4 per cent from mild handicap at age five to nine years (Brimblecombe *et al.* 1978). Of 233 children with mild handicap, 1.3 per cent were of birthweight ≤1500g, 3.9 per cent were 1501 to 2000g and 4.7 per cent were 2001 to 2500g. A further 9.4 per cent of mildly handicapped children were of birthweight >2500g but had required admission to the Special Care Baby Unit. Over 80 per cent of mildly handicapped children were of normal birthweight with no identified neonatal problems. Amongst the 77 children with severe handicaps, none were of birthweight ≤1500g, 2.6 per cent were 1501 to 2000g and 13.0 per cent were 2001 to 2500g. 29.9 per cent were normal birthweight infants admitted to the Special Care Baby Unit. 12 children with severe handicaps were of low birthweight. Of these nine suffered from congenital malformations, one from intra-uterine infection and two from non-specific mild mental retardation. Of the 23 LBW children with mild handicap, a pair of twins of birthweights 1830 and 1860g developed mild diplegia, but in no other case was it considered that handicaps could have been prevented by better neonatal care. Overall, 6.8 per cent of live-born infants weighed ≤2500g; these included 61 per cent of the neonatal deaths but only 16 per cent of the handicaps. The 93.2 per cent of livebirths who weighed >2500g accounted for 39 per cent of neonatal deaths but 84 per cent of handicaps.

Summary

'Handicapping' conditions

The term 'handicap' was applied to primary mental retardation, cerebral palsy, specific conditions and syndromes with mental retardation or physical handicap, visual and hearing defects necessitating special education or use of hearing aid and other NDD of such severity that children were unable to enter normal school at the statutory entrance age of five years or older.

The frequency of 'handicap' was 1.9 per cent of the total population (104 children) and 2.2 per cent of the more stable population. The clinical conditions are listed.

Overall, 43 per cent of these handicaps were attributed to genetic or early intra-uterine factors. In 10 per cent of cases adverse early intra-uterine influences may have been involved. Perinatal factors were considered certainly causative in 4 per cent and possibly so in a further 8 per cent. Postnatal factors were causative in 6 per cent of cases. Adverse social circumstances were causative in 13 per cent and a possible or contributory factor in a further 10 per cent of cases. No cause was found in 15 per cent.

Handicapped children tended to be of small stature and those with multiple minor congenital anomalies were of smaller stature than were handicapped children without multiple anomalies.

After exclusion of children with neurological and other specific conditions, nearly one-half of handicapped children showed definite though minor neurological abnormality.

Moderately severe NDD

Sixty-eight CDC-referred children were considered to have moderately severe NDD. Overall, NDD was associated with probable or possible early intra-uterine insult in 26 per cent of cases. Adverse perinatal situations had occurred in 13 per cent and adverse social circumstances in 35 per cent. No cause could be found in 24 per cent.

Over one-half were neurologically abnormal. Children with multiple minor congenital anomalies were of smaller stature than those without.

REFERENCES

Brimblecombe, F. S. W., Richards, M. P. M., Robertson, N. R. C. (1978) *Separation and Special Care Baby Units. Clinics in Developmental Medicine No. 68.* London: SIMP with Heinemann Medical; Philadelphia: Lippincott.
Great Britain: Department of Health and Social Security (1976) *Fit for the Future. Report of the Committee on Child Health Services* (Chairman: S.D.M. Court). London: HMSO.
—— Parliament: House of Commons Social Services Committee (1980) *Perinatal and Neonatal Mortality. Report of the Committee* (Chairman: R. Short). London: HMSO.
Tanner, J. M., Whitehouse, R. H. (1959) *Height and Weight Standard Charts.* London: Institute of Child Health.
Younghusband, E., Burchall, D., Davie, R., Kellmer Pringle, M. L. (1970) *Living with Handicap: Report of a Working Party on Children with Special Needs.* London: National Bureau for Co-operation in Child Care.

CHAPTER 12

Facilities for Management of Preschool Children with Neurodevelopmental Disabilities

The management of different categories of neurodevelopmental disability (NDD) in the Dundee 1974/75-born research group is described in previous chapters. Here an attempt is made to estimate, from our own experience, what facilities would be required for the assessment, investigation and management of NDD, detected in a screening programme and by other means, in a population of approximately 11,000 children from birth to five years (2200 births per annum). These estimates are based on requirements of children referred to the Child Development Centre (CDC), who comprised two-thirds of all those identified as having some disability between birth and school-entry age and 86 per cent of those referred from the screening programme (see Table 4.5, p. 59). The figures given are minimal since they take no account of children suspected of having NDD but not referred for assessment, nor of additional requirements of children referred to hospital clinics.

ATTENDANCES AT CDC

Table 12.1 details the numbers of attendances at CDC outpatient clinics (for paediatric consultation) of 414 children with NDD of varying severity. 23 children were referred twice making the total of referrals 437.

After the initial attendance (which could be the only one), the mean number of attendances for review was 1.4 for children with minor NDD, 2.7 for those with moderate NDD, 4.8 for those with moderately severe NDD and 3.8 for those classified as having severe or very severe NDD. The smaller number of outpatient attendances for the last group is due to the fact that 19 of the 51 children in this severity grading attended the CDC day nursery and were reviewed there, as were 11 of 108 children graded as having moderately severe NDD. One child with NDD largely due to deprivation improved sufficiently for her problems to be graded as moderate before transfer to a normal day nursery.

Table 12.2 details length of attendance at CDC by severity of NDD and year of life in which the child first attended. As would be expected, the great majority of children with minor disabilities attended for 12 months or less. Mothers' anxiety or concern of paediatricians about social circumstances were the reasons for longer attendance in four of 64 cases. Over one-half of children with moderate NDD attended for one year or less and all but 27 of the total 214 children attended for two years or less. Most of the 27 who attended for longer had problems which changed over a period of time. In contrast, over one-half of children with moderately severe NDD attended for longer than two years as did over two-thirds of those with severe or very severe disabilities.

TABLE 12.1

CDC-referred children (N = 414), number of attendances at CDC consultation clinics

No. attendances	Minor		Moderate		Mod. severe		Severe/very severe		Total referrals		Total attendances
	No.	%	No.	%	No.	%	No.	%	No.	%	No.
1	20	31	35	16	3	3	1	2	59	14	59
2	29	45	58	27	5	5	1	2	93	22	186
3	12	19	41	19	6	6	4	8	63	14	189
4	3	5	33	15	15	14	5	10	56	13	224
5-6	—	—	27	13	30	27	10	19	67	15	366
7-8	—	—	16	8	20	18	7	14	43	10	322
9-10	—	—	1	<1	10	9	3	6	14	3	133
11-12	—	—	2	1	5	5	—	—	7	2	81
13	—	—	—	—	3	3	1	2	4	1	56
NA	—	—	1	<1	11	10	19	37	31	7	—
Total referrals	64 (9)*	100	214 (14)*	100	108	100	51	100	437	100	
Total attendances	126		701		602		187				1616

*In parentheses, no. children referred twice; NA = not applicable, children attending CDC day nursery.

TABLE 12.2

CDC-referred children (N = 414), length of attendance at CDC consultation clinics

Severity of NDD	Length of attendance (yrs.)	No. referrals by year of life first attended					Total referrals		Did not re-attend	
		1st yr.	2nd yr.	3rd yr.	4th yr.	5th yr.	No.	%	No.	%
Minor	<1	17	9	17 (1)*	13	4	60	94	1	2
	1-2	—	—	4	—	—	4	6	—	
Moderate	<1	20 (1)	9	34 (8)	47 (9)	14 (2)	124	58	20	14
	1-2	8	10 (1)	26 (5)	19 (1)	—	63	29	7	
	2-3	—	6 (1)	17 (1)	—	—	23	11	2	
	3-4	2	—	—	—	—	2	1	1	
	4-5	2	—	—	—	—	2	1	—	
Mod. severe	<1	—	3 (3)	5 (3)	7 (2)	4	19	17	8	13
	1-2	—	1	17 (4)	13 (2)	—	31	29	6	
	2-3	2	7	17	5	—	31	29	—	
	3-4	5	11	6	—	—	22	20	—	
	4-5	4	1	—	—	—	5	5	—	
Severe/very severe	<1	3	—	—	1	1	5	10	—	2
	1-2	—	1	1	7	2	11	21	—	
	2-3	1	4 (1)	10	—	—	15	29	1	
	3-4	3	5	2	—	—	10	20	—	
	4 ≥ 5	7	3	—	—	—	10	20	—	
All	<1	40 (1)	21 (3)	56 (12)	68 (11)	23 (2)	208	47	29	11
	1-2	8	12 (1)	48 (9)	39 (3)	2	109	25	13	
	2-3	3	17 (2)	44 (1)	5	—	69	16	3	
	3-4	10	16	8	—	—	34	8	—	
	4 ≥ 5	13	4	—	—	—	17	4	—	
Total referrals		74 (1)	70 (6)	156 (22)	112 (14)	25 (2)	437	100	45	

*In parentheses, children who did not re-attend.

TABLE 12.3
**Some details about CDC-referred children with NDD who were discharged following
failure to attend for review**

		Did not attend (N = 43)		Did attend (N = 371)	
		No.	%	No.	%
Sex	Male	31	72	233	63
	Female	12	28	138	37
Clinical category	Global delay	7	16	70	19
	Mental retardation	2	7	31	8
	Motor disorder	3	5	56	15
	Speech disorder	20	46	105	29
	Behaviour disorder	11	26	72	19
	Other	—	—	37	10
Severity	Minor	1	2	54	15
	Moderate	29	68	171	46
	Moderately severe	12	28	96	26
	Severe	1	2	50	13
Social grade	1	3	7	37	10
	2	2	5	54	15
	3	22	51	176	47
	4	16	37	104	28
Social problems	No	19	44	237	64
	Yes	24	56	134	36
Single parent	No	31	72	317	85
	Yes	12	28	54	15

Non-attendance at review appointments

Table 12.2 also gives the numbers of children who were discharged following
failures to re-attend one of their review appointments. This occurred for 10 per cent
of both the total number of children seen at CDC (N = 414) and for the total number
of referrals (N = 437). Two children did not re-attend following two separate
referrals.

Table 12.3 gives some details about the 43 children who did not re-attend and
about their families, with comparative figures for the 371 children who attended for
all reviews. Some of the latter group needed several appointments and encouragement from health visitors, whose co-operation in ensuring re-attendance was
invaluable.

Seventy-two per cent of those who did not re-attend were male compared with
63 per cent of those who attended for all reviews. This is accounted for by the
proponderance of children with speech or behaviour disorders amongst non-
attenders. In the total sample of 414 CDC-referred children, three-quarters of those
with speech disorders were male, as were two-thirds of those with behaviour
disorders (p. 72). The excess of children with speech or behaviour disorders
amongst non-attenders as compared with attenders is statistically significant (χ^2 =

9.165, p = <0.01). The demands on mothers with children in these two clinical categories are likely to be maximal because of further referrals to speech therapy (this was recommended for all but one of the non-attenders with speech disorder) and the need for active co-operation of parents in the management of behaviour disorders and further referrals to clinical psychology (recommended for one-half of non-attenders). Over two-thirds of non-attenders had NDD considered to be of moderate severity and mothers may have felt that their children's problems were insufficiently severe to merit the efforts required.

The social grade distribution of non-attenders was not significantly different from that of attenders (χ^2 = 3.771, 2df, p = >0.10) but the excess of social problems among the families of the former group was statistically significant. One or more specific social problem was recorded for 56 per cent of non-attenders compared with 36 per cent of attenders (χ^2 = 6.334, p = <0.02). There was also a significant excess of single-parent families amongst non-attenders (χ^2 = 5.126, p = <0.05).

As would be expected, non-attenders at CDC paediatric outpatient clinics were also more likely to disregard recommendations about preschool placements and fail to attend other outpatient appointments. Lack of co-operation obtained in 58 per cent of total recommendations and referrals made for this group, as compared with 8 per cent of the suggestions made about the investigation and management of the disabilities of attending children.

Five children from middle-class or superior working-class homes did not re-attend. Three children had behaviour disorders clearly related to parental mis-handling and mothers were unable to accept this diagnosis. One middle-class mother was extremely resistant to advice about her son's speech problem and would not agree to any further investigation. At a later date hearing loss due to secretory otitis was confirmed and speech therapy instituted in the year before school entry, by which age speech had deteriorated further and behaviour problems had developed. One over-anxious mother of an adopted boy refused further attendance at the Speech and Hearing Clinic and at CDC after the recommendation was made that the child be fitted with a hearing aid. The mother's conviction that hearing loss was not severe may have been justified as, following myringotomy and insertion of grommets, hearing was confirmed as normal.

There was no obvious reason for non-attendance at CDC (and failure to co-operate with other recommendations) of 11 children from average working-class homes. Severe social problems existed in the homes of another 11 children from average working-class backgrounds and in 13 of the 16 from poor working-class homes.

In the only case of a non-attender with a minor problem, the mother hoped to obtain a 'medical note' to bring pressure to bear on her husband who had accepted a short-term contract to work in Saudi Arabia. She did not return after it became evident that this could not be provided.

In all these cases of non-attendance the children's health visitors had attempted to persuade mothers to return to CDC without success. In view of the multiple problems of many of these families, the services of a specialist health visitor or social worker, without a heavy routine workload, could have facilitated the investigation and management of these children by supporting and helping parents with those problems.

DAY PLACEMENTS AND OTHER REFERRALS

Appendix XI details recommendations made about preschool day placements and numbers of referrals to different therapists, clinical and educational psychologists and hospital departments, for the 414 CDC-referred children attending the Centre at different ages. The appendix also details the numbers of referrals and recommendations that were not accepted.

Fifteen per cent of children (N = 63), all but one with moderately severe or severe NDD, were admitted to CDC on a day basis for a period of observation and assessment usually lasting for two weeks. In most cases mothers were present with their children for much of that time. During this period all but one of the children settled sufficiently well to allow reliable assessments to be made by paediatricians, therapists and psychologists. The child's behaviour with and without mother and with other adults and young children was observed, as were spontaneous speech, play behaviour and self-help abilities. Necessary hospital attendances for consultation or investigation could often be accommodated within the period of attendance at CDC. Two mothers were unwilling for their children to be assessed in this way. Of these 63 children admitted for short-term assessment, 31 were provided with a longer-term placement in the CDC day nursery.

The 'did not attend' category for day placements includes non-acceptance of vacancies offered and situations where the child was removed after a short period of attendance or attended infrequently. One or other of these situations obtained in 26 per cent (57 children) of the 220 who were offered nursery class places. In a further nine instances a suitable nursery class vacancy could not be found. Day nursery placement could not be obtained for two children; five others (10 per cent) did not take up or regularly attend a vacancy offered. Vacancies were unavailable for five children who were recommended by educational psychologists for placement in the assessment class. Two of the 46 places offered (4 per cent) were not accepted.

The large number of mothers failing to accept preschool placements, particularly in normal nursery classes, was disappointing. Here again a specialist health visitor, working in the home, might have had more success in persuading parents to accept a vacancy or to attend regularly, after elucidating and helping with domestic and social problems that accompanied non-acceptance of recommendations.

Although an appointment for speech and language assessment was attended by all but nine children (4 per cent) referred for this, 13 of the 104 children (2 per cent) recommended for formal speech therapy did not attend with any regularity or at all.

Ninety-five children were referred to clinical psychology, 81 on account of behaviour disorder (two separate referrals were made for 11 children) and 14 handicapped children for advice on play activities and the development of self-help skills. 31 children did not complete the period of treatment recommended. Referral to the Child Guidance Service was recommended for 123 children. Two mothers did not accept this suggestion and in five cases it was decided to monitor progress in Primary 1 without a formal preschool assessment.

Two hundred and forty referrals were made to other hospital clinics for 143 (35 per cent) of the CDC-referred children, by far the largest number of referrals (37 per cent) being to the Department of Otolaryngology on account of suspected hearing loss and/or suspected secretory otitis media.

Overall, 3.2 actions per child (other than paediatric consultations at CDC) were required in the assessment, investigation, treatment and management of NDD. Few actions were taken on behalf of children attending in the first year of life; 83 per cent attended CDC outpatient clinics only during that period. Thereafter the numbers of recommendations and other referrals increased steadily until the fourth year of life when some action was required for all but 12 per cent of children attending. This was the age when the largest number were recommended for nursery class placements and the numbers of actions fell off somewhat for children attending in the fifth year of life.

FACILITIES REQUIRED FOR ALL PRESCHOOL CHILDREN FROM BIRTH TO FIVE YEARS

The 1974/75-born research-group children were the subjects of special study and the time which could be allotted to individuals was greater than that which could be expected in a routine service commitment. Outpatient clinics were arranged to allow at least one hour for children attending for the first time and 20 to 30 minutes for review attendance. From Table 12.1 it can be calculated that 500 hours were allotted to the children born in one year and 2500 hours would have been needed to cover the age-period birth to five years. With an average clinic time of two and a half hours and a 46-week working year, four to five consultation clinics would be required weekly.

However, scrutiny of the requirements of individual children referred to CDC indicated that most (if not all) children with minor NDD did not need review at CDC and could have been sent back for continued supervision to referring doctors. If screening doctors had become more involved with supervision, the number of recalls for children with moderate NDD might have been cut by one-half and that for children with moderately severe NDD by one-third. Allowing a more realistic average of 40 minutes for initial attendances and 20 minutes for reviews, the calculated hours allotted to children born in any five-year preschool period would be reduced to 1255, requiring two to three clinics per week. This would appear to be the minimum of paediatric consultation clinics necessary for the assessment and supervision of preschool children referred from a screening programme in an area with 2200 births per annum.

We were fortunate in obtaining the close co-operation of clinical and educational psychologists, and in having in Dundee an adequate number of speech therapists to provide assessments for all and therapy for most children requiring this facility. Specialised physiotherapists were also available for the assessment and therapy of children with motor disorders. Occupational therapy assessment was available as well, though treatment facilities were more limited. Other children with motor and perceptual problems would have benefitted from an increase in occupational therapy facilities. We were also fortunate in being able to obtain suitable day placements for the great majority of children likely to benefit from this.

It is not possible to say to what extent (if any) demands on specialist hospital services were increased on account of children with NDD referred from the screening programme, but over a five-year period one would expect at least 600 hospital referrals to be made. This number does not take account of the 206 children initially referred to hospital clinics, some of whom would certainly require further referrals.

Summary

From local experience an attempt was made to estimate what facilities would be required for the assessment, investigation and management of NDD detected in a screening programme in an area with 2200 births per annum.

Attendances at paediatric consultation clinics, day placements and other referrals are considered. Non-attendance and lack of co-operation with recommendations and referrals are discussed.

APPENDIX XI: Recommended day placements and other referrals for children with NDD attending CDC by year of life

	Year of life					Total (N = 414)		0-5 yrs. Did not attend or re-attend	
	1st yr. (N = 74)	2nd yr. (N = 122)	3rd yr. (N = 240)	4th yr. (N = 299)	5th yr. (N = 231)	No.	%	No.	%
Investigations, treatment, management									
Day placement recommendations									
CDC short-term assessment	4	11	26 (2)*	20	2	63	15	2	3
CDC special day nursery	3	8	14	3	3	31	7	—	—
Normal day nursery	2	13	22 (1)	16 (6)	1	54†	13	7†	13
Teacher for the deaf/Deaf nursery class	1	2	1	1		5	1	—	—
Normal nursery class			9 (4)	165 (50)	55 (12)	229†	55	66†	29
Assessment class		2		5	46 (7)	51	12	7	14
Therapy									
Occupational assessment ± therapy		9	8 (1)	22 (3)	17 (1)	56	14	5	9
Physical assessment + therapy	5	11	7	2	5	30	7	—	—
Speech assessment		8	54 (2)	135 (5)	38 (2)	235	57	9	4
therapy		1	6	49 (8)	48 (5)	104	25	13	12
Psychology									
Clinical		3 (1)	21 (4)	40 (15)	31 (11)	95	23	31	32
Educational			3	44	76 (7)	123	30	7	6
Hospital referral									
Paediatric growth clinic		1	4 (1)	7	2	14	3	1	7
other		4	4	5	4	17	4	—	—
Eyes squint ± refractive error	1	3 (1)	13 (2)	19 (1)	5	41	10	4	10
refractive error only			2		6	9	2	—	—
other		6 (1)	2		2	10	2	1	10
ENT hearing ± secretory otitis	2	4	21 (1)	35 (4)	27 (1)	89	21	6	29
other			1	6 (1)		7	2	1	14

cont.

Appendix XI—cont.

| | Year of life | | | | | 0-5 yrs. | |
	1st. yr. (N = 74)	2nd. yr. (N = 122)	3rd. yr. (N = 240)	4th. yr. (N = 299)	5th. yr. (N = 231)	Total (N = 414)	Did not attend or re-attend
Orthopaedic	2	6	8	6	5	27	7 —
Neurosurgery/neurology	2 (1)	6	1	3	3	15	4 1 7
Dentistry (radical)		1	2	2 (1)		5	1 1 20
Child psychiatry			1	1	4	6	1 —
Investigation							
Electrocochleography	1	1	3	3	5	13	3 —
Electroencephalography	1	3	8	15	7 (2)	34	8 2 6
CAT scan		3	3	3		9	2 —
Electromyography ± muscle biopsy	1	2	1	1	1	6	1 —
No actions taken (%)	62 (83)	73 (60)	117 (49)	37 (12)	42 (18)	75 (18)	
Actions per child	0.3	0.9	1.0	2.0	1.7	3.2	

*In parentheses, children not attending or re-attending; †includes children for whom suitable day nursery or nursery class placements could not be found; ENT = Department of Otolaryngology.

220

CHAPTER 13

The Children in School

THE TEACHER QUESTIONNAIRE

In co-operation with past and present educational psychologists of the Child Guidance Service and with advice from some senior infant mistresses, a questionnaire was designed (Appendix IV, see p. 26) for completion by class teachers for all children attending normal primary schools in Dundee in the summer terms of 1981 for 1974-born children and 1982 for those born in 1975. A total of 4004 school-age children were assessed by their teachers. Children were aged six and a half to seven and a half years and most were in the third term of Primary 2. Some early entrants, eligible by date of birth to start school before the age of five years, were in Primary 3 and some children were in Primary 1 because of deferred entry or because they had been retained for two years in that class.

The questionnaire covered levels of attainment in expressive language, reading, number and writing. Since teaching methods and expectations are relatively homogeneous in all Dundee primary schools, it was possible to be specific about levels of attainment of those children considered below average or very much below average in reading, number and writing.

Teachers were asked to comment on some common patterns of troublesome behaviour as 'certainly' or 'somewhat' or 'not applicable', and similarly to comment on intelligibility of speech.

Teachers were also asked to comment on hand function and physical co-ordination by marking 'doesn't apply', 'applies somewhat' or 'certainly applies' to the statements 'poor control of hands (*e.g.* in drawing, handwork, buttoning coat, tying laces)' and 'poor physical co-ordination (*e.g.* in running, jumping, throwing)'. These are aspects of functioning with which class teachers, in the early years, are well acquainted. The term 'clumsy' is used in this chapter as a convenient label to include all those children considered to show poor control of hands and/or poor physical co-ordination.

It is recognised that a teacher's report on clumsiness constitutes at best an imperfect measure of motor dysfunction. Nevertheless, imperfections in the measurements detract from the significance of any differences found and cannot add to them, provided that there is no systematic bias favouring one side or another in the recording of assessments. In this questionnaire the possibility of systematic bias does exist. A child, already in the forefront of the teacher's mind on account of poor school work or troublesome behaviour, might be reviewed more critically (the so-called 'halo effect') than another child who posed no problems.

It was hoped to carry out neurological examinations in school on samples of children described by teachers as clumsy or not clumsy, but time and funding for

TABLE 13.1

TABLE 13.1

Adverse scores applied to children with educational and behavioural problems

Educational progress

Expressive	Above average	0
language	Average for age	0
	Below average	2
	Very poor	4
Reading	Above average	0
	Average for age	0
	Below average	2
	Non-reader	4
Number	Above average	0
	Average for age	0
	Below average	2
	Very poor	4
Writing	Above average	0
	Average for age	0
	Below average	2
	Very poor	4

	Certainly applies	Applies somewhat	Doesn't apply
Behaviour			
Poor attention/concentration	2	1	0
Poor motivation/persistence	2	1	0
Restless, fidgety	2	1	0
Young for age	2	1	0
Unforthcoming, shy	2	1	0
Aggressive	2	1	0
Not much liked by other children	2	1	0

this were not found. However, the assumption that in general teachers' perceptions of clumsiness indicated real evidence of motor (and possibly of neurological) dysfunction was strengthened by finding a relationship between a clumsiness score derived from the questionnaire ('certainly' scored 2 and 'somewhat' scored 1) and a hopping score derived from one item in the neurodevelopmental component of the school medical examination. The majority of medical examinations were carried out between ages five years and five years 11 months, but a few children were as young as four years nine months or as old as six years eight months.

No accepted norms exist for numbers of hops to be expected at different ages. Figures suggested by Touwen and Prechtl (1970) were used to construct arbitrary 'hopping ages'. These ranged from one to two hops at age three years to three years five months, to 15 to 16 hops at age six years seven months to seven years. One point was allotted for each six months 'delay' in hopping on either foot. School medical examination results were scrutinised for all 1974-born children with a school problem grade of 3, 4 or 5 and for 1974-born control group B children in problem grades 1 and 2. No record of hopping was available in 20 per cent of children (usually the number of hops was not recorded); some children refused to attempt hopping and possibly could not do so. Clumsiness and hopping scores were available

TABLE 13.2

Distribution of school problems among children attending normal primary schools

		Score		
			No.	*%*
School problem grade				
1	Nil/minor	0-4	2929	73
2	Moderate	5-9	594	15
3	Moderately severe	10-14	282	7
4	Severe	15-19	138	3
5	Very severe	≥20	61	2
		Total	4004	100

for 303 1974-born children. A highly significant correlation of 0.783 was found between these scores (using the t test, p = <0.001).

An association was also found between clumsiness reported by teachers and abnormal or doubtful neurological signs preschool among children referred to the Child Development Centre (CDC). This is discussed in the next chapter (p. 258).

A further 60 infants who were still attending the hospital infant follow-up clinic at age five months (or real age of five months allowing for prematurity) were examined by the authors at that age and found to have minor transient neurological abnormality. Six years later, one-third of these children were considered clumsy by their teachers, more than twice the proportion reported for the total school population of 4004 children. None of these children had been referred to CDC on account of preschool neurodevelopmental disability (NDD).

A scoring method was used for comparative purposes (Table 13.1). School problems were graded as shown in Table 13.2. Overall, 73 per cent of 1974/75-born children were considered to be problem-free or to have minor problems only, 15 per cent to have moderate problems and 12 per cent to have more severe problems. 15 per cent of children were described as somewhat or certainly clumsy, and 11 per cent as somewhat or certainly difficult to understand because of poor speech.

SOCIAL FACTORS

Type of school

Four educational psychologists from the Child Guidance Service, who work with children of primary school age, rated the social composition of schools on a five-point scale according to the type of residential area from which each one drew its pupils. Gradings were:
(1) good, predominantly middle-class suburbs;
(2) mixed, good/average;
(3) average, predominantly the more favoured council estates;
(4) mixed, average/poor;
(5) poor, predominantly the least favoured council estates.

Social class and severe social problems

Social class was other than I to V or not known for 658 children (16 per cent). Whether or not the child belonged to a social problem group family (p. 51) was not known for 547 children (14 per cent).

In some of the following analyses children are classified as:(1) no known social disadvantage with fathers in social classes I to III and families not recorded as having any severe social problems (N = 1972); (2) known disadvantage with fathers in social classes IV and V (with or without recorded social problems) or in social classes I to III with recorded social problems (N = 1306); and (3) social details incomplete (N = 726). Overall, adequate social details were not known for 18 per cent of children. The most common reason was that the child had transferred into Dundee after the age of three years. However, it is known that this group contained an excess of children from more affluent families. Social details were incomplete for 15 per cent of children from schools in average, average/poor and poor areas of the city, 21 per cent of those in good/average areas and 28 per cent of those in good areas.

It is likely that some children classified as disadvantaged because their fathers were included in occupational social classes IV and V, would be living in materially adequate and problem-free homes, and conversely that some classified as suffering from no known disadvantage would be in poverty, due particularly to rising unemployment, or subjected to other stresses which had not been recorded. At best this is an imperfect division, but it was considered to be the most useful available for the total school population of 4004 children.

More accurate social details were known for selected groups of children. Hospital, clinic, school medical and health visitor records were scrutinised for control group B (p. 10), all children with a school problem grade of 3, 4 and 5 and all children whom CDC wished to see on account of suspected NDD (p. 72). The most complete details were available for children attending CDC.

School problems and social factors

Table 13.3 details the distribution of school problem grades by type of school. As would be expected, children in the poorest areas of town had significantly more schooling problems than did those resident in the most affluent areas (comparing type 1 and type 5 schools, χ^2 = 36.791, 4df, p = <0.001). Nevertheless, the differences are not as great as might be expected. 68 per cent of children from the poorest areas had achieved a satisfactory educational level and had no outstanding problems of behaviour as compared with 83 per cent of children from middle-class areas (a ratio of 0.8:1). The difference in frequency of severe problems was greater (8 per cent in the poorest areas and 3 per cent in the best, a ratio of 2.7:1).

Table 13.4 gives the distribution of school problem grades for those with and without known social disadvantage. Again, as would be expected, the difference in distribution is highly significant (χ^2 = 146, 4df, p = <0.001). Nevertheless the majority of disadvantaged children (61 per cent) appeared to be problem-free and only 9 per cent had severe or very severe problems.

TABLE 13.3

Distribution of school problems among children attending schools in different types of residential area

						Type of school						
	1		2		3		4		5		All	
	No.	%	No.	%	No.	%	No.	%	No.	%	No.	%
School problem grade												
1	545	83	371	77	902	72	777	69	334	68	2929	73
2	62	9	70	15	197	16	181	16	84	17	594	15
3	32	5	25	5	94	8	99	8	32	7	282	7
4	10	2	8	2	43	3	51	5	26	5	138	3
5	8	1	7	1	13	1	20	2	13	3	61	2
Total	657	100	481	100	1249	100	1128	100	489	100	4004	100

TABLE 13.4

Distribution of school problems by social class of father and severe social problems

	S.Cl. I-III, no SP		S.Cl. IV-V, or SP		S.Cl./SP incomplete		Total	
	No.	%	No.	%	No.	%	No.	%
School problem grade								
1	1571	80	801	61	557	77	2929	73
2	232	12	230	18	132	18	594	15
3	104	5	161	12	17	2	282	7
4	49	2	74	6	15	2	138	3
5	16	1	40	3	5	1	61	2
Total	1972	100	1306	100	726	100	4004	100

S.Cl. = social class; SP = social problem.

SCHOOL PROBLEMS AND MOTOR DYSFUNCTION

Poor ability in hopping was related to school problems 18 months after the school medical examination, as shown in Table 13.5. Children in school problem grades 3 to 5 had been significantly worse at hopping than control group B children in problem grade 1 (χ^2 = 22.019, p = <0.001). 13 control children in problem grade 2 were omitted because of the small number.

Table 13.6 gives the distribution of school problems among children who were not or were considered somewhat or certainly clumsy by their teachers. The difference in distribution is even greater than that noted in Table 13.4 for children without and with known social disadvantage. Only 29 per cent of clumsy children were problem-free and 23 per cent had severe problems. The difference in distribution of school problems betweeen children who were not or were considered clumsy is overwhelmingly significant (χ^2 = 929, 4df).

CDC-referred children from poor homes with preschool NDD were not more likely to show minor abnormal neurological signs than children from better homes

TABLE 13.5

1974 births. Hopping ability among 300 children without and with school problems

| | School problem grade | | | |
| | 1 | | 3-5 | |
	No.	%	No.	%
Hopping score				
0-3	73	89	127	61
4-7	7	9	48	23
≥8	2	2	33	16
Total	82	100	208	100

TABLE 13.6

Distribution of school problems among children who were not or were considered clumsy by their teachers

| | Not clumsy | | Clumsy | | Total | |
	No.	%	No.	%	No.	%
School problem grade						
1	2750	81	179	29	2929	73
2	420	12	174	28	594	15
3	158	5	124	20	282	7
4	48	2	90	15	138	3
5	11	1	50	8	61	2
Total	3387	100	617	100	4004	100

TABLE 13.7

Distribution of school problems by social factors and motor dysfunction among children with complete social details (N = 3278)

| | S.Cl. I-III, no SP | | | | S.Cl. IV-V, or SP | | | |
| | Not clumsy | | Clumsy | | Not clumsy | | Clumsy | |
	No.	%	No.	%	No.	%	No.	%
School problem grade								
1	1479	87	92	34	751	71	50	20
2	157	9	75	27	168	16	62	25
3	52	3	52	19	96	9	65	26
4	11	1	38	14	31	3	43	17
5	—	—	16	6	10	1	30	12
Total	1699	100	273	100	1056	100	250	100

S.Cl. = Social class; SP = social problem.

(p. 101). However, in this total population school-age group, disadvantaged children were more likely to be described as clumsy (20 per cent) than were those with no known social disadvantage (14 per cent). This excess of clumsiness reported for socially disadvantaged children is statistically significant ($\chi^2 = 10.007$, p = <0.01). However, the increase in school problems for those described as clumsy cannot be accounted for by the increased number from disadvantaged homes described thus, since highly significant and comparable differences between children described as clumsy or not clumsy existed in both social groups (Table 13.7). There were highly significant differences in distribution of problems for both the social group with no known social disadvantage ($\chi^2 = 528$, 4df, p = <0.001) and the disadvantaged social group ($\chi^2 = 291$, 4df, p = <0.001).

Educational attainment, behaviour, social factors and motor dysfunction

Preliminary analysis indicated that educational attainment was especially related to the occupational social class of the father, and that behaviour in school was especially related to the presence or absence of severe social problems. The two main sections of the teacher questionnaire on education and behaviour were analysed separately.

Educational attainment

Performance in expressive language, reading, number and writing was scored 0 for average and above average attainment, 2 for below average and 4 for very much below average, giving a possible range of 0 to 16 adverse points in the questionnaire section dealing with educational attainment (Table 13.1). Table 13.8 gives education scores for children who were not or were reported as clumsy by social class of father.

As would be expected, adverse education scores decreased as social class became higher. The difference in distribution of scores between children with fathers in social classes I and II and social class III is significant at a p value of <0.001 ($\chi^2 = 24.308$, 7df). The difference between social class III and social classes IV and V is significant at a p value of <0.001 ($\chi^2 = 58.469$, 7df).

A highly significant difference in distribution of education scores for those who were not or were considered clumsy by their teachers is found when comparing children in social classes I and II ($\chi^2 = 137$, 7df), social class III ($\chi^2 = 429$, 7df) and social classes IV and V ($\chi^2 = 236$, 7df), (all p values = <0.001).

Behaviour

Table 13.9 gives adverse behaviour scores for children who were not or were described as clumsy, coming from families reported as having or not having severe social problems. Troublesome behaviours marked 'certainly applies' scored 2 and those marked 'applies somewhat' scored 1. Children scoring 0 to 3 were considered to have no problems of behaviour or minor problems only, 4 to 7 to have moderate problems and ≥8 to have severe problems.

Again, as would be expected, children coming from social problem families were much more likely to show disturbed behaviour in school. 60 per cent were problem-free, 29 per cent had moderate problems and 11 per cent had severe problems as compared with 86, 12 and 2 per cent of children with no severe social

TABLE 13.8

Education score by social class of father and motor dysfunction (N = 3346)

Education score	I and II Not clumsy No.	%	I and II Clumsy No.	%	I and II All No.	%	Social class III Not clumsy No.	%	Social class III Clumsy No.	%	Social class III All No.	%	IV and V Not clumsy No.	%	IV and V Clumsy No.	%	IV and V All No.	%	Total Not clumsy No.	%	Total Clumsy No.	%
0	374	84	23	33	397	77	1135	78	50	19	1185	68	600	67	36	18	636	58	2109	75	109	20
2	39	9	16	23	55	11	145	10	58	22	203	12	103	11	25	12	128	12	287	10	99	18
4	19	4	10	14	29	6	82	6	50	19	132	8	71	8	31	16	102	9	172	6	91	17
6	7	2	4	6	11	2	50	3	32	12	82	5	65	7	24	12	89	8	122	4	60	11
8	4	1	5	7	9	2	33	2	34	13	67	4	31	3	33	17	64	6	68	3	72	13
10	—	—	5	7	5	1	10	1	25	9	35	2	17	2	19	9	36	3	27	1	49	9
12	—	—	2	3	2	<1	6	1	11	4	17	<1	9	1	16	8	25	2	15	1	29	6
≥14	—	—	5	7	5	1	1	1	7	2	9	<1	7	1	16	8	23	2	9	1	28	6
Total	443	100	70	100	513	100	1463	100	267	100	1730	100	903	100	200	100	1103	100	2809	100	537	100

TABLE 13.9

Behaviour score by severe social problems and motor dysfunction (N = 3457)

	Behaviour score 0-3		4-7		$\geqslant 8$		Total	
	No.	%	No.	%	No.	%	No.	%
No social problems								
Not clumsy	2290	90	240	9	24	1	2554	100
Clumsy	236	61	108	28	40	11	384	100
All	2526	86	348	12	64	2	2938	100
Social problems								
Not clumsy	263	70	88	24	24	6	375	100
Clumsy	50	35	64	44	30	21	144	100
All	313	60	152	29	54	11	519	100
Total								
No	2553	87	328	11	48	2	2929	100
Yes	286	54	172	33	70	13	528	100
All	2839	82	500	14	118	4	3457	100

problems. This difference is highly significant (χ^2 = 212, 2df). A bigger difference was noted for all children who were clumsy compared with all those who were not (χ^2 = 371, 2df).

In both social sub-divisions there were marked differences between children who were not and were clumsy. The distributions in behaviour scores were significantly different for both groups (no reported social problems, χ^2 = 371, 2df, p = <0.001; social problems, χ^2 = 58, 2df, p = <0.001).

School problem grades, sex and motor dysfunction

Table 13.10 gives the distribution of school problem grades for boys and girls further subdivided into those who were not or were considered clumsy by their teachers.

Boys had more problems in school than girls. 67 per cent of boys were problem-free, 18 per cent had moderate problems and 15 per cent had more severe problems compared with 80, 11 and 9 per cent of girls in these three groups. The difference in distribution of problem grades is highly significant (χ^2 = 80, 3df, p = <0.001). Boys were almost twice as likely to be considered clumsy (20 per cent) as were girls (11 per cent). This difference is also highly significant (χ^2 = 64, p = <0.001).

The advantage of female sex was confined to those children without motor dysfunction. There is a highly significant difference in problem grades distribution between girls and boys not considered clumsy (χ^2 = 40, 3df, p = <0.001), but the difference in problem grades between clumsy girls and clumsy boys is not statistically significant (χ^2 = 7.630, 3df, p = >0.05).

Education grades and behaviour scores for boys and girls

Table 13.11 gives the numbers of boys and girls who were graded as (1) above average, (2) average, (3) below average and (4) very much below average in

TABLE 13.10

School problems by sex and motor dysfunction

	School problem grade									
	1		2		3		4 and 5		Total	
	No.	%	No.	%	No.	%	No.	%	No.	%
Male										
Not clumsy	1268	77	249	15	100	6	35	2	1652	100
Clumsy	115	28	122	30	71	17	100	25	408	100
All	1383	67	371	18	171	8	135	7	2060	100
Female										
Not clumsy	1482	85	171	10	58	3	24	1	1735	100
Clumsy	64	31	52	25	53	25	40	19	209	100
All	1546	80	223	11	111	6	64	3	1944	100

expressive language, reading, number and writing. It also gives the numbers of boys and girls reported as having no problems of behaviour or minor problems only, moderate problems and severe problems. In number work the distribution of grades was almost the same for boys and girls. In all other areas of educational ability girls performed significantly better than boys. They also had fewer problems of behaviour. (Expressive language, $\chi^2 = 38$, 3df; reading, $\chi^2 = 65$, 3df, writing, $\chi^2 = 98$, 3df; behaviour, $\chi^2 = 64$, 2df. All p values are <0.001.)

Motor dysfunction and specific problems

Children with severe problems of behaviour or education were both more likely to be reported as somewhat or certainly clumsy and also to show more marked degrees of clumsiness than children in a control group. Clumsiness scores and distributions were similar for boys and girls with severe problems of education and behaviour.

Table 13.12 details clumsiness scores for all control group B children (whether or not they had school problems), for children reported as very much below average in expressive language, reading, number and writing and for those with an adverse behaviour score of 8 or more.

Only 12 per cent of the control group were described as clumsy and over two-thirds of these children were described as somewhat clumsy in either hand function or physical co-ordination only. Children with severe educational and behavioural problems were much more likely to be described as clumsy and also to have more obvious degrees of clumsiness than control children.

It was not surprising to find that children experiencing great difficulty in copying were particularly likely to show marked clumsiness, but it was more surprising to find an equally high frequency of clumsiness among those children with severe expressive language difficulties. The frequency of clumsiness and distribution of clumsiness scores was roughly similar for those with severe problems of reading, number and behaviour.

230

TABLE 13.11

Education and behaviour scores by sex

		Male		Female		All	
		No.	%	No.	%	No.	%
Language grade	1	438	21	504	26	942	24
	2	1279	62	1238	63	2517	63
	3	287	14	169	9	456	11
	4	56	3	33	2	89	2
	Total	2060	100	1944	100	4004	100
Reading grade	1	383	19	527	27	910	23
	2	1185	57	1122	58	2307	58
	3	436	21	261	13	697	17
	4	56	3	34	2	90	2
	Total	2060	100	1944	100	4004	100
Number grade	1	330	16	303	16	633	16
	2	1309	64	1292	66	2601	65
	3	312	15	262	13	574	14
	4	109	5	87	5	196	5
	Total	2060	100	1944	100	4004	100
Writing grade	1	233	11	395	20	628	16
	2	1339	65	1270	66	2609	65
	3	438	21	257	13	695	17
	4	50	3	22	1	72	2
	Total	2060	100	1944	100	4004	100
Behaviour score	0-3	1571	76	1676	86	3247	81
	4-7	387	19	223	12	610	15
	≥8	102	5	45	2	147	4
	Total	2060	100	1944	100	4004	100

TABLE 13.12

Clumsiness scores for children with severe behavioural or educational problems and for control group B children

	Clumsiness score										Total	
	0		1		2		3		4			
	No.	%	No.	%	No.	%	No.	%	No.	%	No.	%
Severe problems in:												
Language	23	26	27	31	18	20	10	11	11	12	89	100
Reading	40	44	25	27	15	17	4	4	6	7	90	100
Number	81	41	49	25	39	20	13	7	14	7	196	100
Writing	18	25	19	26	14	20	8	11	13	18	72	100
Behaviour	50	34	42	29	30	20	12	8	13	9	147	100
Control group B	252	88	24	8	8	3	2	1	1	<1	287	100

Motor dysfunction and overactivity

In recent years a large number of publications have reported on children with overactivity and distractibility combined with motor or visuo-motor difficulties. This combination of problems is commonly called minimal brain dysfunction (p. 247). The characteristics of children exhibiting this type of behaviour and its frequency were examined for the 1974/75-born school population (Table 13.13). Children were considered to show definite evidence of overactivity/distractibility when their total adverse score was ≥ 4 (maximum possible = 6) for the three items poor attention/concentration, poor motivation/persistence, restless fidgety child. This type of behaviour was recorded for 11 per cent of boys and 5 per cent of girls. In 6 per cent of boys and 2 per cent of girls (4 per cent overall) this behaviour was combined with motor dysfunction. A large part of the sex difference was accounted for by the excess of motor dysfunction reported for boys. Of all children reported as clumsy, 29 per cent of boys and 21 per cent of girls were markedly overactive and distractible. This difference, though not very great, is statistically significant (χ^2 = 5.553, p = <0.02).

Overactive behaviour was more commonly reported for children from disadvantaged families (12 per cent) than from better homes (6 per cent). However, of all children reported as clumsy, 25 per cent of those from homes with no known disadvantage and 32 per cent of those from disadvantaged homes were markedly overactive. This difference is not statistically significant (χ^2 = 2.892, p = >0.10).

As would be expected, children with marked overactivity had considerable educational difficulties. 48 per cent had an adverse education score of ≥ 8 as compared with 9 per cent in the total school population. There was also a marked increase in educational failure for those with associated motor dysfunction as compared with overactive children who were not considered clumsy. Only 12 per cent of clumsy, overactive children were making satisfactory educational progress and 67 per cent had severe educational problems.

Motor dysfunction and squint

School medical and hospital records were scrutinised for all 1974/75-born children with school problems (grades 3 to 5) and all control group B children. School medical records were not obtained for 59 children with problems, 23 of whom were described as clumsy. These 59 children were excluded.

Table 13.14 gives numbers of confirmed squints among children in school problem grade 3 to 5 and among group B children in problem grades 1 and 2. So-called 'latent squint' was not included.

The frequency of squint (5 per cent) was identical for problem children (grades 3 to 5) who were not considered clumsy and control group B children in problem grades 1 and 2. In contrast, 14 per cent of children with significant school problems and evidence of motor dysfunction were identified as having squint. Squint had been treated in the majority of cases and would not have been evident to teachers, although glasses were worn by some children with refractive errors. The difference in frequency of squint between children with school problems who were or were not clumsy is highly significant (χ^2 = 8.954, p = <0.01). Amongst CDC-referred

TABLE 13.13

Marked overactivity with and without motor dysfunction by sex, social factors and educational progress (N = 322)

Education score	Male					Female				
	S.Cl. I-III, no SP	S.Cl. IV-V, or SP	S.Cl./SP incomplete	All		S.Cl. I-III, no SP	S.Cl. IV-V, or SP	S.Cl./SP incomplete	All	
	No.	No.	No.	No.	%	No.	No.	No.	No.	%
Overactivity + motor dysfunction										
0-2	6	7	5	18	15	2	—	1	3	7
4-6	12	9	1	22	18	5	5	—	10	23
≥8	38	43	7	80	67	13	14	2	30	70
Total	48	59	13	120	100	20	20	3	43	100
Overactivity no motor dysfunction										
0-2	17	14	6	37	35	10	9	6	25	45
4-6	18	19	1	38	37	5	7	1	13	24
≥8	7	18	4	29	28	3	14	—	17	31
Total	42	51	11	104	100	18	30	7	55	100

S.Cl. = social class; SP = social problem.

TABLE 13.14

Confirmed squint among children with school problems (N = 422) and control group B children

	Clumsy	No squint		Squint		Total	
		No.	%	No.	%	No.	%
1974/75-born children,	No	173	95	9	5	182	100
school problem grades 3-5	Yes	207	86	33	14	240	100
Control group B,	No	220	95	12	5	232	100
school problem grades 1-2	Yes	16	94	1	6	17	100

TABLE 13.15

Children with known social details, speech problems by school problem grades (N = 3274)

	Speech											
	S.Cl. I-III, no SP						S.Cl. IV-V, or SP					
	Satisfactory		Poor		All		Satisfactory		Poor		All	
	No.	%	No.	%	No.	%	No.	%	No.	%	No.	%
School problem grade												
1	1522	84	49	31	1571	80	754	70	47	21	801	62
2	194	11	37	24	231	12	175	16	53	24	228	17
3	68	4	36	23	104	5	101	9	60	27	161	12
4	25	1	24	15	49	2	39	4	34	16	73	6
5	5	<1	11	7	16	<1	13	1	27	12	40	3
Total	1814	100	157	100	1971	100	1082	100	221	100	1303	100

S.Cl. = social class; SP = social problem.

children confirmed squint was significantly associated with minor neurological abnormality preschool (p. 195).

Articulatory disorder, motor dysfunction and school problems

Teachers were asked to comment on intelligibility of speech by marking 'doesn't apply', 'applies somewhat' or 'certainly applies' to the statement 'difficult to understand because of poor speech'. Overall, 'applies somewhat' was recorded for 372 children (9 per cent) and 'certainly applies' for 69 (2 per cent). 10 immigrant children with little command of English were excluded, social details were incomplete for six. Other immigrant children, who had benefited from nursery class placement and inclusion in a Primary 1 group for those whose first language was not English, had no more problems with language at the end of Primary 2 than did their classmates.

Table 13.15 gives the distribution of school problem grades for children with no known social disadvantage and for those from disadvantaged homes, subdivided into those who were not difficult to understand and those who were somewhat or certainly unintelligible. The distribution of problem grades for all children in the

TABLE 13.16

Children with known social details, speech problems
by motor dysfunction (N = 3274)

| | Speech | | | |
| | Satisfactory | | Poor | |
	No.	%	No.	%
S.Cl. I-III, no SP				
Not clumsy	1583	87	76	48
Clumsy	231	13	81	52
Total	1814	100	157	100
S.Cl. IV-V, or SP				
Not clumsy	941	86	112	51
Clumsy	141	14	109	49
Total	1082	100	221	100

S.Cl. = social class; SP = social problem.

two social groups is also given. As would be expected, children from disadvantaged homes were more likely to have unintelligible speech (17 per cent) than were children from better homes (8 per cent). This difference is highly significant ($\chi^2 = 62$, p = <0.001).

In both social groups poor speech was significantly associated with school problems. χ^2 (4df) for the differences in distributions of problem grades for children with and without poor speech is 354 for the social group without known disadvantage and 241 for the disadvantaged (p values = <0.001).

Although children from better homes with no speech disorder had significantly fewer school problems than did children from disadvantaged homes with no speech disorder, there was no significant difference in the distribution of school problem grades for children from different home backgrounds with speech disorder ($\chi^2 = 6.700$, 4df, p = >0.10). Thus, relatively speaking, articulatory disorder among children from better homes was more often associated with school problems than among disadvantaged children.

Table 13.16 divides children by social factors, intelligibility of speech and whether or not they were considered clumsy. Since the articulation of speech is a motor function, it is not surprising to find that clumsy children were four times as likely to have disordered articulation as children with no evidence of motor dysfunction. The excess of unintelligible speech among clumsy children was similar in both social groups. The difference in proportions of satisfactory speakers and poor speakers amongst all children considered or not considered clumsy is overwhelmingly significant ($\chi^2 = 329$).

School problems, motor dysfunction, perinatal and postnatal history

Table 13.17 gives some details of perinatal histories of Dundee-born children in the 1974/75 school population group with significant school problems (grades 3 to 5) divided into those who were not or were considered clumsy, and of children in control group B who had no school problems (grade 1). The scoring system

TABLE 13.17

Perinatal and postnatal histories of children with school problems
(N = 399) and control group B children

		1974/75-born children, school problem grade 3-5				Control group B, school problem grade 1	
		Not clumsy (N = 174)		Clumsy (N = 225)		(N = 210)	
		No.	%	No.	%	No.	%
Complications							
Pregnancy	0	118	68	147	65	151	72
	1	56	32	78	35	59	28
Delivery	0	132	76	146	65	138	66
	1	42	24	79	35	72	33
Neonatal	0	154	89	190	84	187	89
	1	14	8	26	12	19	9
	2	5	3	7	3	4	2
	3	1	<1	2	1	—	—
Total	0	87	50	97	43	100	48
	1	59	34	71	31	68	32
	2	24	14	42	19	36	17
	3/4	4	2	15	7	6	3
LBW/SFD		21	12	40	18	10	5
Postnatal incidents		7	4	33	15	5	2

LBW = low birthweight; SFD = small for date.

described in Chapter 5 (p. 90) was applied. Hospital records of all children were scrutinised. Initially findings were analysed separately for children known or not known to have suffered some social disadvantage. Surprisingly, no differences were found by social factors in perinatal histories or in the numbers of low birthweight (LBW) or small-for-date (SFD) infants. Virtually all infants in Dundee are delivered in one hospital unit and inadequate antenatal care is rare. This may account for the absence of differences by social status of mothers. Figures are given in the table for both social groups combined.

Differences in perinatal histories between children with and without schooling problems and between problem children who were not or were considered clumsy were not marked. A statistically significant difference exists only in the excess of LBW/SFD infants amongst those who later presented with school problems (χ^2 = 14.802, p = <0.001).

When scrutinising hospital and school medical records, note was taken of postnatal incidents which might have resulted in cerebral insult. Those found were convulsions, meningitis or encephalitis and skull fracture. One or other of these were reported for 2 per cent of control children, 4 per cent of problem children who were not clumsy and 15 per cent of children with school problems and clumsiness. The difference in these postnatal incidents between problem children who were not or were considered clumsy is highly significant (χ^2 = 12.323, p = <0.001).

RECOGNITION OF PRESCHOOL NEURODEVELOPMENTAL DISABILITY AND TAKE-UP OF DEVELOPMENT SCREENING AMONG CHILDREN WITH SCHOOL PROBLEMS

Appendix XII shows for all 1974/75-born children with school problem grade 3 whether or not any preschool NDD had been identified or suspected, and if not, details of screenings missed or carried out at two and three years by doctor or health visitor. The children are further subdivided into the three social groups used previously. Appendix XIII gives the same details for all children with school problem grades 4 and 5.

A further control group (control group C) was constructed by matching each child in school problem grades 3 to 5 who had not been identified (or suspected of) having NDD preschool (grade 3, N = 192, grade 4 and 5, N = 115) with the nearest-aged child of the same sex attending the same school who had no school problems (grade 1). Controls could not be found for two problem boys in grade 3 and one problem boy in grade 4 because the number of boys in their classes with problem grades 3 to 5 exceeded the number without problems. Thus 190 controls were matched with the grade 3 school problem children and 114 controls with the grade 4 to 5 problem children.

Scrutiny of the records of control group C children revealed that 21 matched with grade 3 problem children and 11 matched with grades 4 to 5 problem children had been identified (or suspected of) having preschool NDD. These were omitted from the comparisons of screening patterns of children with school problems (grades 3 to 5) who had not been identified as (or suspected of) having NDD preschool with control children (grade 1) who had similarly been considered developmentally and behaviourally normal preschool, leaving a total of 169 controls for comparison with 190 problem group 3 children and 103 controls for comparison with 114 problem group 4 to 5 children.

Children with moderately severe school problems (grade 3)

Only 90 (32 per cent) of the 282 grade 3 children had been identified (or suspected of) having NDD preschool; 50 (18 per cent) had been referred to hospital clinics or CDC, and in 40 cases (14 per cent) screening results had been sufficiently suspect for CDC referral to have been recommended.

The other 192 grade 3 children had not been identified as (or suspected of) having NDD preschool: 40 (21 per cent of subgroup) had not been screened at either two or three years (all but seven transferred into the city after the last screening age of three years); 102 (53 per cent) had been screened at two and/or three years by doctors and no problem had been suspected; and 50 (26 per cent) had been screened by health visitors only. The distribution of screening (missed, health visitor only, doctor) for grade 3 children was significantly different from that of their controls, particularly for the increase of doctor screening of controls ($\chi^2 = 16.431$, 2df, p = <0.001). However, this difference was largely confined to the social group with no known disadvantage. The excess of grade 3 children from these homes screened by health visitor only was statistically significant ($\chi^2 = 7.424$, p = <0.01) but not for children from disadvantaged homes ($\chi^2 = 2.955$, p = >0.05).

Children with severe or very severe school problems (grades 4 and 5)

A greater proportion (43 per cent) of the 199 grade 4 and 5 children had been identified as (or suspected of) having NDD preschool; 60 (30 per cent) had been referred to hospital clinics or to CDC, and CDC had wished to see a further 25 children (13 per cent).

Of the other 114 grade 4 and 5 children who had not been identified or suspected preschool, 41 (36 per cent of subgroup) had not been screened at either two or three years (all but 10 had transferred in after the last screening age of three years), 43 (38 per cent) had been screened by doctors and 30 (26 per cent) by health visitors only.

Again, the distribution of screening of grade 4 and 5 children was significantly different from that of their controls ($\chi^2 = 27.724$, 2df, p = <0.001). Only two problem children and four control children from homes with no known social disadvantage had been screened by doctors. However, unlike the grade 3 group there was a significant excess of grade 4 and 5 children from disadvantaged homes who had been screened by health visitors only ($\chi^2 = 4.887$, p = <0.05).

As compared with grade 3 children, a larger proportion (+ 15 per cent) of grade 4 and 5 children had not been screened at either two or three years, and 15 per cent fewer had been screened by doctors.

Although significantly more grade 3 to 5 than grade 1 children had been screened by health visitors only, in terms of absolute numbers more children who proved to have school problems had been 'missed' by doctors (102 in grade 3 and 43 in grades 4 and 5) than by health visitors (50 in grade 3 and 30 in grades 4 and 5). Scrutiny of individual screening cards indicated an undue reliance by some doctors on the mothers' histories, particularly in the cases of those who appeared later in school problem grades 4 and 5. Of all those grade 3 to 5 children whose preschool progress had given cause for concern, one-third had not been referred for further assessment.

Overall, it appears that health visitor screening in the home gives a less accurate prediction of school difficulties than does doctor screening in a clinic situation. Children from disadvantaged homes are more likely to be screened by health visitors. In control group C only 4 per cent of children from homes with no known social disadvantage had been screened only by health visitors after the age of 15 months, compared wth 32 per cent of disadvantaged children. Nevertheless, in both social groups, health visitor screening had been significantly more common for children with school problems graded 3 to 5 than for those who had no school problems. Screening in the home, after infancy and early toddler age, poses considerable problems for the health visitor. The environment may be unsuitable for even simple formal testing. The parent is unlikely to appreciate the point or possible value of screening, since clinic appointments have not been kept. In many instances the health visitor has to rely largely on the parent's history. Although no child with overt handicap (*i.e.* admitted to special education on school entry) was missed on

238

health visitor screening, it seems likely that less serious impairment would be more evident to a screening doctor in the structured environment of a clinic room than to the health visitor at home.

Of course it could be argued that it is the type of child and the unsuitable environment, rather than the person doing the screening, that account for the poorer predictive value of home screening. In the Dundee screening programme, health visitors screen a larger proportion of high-risk children than do doctors, and often in unfavourable surroundings. Children who do not attend for screening, rather than those who are brought regularly to clinics, could constitute a priority group for developmental surveillance by doctors. This is discussed further in Chapter 15.

Acceptable frequency of screening

A minimum acceptable frequency of screening has been defined (p. 34). This could only be applied to children available for all six screenings. The minimum frequency was not achieved for 13 per cent of 89 grade 3 to 5 children who had not been suspected of having NDD preschool and had come from homes with no known disadvantage. Screening was inadequate in 6 per cent of 148 control children from similar homes. Frequency of screening was considered inadequate in 19 per cent of 135 problem children from disadvantaged homes and in 10 per cent of 73 controls. Overall, the excess of acceptable frequency of screening among control children was highly significant ($\chi^2 = 9.128$, p = <0.01).

READING SCREEN

In mid-September 1981 all available children in Dundee primary schools, whose birthdays fell between 1 January and 31 December 1974, attempted the Young Group Reading Test (1977). Most children were in the first term of Primary 3. A reading quotient (RQ) was obtained for 1995 of the 2070 1974-born children for whom teacher questionnaires were completed. In most schools the test was applied by teachers other than those who had completed questionnaires for the same children.

Norms were constructed in 1976 for the Tayside region (*i.e.* Dundee and the adjacent counties of Perthshire and Angus) and the RQs were derived from these rather than from national norms. At this age, the Young Group Reading Test measures attention, listening skills, ability to follow adult directions and to maintain concentration, as well as reading skills. In Dundee the test is used as the first of a two-stage identification process: children with RQs of 85 or less are subjected to further review. In the current group of children this score represented the 10th centile, the 3rd centile being a score of 75 and the 50th a score of 105. Table 13.18 compares results on the reading test with teachers' estimates in the previous term. In general the agreement was good.

In all areas examined, associations with the distribution of reading scores were similar to those for the distribution of school problem grades derived from the teacher questionnaires. Thus there were highly significant differences by social dis-

239

TABLE 13.18
1974-born children screened for reading (N = 1995), teachers' estimates of reading ability compared with results of reading screen

	≥116		Reading quotient score 96-115		86-95		≤85		Total
	No.	%	No.	%	No.	%	No.	%	No.
Teachers' estimates of reading ability									
1	275	62	186	16	3	1	—	—	464
2	169	38	898	77	33	17	27	14	1127
3	2	<1	79	7	158	78	117	64	356
4	—	—	—	—	8	4	40	22	48
Total	446	100	1163	100	202	100	184	100	1995

advantage and motor dysfunction, and girls scored significantly higher on the reading test than did boys.

Fifty-seven children (3 per cent) scored at or below an RQ of 75 and were considered to be non-readers. Of these children, 26 (46 per cent) had been identified as (or suspected of) having NDD preschool, 14 (24 per cent) had not been screened at two or three years and 17 (30 per cent) had been screened (but not suspected) at two and/or three years. One third had been screened by health visitors only. A further 117 children (6 per cent) had RQs in the range 76 to 85 and were considered to be very poor readers. Of these children, only 31 (27 per cent) had been detected as having had NDD preschool, 19 (16 per cent) were not screened at two or three years and 67 (57 per cent) had been screened (but not suspected) at one or both ages. Nearly one-half were screened by health visitors only.

COMPARISON OF SCHOOL STATUS OF RESEARCH-GROUP CHILDREN WITH THOSE BORN 1973 AND 1976

The main aim of development screening is the 'earliest identification of any disabilities likely to have an educational implication, in order that appropriate measures may be taken to ameliorate or minimise the disabilities detected' (p. 3). Identification without intervention is of little practical value, but it remains to be demonstrated that preschool intervention reduces the frequency of problems at early school age. Some comparative information is available about school performance of all Dundee children born 1973 to 1976. Teacher questionnaires for 1973- and 1976-born children were completed in the summer terms of 1980 and 1983, when children were six and a half to seven and a half years. At those dates 2067 1973-born children and 1806 1976-born children were attending normal primary schools.

In 1973, the screening programme was fully operational and children with suspected NDD could be referred to CDC which opened in 1972. Initially facilities for management of children with disabilities not amounting to 'handicap' (p. 199) were limited. These improved and expanded over the next five years. Thus facilities at

TABLE 13.19

1973 to 1976 births. Distribution of school problem grades among all children and those without and with motor dysfunction by date of birth

Date of birth	School problem grade 1 No.	1 %	2 No.	2 %	3 No.	3 %	4 No.	4 %	5 No.	5 %	Total No.	Total %
Not clumsy												
1973	1438	82	223	13	73	4	14	1	7	<1	1755	100
1974	1404	80	206	12	99	6	30	2	8	<1	1747	100
1975	1346	82	214	13	59	4	18	1	3	<1	1640	100
1976	1199	78	211	14	98	6	24	2	3	<1	1535	100
Clumsy												
1973	76	24	84	27	66	21	53	17	33	11	312	100
1974	92	28	95	29	64	20	47	15	25	8	323	100
1975	87	30	79	27	60	20	43	15	25	8	294	100
1976	51	19	80	29	82	30	29	11	29	11	271	100
All												
1973	1514	73	307	15	139	7	67	3	40	2	2067	100
1974	1496	72	301	14	163	8	77	4	33	2	2070	100
1975	1433	74	293	15	119	6	61	3	28	2	1934	100
1976	1250	69	291	16	180	10	53	3	32	2	1806	100

TABLE 13.20

Significances of differences in distributions of school problem grades by date of birth using χ^2 test (2df)

		Children attending normal primary schools		
		Not clumsy	Clumsy	All
Comparisons by date of birth				
1973	1974	NS	NS	NS
1973	1975	NS	NS	NS
1973	1976	p = <0.01	NS	p = <0.02
1974	1975	p = <0.01	NS	NS
1974	1976	NS	p = <0.02	NS
1975	1976	p = <0.001	p = <0.01	p = <0.001

NS = not statistically significant.

CDC were least well developed for 1973-born children and best developed for those born 1975. Of the 1973-born children, 112 were referred to CDC and identified as having NDD, compared with 414 children born 1974/75. The number of 1973-born children referred to hospital clinics is not known.

Children born 1976 with developmental and behavioural problems not amounting to 'handicap' were seldom referred to CDC. Only nine 1976-born children, attending normal school in 1983, had been referred. 8 per cent had been referred to hospital clinics. It seems likely that screening doctors (particularly community child health doctors) became more actively involved in the assessment and management of children with less severe disabilities born after 1975.

Table 13.19 details the distribution by school problem grades of children born 1973 to 1976, subdivided into those who were not or were considered clumsy. The proportion of children considered by their teachers to be certainly or somewhat clumsy remained constant (15 per cent) throughout the four-year period. Table 13.20 gives the result of tests of significance of differences in the distributions of school problem grades among children born in different years.

The interpretation of the findings is complicated by the fact that 1974-born children entered school in 1979, at the beginning of a period of sharply increasing social difficulties resultant on an unprecedented rise in unemployment. In 1980 to 1983 the social situation deteriorated further. Cuts in education spending have also posed considerable problems in maintaining school standards. In 1979 some disruption was also caused by industrial action taken by Scottish teachers.

It has already been demonstrated that social disadvantage and motor impairment appear to have roughly equal effects on school progress, with the effects being independent and additive. Children from disadvantaged homes were more likely to be described as clumsy by their teachers (p. 225). Thus it is probable that social factors played some part in the poor school performance of children with apparent motor dysfunction. Nevertheless, in general, one may hypothesise that environmental factors predominated in the school progress of children not described as clumsy and that innate factors were more important in the progress of children who were described as clumsy.

242

Children not described as clumsy

Children born 1974 did rather worse than those born 1973, although the difference in distribution of school problem grades was not statistically significant. However, there was a significant improvement in those born 1975 (as compared with the 1974-born) and a return to the distribution observed in 1973.

Furthermore, children born in 1976 had significantly more school problems than those born in both 1973 and 1975.

It seems reasonable to suppose that the deterioration in school performance, at age six and a half to seven and a half years, between those born in 1976 and 1973 was due to increasing social disadvantage and that the facilities which became available for research-group children (particularly preschool placements for those from poor homes) tended to cancel out the effects of environmental deterioration for some disadvantaged children.

Children described as clumsy

The distribution of school problems in 1973-born children did not differ significantly from those born in 1974 or 1975, although there were fewer problem-free 1973-born and more with severe and very severe school problems. The excess of severe and very severe problems in the 1973-born as compared with those born 1974/75 borders on statistical significance ($\chi^2 = 3.650$; $p = 0.05$ when $\chi^2 = 3.841$).

There was no significant difference in the distribution of school problems between clumsy children born 1973 and 1976. This lends support to the hypothesis that innate rather than environmental factors are primarily involved in the school progress of children with motor dysfunction.

However, clumsy children born 1976 had significantly more school problems than had clumsy children born in both 1974 and 1975. Only 19 per cent of clumsy children born 1976 were problem-free in school compared with 29 per cent of those children born 1974/75, whereas 52 per cent of the 1976-born children had moderately severe and more severe school problems compared with 43 per cent of those born 1974/75.

All children

The most highly significant differences noted in Table 13.19 are between all research-group children born 1975 and all children born 1976, of whom 5 per cent fewer were included in school problem grade 1 and 5 per cent more in grades 3 to 5. This represents a decrease in moderately severe or more severe school problems of 36 per cent in those born 1975 as compared with those born one year later.

Overall, these findings suggest that efforts to intervene in the developmental and behavioural disabilities of disadvantaged children helped to offset the damaging effects of increasing poverty and also that children at-risk of developing schooling difficulties because of innate rather than environmental factors clearly benefited from the assessment and management facilities which were available at CDC for research-group children.

The effectiveness of preschool intervention is also discussed in Chapter 14.

COMPARISON WITH OTHER STUDIES

National Child Development (1958) Study

The form of the Dundee teacher questionnaire was similar to that used in the National Child Development Study (NCDS) of seven-year-old children born 3 to 9 March 1958 in England, Scotland and Wales (Kellmer Pringle *et al.* 1966). We are grateful for permission to use the latter as a framework in the construction of the Dundee questionnaire.

The NCDS questionnaire asked teachers to rate each pupil on a 1- to 5-point scale (well abve average to well below average) in oral ability, awareness of the world around him, reading, creativity and number work. In Dundee teachers were asked to rate pupils on a 4-point scale (above average to well below average) in expressive language, reading, number and writing. Similar questions were asked in both questionnaires about unintelligible speech, poor control of hands and poor physical co-ordination. In addition, the overall description of 'clumsy' was included as a separate item in the NCDS questionnaire. This was omitted in Dundee because (as stressed by Henderson and Hall 1982) this description may be used not only for children with motor difficulties but for those who knock things over and fall frequently because they are impulsive, distractible or hyperactive. Three items on troublesome behaviour (squirmy, fidgety child; often running or jumping about, hardly ever still; over-dependent upon mother) included in the NCDS questionnaire are comparable to two of the seven items used in Dundee. However, in the national study a separate behaviour schedule, the Bristol Social Adjustment Guide (Stott 1963), was completed for each pupil.

In the national study head-teachers in ordinary primary schools were asked, for each child, if they considered that he or she would benefit now, or in the next two years, from special educational help. Overall, 5 per cent of children (6.3 per cent of boys; 3.4 per cent of girls) were identified as needing such help. In a further 3.5 per cent of children head-teachers felt unable to commit themselves. Of these children, three-quarters were poor or very poor readers and it was assumed that at least one-half would need special help, making a total of at least 7 per cent in the whole study. In Dundee 4.9 per cent of children (6.5 per cent of boys; 3.3 per cent of girls) had severe problems (grades 4 and 5) and all had received, or were said to need, special help in reading and/or number work. These figures are almost identical to the estimates of NCDS boys and girls definitely needing special help.

Forty-eight NCDS children (0.4 per cent) were known to be in special schools. A further 73 children (0.6 per cent) were attending 'unclassified' schools which might have been providing special education. In the Dundee 1974/75 population 1.3 per cent were attending or had been recommended for special schools (p. 265).

Table 13.21 compares levels of attainment in expressive language, reading and number among boys and girls in the two studies. In both studies girls scored significantly better than boys in language and reading but not in number work. The superiority of NCDS girls in reading was further demonstrated by results on the Southgate Group Reading Test (1962) as it was in Dundee using the Young Screening Test. In the NCDS a problem arithmetic test was devised which indicated

TABLE 13.21

Comparison of levels of attainment by sex in National Child Development Study
(1958 cohort) and Dundee children born 1974/75

	Attainment	NCDS 1958			Dundee 1974/75		
		M	F	All	M	F	All
		%	%	%	%	%	%
Ability in:							
Expressive	1	24	28	26	21	26	24
language	2	51	55	53	62	63	63
	3	21	15	18	14	9	11
	4	4	2	3	3	2	2
Reading	1	26	39	30	19	27	23
	2	43	44	43	57	58	58
	3	28	16	24	21	13	17
	4	3	1	2	3	2	2
Number	1	22	19	20	16	16	16
	2	42	45	43	64	66	65
	3	32	33	33	15	13	14
	4	4	3	4	5	5	5

that boys were significantly superior to girls in the particular aspect of arithmetic ability assessed by this test.

In the national study 15.6 per cent of boys and 8.1 per cent of girls (including children in special schools) had an adverse score of 20 or over on the Bristol Social Adjustment Guides, which Stott considered to be an indication of severe behaviour disorder. In Dundee 5 per cent of boys and 2 per cent of girls were considered to have severe behaviour disturbance in school, but children in special education were not included. Although not strictly comparable, the frequency of severe behaviour disturbance in Dundee children would appear to be significantly less than in the national study.

Butler *et al.* (1973) reported on the speech aspects of the NCDS. 8 per cent of children were described as somewhat and 2 per cent as certainly difficult to understand because of poor speech, frequencies very similar to the 9 and 2 per cent found in Dundee. After excluding all those with hearing defect and recognised educational difficulty, 11 per cent of NCDS children who were certainly difficult to understand were also described as certainly clumsy and 28 per cent as somewhat clumsy. In the rest of the sample the proportions considered certainly or somewhat clumsy were 2 and 11 per cent. Children with speech defects were described as more often male and from a poor family background, more often at a disadvantage educationally, showing more clumsiness and behaviour difficulties and more defects of vision and visuo-motor co-ordination.

Newcastle Survey of Child Development (1960/62)

Information was obtained about the subsequent progress of 98 per cent of surviving children born to mothers resident in Newcastle upon Tyne in the years 1960/62 (Neligan and Prudham 1976). Health visitors had completed a detailed *pro forma* for over 4000 children at three years of age, which recorded the quality of the mother's care for the child and other family factors. Social class derived from the father's occupation was also known. The Goodenough Draw-a-man Test was administered by class teachers at age five years. At 10 years non-verbal intelligence quotient (IQ) was estimated (National Foundation for Educational Research Test 5/BD) and a behaviour *pro forma* completed by teachers. The effect of family factors on later development (the most important being the quality of the mother's care) far outweighed that of occupational social class, except in the case of IQ at 10 years. However, unfavourable family gradings were markedly increased in social classes IV and V, especially with regard to maternal care, and it was conceded that social class could act as 'a very effective label' for different aspects of the children's immediate environment. Neligan and Prudham suggest that quality of care seems to be the factor most accessible to modification by extra support from a health visitor or social worker coming into the home and by nursery facilities outside the home.

Motor dysfunction and school progress

In a small group of 16 children, Henderson and Hall (1982) examined the ability of teachers to recognise motor impairment accurately, by correlating their observations with those of a psychologist who administered the Motor Impairment Test (Stott *et al.* 1972) and of a paediatrician who carried out a 16-point neuro-developmental battery of test items as well as a conventional neurological examination. The agreement between the various measures of motor skills was high (92 per cent average) while the agreement between teacher observations and the Motor Impairment Test was 100 per cent. Henderson and Hall concluded that teachers are well able to recognise motor impairment and pointed out that activities in the neurodevelopmental battery such as hopping, balancing, threading beads and controlling a pencil, are exactly what the infant teacher is observing in the classroom.

In a validity study of the Motor Impairment Test (Moyes 1969) teachers were asked to pick out children aged six to eight years whom they thought showed motor impairment. The test was administered to 60 of these children and to 60 controls matched for age, sex and social class. Test scores and teacher assessments agreed significantly. Disagreement amounted to 17.5 per cent.

In an early study from Cambridgeshire (Brenner *et al.* 1967) 810 school children aged eight to nine years were sampled by means of a group test battery of 11 items which examined dexterity, perceptual analysis, constructional skill and verbal intelligence (National Foundation for Educational Research, Verbal Test I). High correlations were found between visuo-motor items and verbal IQ. 54 children (6.7 per cent of those with IQs ≥90) deviated more than one standard deviation from the mean on the visuo-motor tests. School performance of these children was in general found to be poor for IQ level, especially in spelling, writing and arithmetic, though reading was usually adequate. The characteristic of these children most frequently remarked on by teachers was clumsiness in gait, in movement or in fine motor control.

In the NCDS group 3.1 per cent of boys were described as certainly and 14.9 per cent as somewhat clumsy (overall, 18.0 per cent) compared with 1.1 and 7.2 per cent of girls (overall, 8.3 per cent). Clumsiness was significantly associated with occupational social class of fathers. 11 per cent of those with fathers in social classes I and II, 12 per cent in social class III and 16 per cent in social classes IV and V were described as clumsy (Davie *et al.* 1972).

The proportions of boys and girls considered to show poor control of hands and poor physical co-ordination were higher. Poor hand control was reported for 26.0 per cent of boys and 14.2 per cent of girls and poor physical co-ordination for 15.8 per cent of boys and 10.3 per cent of girls. The total numbers exhibiting poor hand control and/or poor physical co-ordination are not given. The proportions reported as having evidence of motor dysfunction are considerably higher in the national study than in Dundee (Table 13.22). Differences between boys and girls are similar but in both sexes and both areas of functioning the proportions were 1.6 times higher in the NCDS sample. Overall, in Dundee 15.4 per cent of children were described as certainly or somewhat showing poor control of hands and/or poor physical co-ordination.

In the study by Henderson and Hall (1982), 20 (5 per cent) of 400 children in infant schools were described by teachers as having poor motor co-ordination for age and that this was significantly affecting school progress. All but three of the 16 children examined were boys. The motor impairment group had a significantly higher incidence of additional problems than did a matched control group. They were also more likely to be considered socially immature and to have poor speech; reading test scores and drawing skills were depressed. Significant differences on the Wechsler Intelligence Scale for Children (WISC) were not found.

The relationship of motor impairment (using the Motor Impairment Test) and behaviour disturbance in school (using the Bristol Social Adjustment Guide) was explored in a random sample of six to 14 year olds in Ontario (Stott 1978). Mean behaviour disturbance scores rose with increasing motor impairment. The type of behaviour called 'inconsequence' (*i.e.* a failure to restrain first impulses and hence to monitor their consequences) stood out as the type of maladjustment most closely associated with motor impairment. Stott cautions against the too-ready assumption that the common association between learning disabilities and clumsiness implies a causal relationship. He suggests that the learning disability may be chiefly one of faulty learning style as an aspect of behaviour disturbance, with motor impairment a concomitant rather than a cause of the learning disability.

In a study from Göteborg, Sweden (Gillberg *et al.* 1982), detailed question-naires were submitted to teachers of 4797 six year olds. These were completed for 72 per cent of the children. Questions were asked about six areas of functioning: poor attention, distractibility, conceptualisation, conduct problems, gross motor dysfunction, fine motor dysfunction. The term minimal brain dysfunction (MBD) was applied to non-retarded, non-cerebral-palsied children showing signs of attentional deficits or hyperactivity in combination with either problems of motor control or perceptual difficulties. Neurological, psychiatric and psychological assessment was carried out for 82 randomly selected children with suggestive symptoms of MBD and 59 control children without these symptoms. A diagnosis of

TABLE 13.22

Comparison of teacher ratings of control of hands and physical co-ordination by sex in the NCDS (1958 cohort) and Dundee children born 1974/75

Teacher rating	NCDS 1958			Dundee 1974/75		
	M	F	All	M	F	All
Poor control of hands	(N = 7665)	(N = 7284)	(N = 14,949)	(N = 2060)	(N = 1944)	(N = 4004)
	%	%	%	%	%	%
Applies certainly	5.6	2.7	4.2	3.2	1.0	2.1
somewhat	20.4	11.5	16.1	13.2	7.3	10.3
not at all	74.0	85.8	79.7	83.6	91.7	87.6
Poor physical co-ordination	(N = 7623)	(N = 7250)	(N = 14,837)	(N = 2060)	(N = 1944)	(N = 4004)
	%	%	%	%	%	%
Applies certainly	3.2	1.7	2.5	1.6	0.7	1.1
somewhat	12.6	8.6	10.6	8.4	5.6	7.0
not at all	84.2	89.7	86.9	90.0	93.7	91.9

MBD was confirmed in 41 per cent of those with suggestive symptoms on the teacher questionnaire and in 3 per cent of control children. Extrapolation procedures gave a total population frequency of 1.2 per cent with severe MBD and 5.9 per cent with mild to moderate MBD.

A special neurological examination devised by Peters (Peters *et al.* 1975) was applied to 82 boys, aged eight to 11 years, with learning and/or behaviour problems but normal intelligence (WISC verbal or performance IQ ≥90) and 45 control boys. The procedures included items from the conventional neurological examination and tests of integrated motor acts. In 44 of 80 neurological items, problem children were significantly different from control children. The authors state that at least 26 of these 44 items could be placed in the category of motor awkwardness or clumsiness. The younger problem children showed a much greater number of discriminatory signs than did the older children. A reduction in abnormal neurological signs with increasing age but retention of school difficulties was reported by Köhler and colleagues (1979) from Lund, Sweden. In a general health examination of 95 per cent of a total population of four year olds, 52 (2.1 per cent) were diagnosed as having MBD on the basis of general clumsiness and lack of fine motor co-ordination in combination with excessive mobility, restlessness and short attention span. The majority of these children were boys (N = 43). All but one were traced and re-examined seven to nine years later. By that age only one-third had 'minor neurological disturbance' (*e.g.* clumsiness, tremors, co-ordination difficulties) but 10 were in special education (20.4 per cent) compared with 2.7 per cent of all children in the city. Only six had no problems of behaviour.

A long-term study (birth to 12 years) from one of the hospital groups participating in the US Collaborative Perinatal Research Project (Rubin and Balow 1980) demonstrated that children identified as neurologically suspect or abnormal on two or more of three examinations in the first year of life (1.7 per cent) were at high risk of later impairment of perceptuo-motor, cognitive and academic performance. Children who had been abnormal/suspect on one examination (12.5 per cent) showed significant impairment of a lesser degree. At four years highly significant differences were found on tests of gross and fine motor skills between children who had shown neurological abnormality in the first year and those who had not. At seven years, 50 per cent of those who were abnormal/suspect on more than one first-year examination and 9 per cent of those abnormal/suspect on one examination continued to show definite clinical signs of neurological abnormality, compared with 1 per cent of those considered neurologically normal throughout the first year of life.

Effect on families of unemployment and maternal depression

It has been suggested that the deteriorating social situation, consequent upon sharply rising unemployment in the period 1979/82, might have been expected to result in an increase in early schooling problems for those Dundee children born 1974/75. The effect of unemployment on family health was studied in 22 families by Fagin (1981). Health deteriorated after unemployment and this deterioration (principally a moderate or severe depression) was not confined to the ex-worker but also occurred among wives and children. Children's school performance declined and their behaviour became disturbed. Another study (Cochrane and Stopes-Roe 1981) examined the relationship between mental health in women and employment. Women who worked outside the home had fewer psychological symptoms (particularly symptoms of depression) than did those not in paid employment.

That depression among women in widespread was indicated by a study of a randomly selected sample of women living in inner London (Brown *et al.* 1975). Overall, the prevalence rate, using a standardised interview, was calculated to be 16 per cent, with big differences by social class and 'life stage'. The highest rate was 42 per cent for working-class women who had children under six years of age. In another study (Richman 1974) a similar incidence rate was found for mothers of pre-school children living in a different working-class area of London.

A group of 250 preschool children living in Camden, London, was studied by Bax and Hart (1976). This was a more favoured area with a significant excess, as compared with the general population, of social classes II and III (non-manual) families. Nevertheless, 21 per cent of mothers had taken pills for depression in the previous year, 10 per cent reported that life was not worth living and two mothers had attempted suicide.

These studies were carried out in the early 1970s. It would be surprising if the prevalence of maternal depression had not increased significantly in the early 1980s. A recent report from a working party appointed by the Royal College of General Practitioners (1982) summarised the current situation as follows: 'At the time of writing, about three million people are unemployed and the country faces one of the two greatest economic recessions of the century. This must act as a major stress on families and have a substantial impact on children'.

Summary

A teacher questionnaire was designed for completion by teachers of children aged six and a half to seven and a half years attending normal primary schools in Dundee. The questionnaire contained items about educational attainment, behaviour, speech and motor abilities. A scoring method was used for analysis of results and children graded for school problems according to this score. Measures of social disadvantage are described.

School problems, social factors and motor dysfunction

Highly significant differences in the distribution of school problem grades was found by area of residence and by the absence or presence of known social disadvantage.

Differences in distribution of school problem grades for children who did not or did have evidence of motor dysfunction ('clumsiness') were even greater than those mentioned above. Clumsy children were more likely to come from disadvantaged homes but, whatever the home background, clumsy children had significantly more school problems than those not so described.

Adverse education scores were significantly associated with occupational social class of fathers. Within each social class group clumsy children were significantly more likely to have problems of education. Adverse behaviour scores were significantly increased among children from social problem families. Whether or not severe social problems were reported, clumsy children were significantly more likely to show disturbed behaviour in school.

School problems in boys and girls

Overall, boys had significantly more school problems than girls and were more likely to be described as clumsy. The difference in distribution of school problem grades was confined to those not reported as clumsy. Clumsy girls had as many school problems as clumsy boys.

Levels of attainment in number work were not dissimilar but girls excelled in expressive language, reading and writing and had less disturbed behaviour than boys.

Motor dysfunction and specific problems

Children with severe problems of behaviour or making very poor progress in the different areas of educational attainment were both more likely to be described as clumsy and also to show more marked degrees of clumsiness than were children in a control group.

Motor dysfunction and overactivity

Motor dysfunction was combined with marked overactivity/distractibility in 6 per cent of boys and 2 per cent of girls. Only 12 per cent of children with this combination of problems were making satisfactory educational progress and 67 per cent had serious educational difficulties.

Motor dysfunction and squint

The frequency of squint was identical for children with school problems who were not considered clumsy and for control children. The excess incidence of squint in children described as clumsy was nearly three-fold.

Articulatory disorder, motor dysfunction and school problems

Overall, unintelligble speech was significantly increased among children from disadvantaged homes and significantly associated with school problems and with clumsiness in children from homes without and with known disadvantage. There was little difference in the distribution of school problems for speech-disordered children from different social backgrounds, indicating a relative excess of school problems among speech-disordered children from better homes.

School problems, motor dysfunction, perinatal and postnatal histories

Differences in perinatal histories between children with and without schooling problems and between problem children who were not or were considered clumsy were not marked. The only significant difference was an increase in school problems for those who had been low birthweight or small for date. A significant excess of

251

postnatal incidents, which might result in cerebral insult, was recorded for problem children considered clumsy.

Recognition of preschool NDD and take-up of development screening among children with school problems

Only 32 per cent of 282 children with moderately severe school problems were identified as (or suspected of) having NDD preschool. Of the rest, 53 per cent were screened by doctors at two and/or three years, 26 per cent by health visitors only and 21 per cent were not screened at either age. Of those with severe school problems, 43 per cent were identified or suspected preschool and, of the rest, 38 per cent were screened by doctors, 26 per cent by health visitors only and 36 per cent were not screened. There was a significant excess of health visitor screening of problem children who had not been suspected or identified preschool as compared with a control group without school problems. Of all children with school problems, whose preschool progress gave cause for concern, one-third were not referred for further assessment.

The minimum acceptable frequency of screening (previously defined) was not achieved among significantly more children with school problems than in a control group without school problems.

Reading screen

The Young Group Reading Test was applied to 1974-born children; 3 per cent were considered non-readers and 6 per cent very poor readers. Reading failure was significantly associated with social disadvantage and motor dysfunction. Girls scored higher than boys.

Comparison of school status of research-group children with those born 1973 and 1976

This issue was complicated by the deteriorating social situation throughout 1979 to 1983. The findings suggest that preschool intervention may help to offset the adverse effects of increasing poverty and also directly benefit those at risk of early schooling difficulties because of innate rather than environmental factors.

APPENDIX XII: **Recognition of preschool NDD among 1974/75-born children with school problems grade 3 and matched control group C children**

Take-up at 2 yr. and 3 yr. D/S	School problem grade 3				Control group C (school problem grade 1)			
	S.Cl. I-III, no SP (N = 104)	S.Cl. IV-V, and/or SP (N = 161)	S.Cl./SP NK (N = 17)	Total (N = 282)	S.Cl. I-III, no SP (N = 116)	S.Cl. IV-V, and/or SP (N = 58)	S.Cl./SP NK (N = 16)	Total (N = 190)
Preschool NDD identified/suspected								
Ref. hospital	5	6	—	11	3	2	—	5
Ref. CDC	13	26	1	39	5	6	—	11
CDC wished to see	15	24	1	40	1	3	1	5
Total identified/suspected (%)	33 (32)	56 (35)	1 (6)	90 (32)	9 (8)	11 (19)	1 (6)	21 (11)
No preschool NDD identified/suspected								
Missed both D/S	3	4	—	7	2	2	—	4
Transferred in after 3 yrs., missed both D/S	8	11	14	33	12	4	8	24
All (%)	11 (10)	15 (9)	14 (82)	40 (14)	14 (12)	6 (10)	8 (50)	28 (15)
D/S by doctor or health visitor:								
2 yr. D/S—doctor; 3 yr. D/S—health visitor/missed	3	15	—	18	10	8	1	19
2 yr. D/S—health visitor/missed; 3 yr. D/S—doctor	10	12	—	22	16	5	2	23
Both D/S—doctor	31	30	1	62	58	19	3	80
All (%)	44 (43)	57 (35)	1 (6)	102 (36)	84 (72)	32 (55)	6 (38)	122 (64)
D/S by health visitor only:								
2 yr. D/S—health visitor; 3 yr. D/S—missed	6	9	—	15	4	3	—	7
2 yr. D/S—missed; 3 yr. D/S—health visitor	9	14	—	23	5	5	—	10
Both D/S—health visitor	1	10	1	12	—	1	1	2
All (%)	16 (15)	33 (21)	1 (6)	50 (18)	9 (8)	9 (16)	1 (6)	19 (10)
Total not identified/suspected (%)	71 (68)	105 (65)	16 (94)	192 (68)	107 (92)	47 (81)	15 (94)	169 (89)
Total (%)	104 (100)	161 (100)	17 (100)	282 (100)	116 (100)	58 (100)	16 (100)	190 (100)

S.Cl = social class; SP = social problem; D/S = development screening; NK = not known.

APPENDIX XIII: Recognition of preschool NDD among 1974/75-born children with school problems grade 4 and 5 and matched control group C children

Take-up at 2 yr. and 3 yr. D/S	School problem grade 4 and 5				Control group C (school problem grade 1)			
	S.Cl. I-III, no SP (N = 65)	S.Cl. IV-V, and/or SP (N = 114)	S.Cl./SP NK (N = 20)	Total (N = 199)	S.Cl. I-III, no SP (N = 66)	S.Cl. IV-V, and/or SP (N = 31)	S.Cl./SP NK (N = 17)	Total (N = 114)
Preschool NDD identified/suspected								
Ref. hospital	—	5	—	5	3	1	—	4
Ref. CDC	22	32	1	55	3	1	—	4
CDC wished to see	11	13	1	24	1	2	—	3
Total identified/suspected (%)	33 (51)	50 (44)	2 (10)	84 (43)	7 (10)	4 (13)	—	11 (9)
No preschool NDD identified/suspected								
Missed both D/S	2	7	1	10	1	—	1	2
Transferred in after 3 yrs., missed both D/S	8	7	16	31	2	2	10	14
All (%)	10 (15)	14 (12)	17 (85)	41 (21)	3 (5)	2 (6)	11 (65)	16 (14)
D/S by doctor or health visitor:								
2 yr. D/S—doctor; 3 yr. D/S—health visitor/missed	3	7	—	10	7	3	2	12
2 yr. D/S—health visitor/missed; 3 yr. D/S—doctor	2	8	—	10	7	4	2	13
Both D/S—doctor	15	7	1	23	38	11	2	51
All (%)	20 (31)	22 (19)	1 (5)	43 (21)	52 (79)	18 (58)	6 (35)	76 (67)
D/S by health visitor only:								
2 yr. D/S—health visitor; 3 yr. D/S—missed	1	8	—	9	1	3	—	4
2 yr. D/S—missed; 3 yr. D/S—health visitor	—	16	—	16	3	4	—	7
Both D/S—health visitor	1	4	—	5	—	—	—	—
All (%)	2 (3)	28 (25)	—	30 (15)	4 (6)	7 (23)	—	11 (10)
Total not identified/suspected (%)	32 (49)	64 (57)	18 (90)	114 (58)	59 (89)	27 (87)	17 (100)	103 (90)
Total (%)	65 (100)	114 (100)	20 (100)	199 (100)	66 (100)	31 (100)	17 (100)	114 (100)

S.Cl = social class; SP = social problem; D/S = development screening; NK = not known.

REFERENCES

Bax, M., Hart, H. (1976) 'Health needs of preschool children' *Archives of Disease in Childhood,* **51,** 848-852.

Brenner, M. W., Gillman, S., Zangwill, O. L., Farrell, M. (1967) 'Visuo-motor disability in school children.' *British Medical Journal,* **4,** 259-262.

Brown, G. W., Ni Brolchain, M., Harris, T. O. (1975) 'Social class and psychiatric disturbance among women in an urban population.' *Sociology,* **9,** 225-254.

Butler, N. R., Peckham, C., Sheridan, M. (1973) 'Speech defects in children aged 7 years: a national study.' *British Medical Journal,* **1,** 253-257.

Cochrane, R., Stopes-Roe, M. (1981) 'Women, marriage, employment and mental health.' *British Journal of Psychiatry,* **139,** 373-381.

Davie, R., Butler, N., Goldstein, H. (1972) *From Birth to Seven.* London: Longman for the National Children's Bureau.

Fagin, L. (1981) *Unemployment and Health in Families:* Case Studies Based on Family Interviews—a Pilot Study. London: DHSS.

Gillberg, C., Rasmussen, P., Carlstrom, G., Svenson, B., Waldenström, E. (1982) 'Perceptual, motor and attentional deficits in six-year-old children: epidemiological aspects.' *Journal of Child Psychology and Psychiatry,* **23,** 131-144.

Henderson, S. E., Hall, D. (1982) 'Concomitants of clumsiness in young schoolchildren.' *Developmental Medicine and Child Neurology,* **24,** 448-460.

Kellmer Pringle, M. L., Butler, N. R., Davie, R. (1966). *11,000 Seven-Year-Olds.* London: Longman for the National Children's Bureau.

Köhler, E., Köhler, L., Regefalk, C. (1979) 'Minimal brain dysfunction in pre-school age: risk for trouble in school?' *Paediatrician,* **8,** 219-277.

Moyes, F. A. (1969) *A Validation Study of the Test of Motor Impairment.* M.Ed. Thesis, University of Leicester.

Neligan, G. A., Prudham, D. (1976) 'Family factors affecting child development.' *Archives of Disease in Childhood,* **51,** 853-858.

Peters, J. E., Romine, J. S., Dykeman, R. A. (1975) 'A special neurological examination of children with learning disabilities.' *Developmental Medicine and Child Neurology,* **17,** 63-78.

Richman, N. (1974) 'The effects of housing on preschool children and their mothers.' *Developmental Medicine and Child Neurology,* **16,** 53-58.

Royal College of General Practitioners (1982) 'Healthier children—thinking prevention.' *Report from General Practice,* **22.**

Rubin, R. A., Balow, B. (1980) 'Infant neurological abnormalities as indicators of cognitive impairment.' *Developmental Medicine and Child Neurology,* **22,** 336-343.

Southgate, V. (1962) *Southgate Group Reading Tests: Manual of Instructions.* London: University of London Press.

Stott, D. H. (1962) *The Social Adjustment of Children, Manual to the Bristol Social Adjustment Guides.* London: University of London Press.

——(1978) 'Association of motor impairment with various types of behaviour disturbance.' *Journal of Learning Disabilities,* **11,** 34-41.

——Moyes, F. A., Henderson, S. E. (1972) *A Test of Motor Impairment.* London: National Foundation for Educational Research.

Towen, B. C. L., Prechtl, H. F. R. (1970) *The Neurological Examination of the Child with Minor Nervous Dysfunction. Clinics in Developmental Medicine No. 38.* London: SIMP with Heinemann Medical; Philadelphia: Lippincott.

Young, D. (1977) *Manual for the Group Reading Test, Tenth Impression.* Sevenoaks, Kent: Hodder and Stoughton Educational.

CHAPTER 14

School Status of Children with Identified or Suspected Preschool Neurodevelopmental Disabilities

CDC-REFERRED CHILDREN IN SCHOOL

Of 446 1974/75-born children referred to CDC preschool (414 with NDD and 32 considered acceptably normal), 377 remained in Dundee at age six and a half to seven and a half yers. 34 children were admitted to special education at school-entry age (two of these were later transferred to normal school), four were transferred to special education from primary school and 339 attended normal primary schools throughout.

Preschool severity grading and early school status

A severity grading was applied to all children with preschool NDD based on the likely implication of their disabilities for educational progress and behaviour at early school age (p. 48). Social circumstances *per se* were not taken into account when deciding whether or not severity of preschool NDD was likely to be associated with later schooling problems.

Of the 377 CDC-referred children remaining in Dundee at six and a half to seven and a half years, 28 had been considered within normal limits and 349 were considered to have had neurodevelopmental or behavioural problems ranging from minor to severe. Table 14.1 details the problem grades allotted at school age by severity of preschool problems. For the purpose of calculating correlation coefficients, numerical scores were applied to both preschool and school gradings as detailed in the table. An additional school problem grade was included for children who had attended or were attending special schools. Correlation coefficients were calculated between preschool and school scores for the total group and separately for those who were or were not known to come from social class IV or V families or to have experienced severe social problems preschool. The correlation coefficient between preschool and school problem scores is 0.593 for the total group, with a rather higher correlation for children with no known social disadvantage (0.608) than for those known to come from disadvantaged backgrounds (0.584). All correlation coefficients are highly significant (using the t test, all p values = <0.001).

In 39 (12 per cent) of the 339 CDC-referred children attending normal schools, educational progress and school behaviour were very different from what had been anticipated preschool.

The school performance of eight children was much worse. One considered to be within normal limits and seven rated as having minor neurodevelopmental disability (NDD) only had significant problems in school (problem grade 3 or higher). Three had presented preschool with motor delay and minor abnormal neurological

256

TABLE 14.1
School problems at 6½-7½ years of 377 CDC-referred children by severity of preschool NDD

| | | Severity of preschool NDD | | | | | | | | | | | |
| | | 0 WNL | | 1 Minor | | 2 Moderate | | 3 Mod. severe | | 4 Severe | | Total | |
School problem grade	Social disadvantages	No.	%	No.	%	No.	%	No.	%	No.	%	No.	%
1/0	No	13	93	21	81	61	62	15	30	—	—	110	52
	Yes	11	79	7	41	26	39	9	21	1	4	54	33
	All	24	86	28	65	87	53	24	26	1	2	164	44
2/1	No	1	7	3	11	22	23	15	30	2	9	43	20
	Yes	2	14	4	24	17	26	11	26	4	15	38	23
	All	3	11	7	16	39	24	26	28	6	12	81	22
3/2	No	—	—	1	4	5	5	6	12	—	—	13	6
	Yes	1	7	2	12	12	18	10	23	1	4	25	15
	All	1	3	3	7	17	10	16	17	1	2	38	10
4/3	No	—	—	1	4	10	10	9	18	2	9	22	11
	Yes	—	—	3	19	8	12	8	18	2	7	21	13
	All	—	—	4	10	18	11	17	18	4	8	43	11
5/4	No	—	—	—	—	—	—	3	6	1	5	4	2
	Yes	—	—	—	—	4	6	3	7	2	7	9	5
	All	—	—	—	—	4	3	6	7	3	6	13	3
Sp.Ed./5	No	—	—	—	—	—	—	2	4	17	77	19	9
	Yes	—	—	—	—	—	—	2	5	17	63	19	11
	All	—	—	—	—	—	—	4	4	34	70	38	10
Total	No	14	100	26	100	98	100	50	100	22	100	211	100
	Yes	14	100	16	100	67	100	43	100	27	100	166	100
	All	28	100	42	100	165	100	93	100	49	100	377	100

Sp.Ed./5 = special education; WNL = within normal limits.

signs (p. 127), two with minor speech delays, one with a minor behaviour problem (her school failure was attributed to poor attendance rather than lack of ability) and one with minor global delay. This child was last seen in foster care where he made good progress before being returned to a very poor home at five years. All but two of these eight children came from poor homes with severe social problems.

The school performance of 31 children was much better than had been anticipated. 24, graded as having moderately severe NDD preschool, had no school problems (grade 1) and seven, graded as severe, had no problems (one child) or moderate problems only (grade 2).

Of these 31 children, 12 were considered preschool to be borderline retarded (four) or very dull (eight). In eight cases Primary 1 entrance was deferred on recommendation of the Child Guidance Service and/or the child attended the assessment class. Primary 1 entrance was deferred for four of the nine children who had severe primary communication disorders (p. 152). All made acceptable educational progress and had no problems of behaviour in their first year of primary school, although three were still difficult to understand because of poor speech at six and a half to seven and a half years. Three other children with moderately severe preschool speech disorders had no problems in school; two were still difficult to understand. Five cerebral-palsied children, graded preschool as moderately severe, had no educational or behavioural problems in Primary 2 although all were noted to be clumsy, as were two children with moderately severe preschool motor disorder.

Two children with 'handicapping' behaviour disorder preschool (p. 171) were coping in normal school with only moderate problems; both had attended the assessment class. Two other children with moderately severe preschool behaviour disorder had no problems in school; both came from good homes.

The last child, whose school questionnaire did not confirm preschool expectations, has a hemimelia, is of very small stature, was markedly overactive and appeared generally delayed preschool. School entrance was deferred and he is managing well in a class of younger children.

Preschool neurological findings and motor dysfunction in school

Table 14.2 details clumsiness scores derived from teachers' reports for 331 CDC-referred children who were examined neurologically preschool and classified as neurologically normal, doubtful or abnormal. 10 children with cerebral palsy are excluded and one who was inadequately examined preschool. The two children who transferred to normal school from special education and one who transferred to special school after his questionnaire was completed in normal school are included.

Of those CDC-attenders considered neurologically normal preschool, 20 per cent were considered clumsy by their teachers, as were 46 per cent of the neurologically doubtful and 51 per cent of the abnormal children. The difference in frequency of reported clumsiness among those who were neurologically normal preschool and those who were doubtful or abnormal is overwhelmingly significant ($\chi^2 = 31$). In addition, clumsy children who were neurologically doubtful or abnormal preschool were likely to show more marked evidence of clumsiness, as indicated by the clumsiness score, than were clumsy children who had been neurologically normal.

TABLE 14.2

Clumsiness and preschool neurological status of CDC-referred children attending normal primary schools (N = 331)

| | Neurological status | | | | | |
| | Normal | | Doubtful | | Abnormal | |
	No.	%	No.	%	No.	%
Clumsiness score						
0	125	80	37	54	52	49
1	22	14	14	20	22	21
2	8	5	8	12	24	22
3/4	1	1	10	14	8	8
Total	156	100	69	100	106	100
% clumsy	20		46		51	

TABLE 14.3

CDC-referred children, school problems by preschool neurological status and social disadvantage

| Neurological status | Social disadvantages | School problem grade | | | | | | | | Total | |
| | | 1 (N = 159) | | 2 (N = 81) | | 3 (N = 38) | | 4/5 (N = 53) | | (N = 331) | |
		No.	%	No.	%	No.	%	No.	%	No.	%
Normal	No	60	72	13	16	5	6	5	6	83	100
	Yes	31	42	18	25	10	14	14	19	73	100
	All	91	58	31	20	15	10	19	12	156	100
Doubtful	No	20	61	4	12	2	6	7	21	33	100
	Yes	13	36	7	19	7	19	9	25	36	100
	All	33	48	11	16	9	13	16	23	69	100
Abnormal	No	24	40	25	40	4	6	10	16	63	100
	Yes	11	26	14	32	10	23	8	19	43	100
	All	35	33	39	37	14	13	18	17	106	100

TABLE 14.4

School problems of CDC-referred children who did or did not exhibit multiple minor congenital anomalies

| | School problem grades | | | | | | | |
| | 1 | | 2 | | 3-5 | | Total | |
	No.	%	No.	%	No.	%	No.	%
MCA 0-2								
Not clumsy	123	66	39	21	23	13	185	100
Clumsy	14	19	20	27	39	54	73	100
All	137	52	59	23	62	24	258	100
MCA ⩾ 3								
Not clumsy	16	55	8	28	5	17	29	100
Clumsy	6	14	14	32	24	54	44	100
All	22	30	22	30	29	40	73	100

MCA = minor congenital anomalies.

259

The difference in distribution of clumsiness scores is highly significant ($\chi^2 = 9.160$, 2df, p. = <0.01).

These findings lend support to the hypothesis that clumsiness as reported by teachers is a measure, albeit crude, of neurological dysfunction.

Preschool neurological status and early school problems

Table 14.3 details school problem grades for CDC-referred children, who did or did not suffer some social disadvantage, by preschool neurological status. There is a trend for those considered neurologically doubtful or abnormal to have more school problems than those considered to be neurologically normal. The difference in distribution of school problem grades for the neurologically normal and the doubtful/abnormal children is statistically highly significant ($\chi^2 = 12.662$, 3df, p = <0.01). However, this is acounted for only by those children without known social disadvantage ($\chi^2 = 14.324$, 3df, p = <0.01) and not for those from disadvantaged families ($\chi^2 = 3.001$, 3df, p = >0.3) where, one presumes, extrinsic rather than intrinsic factors were of more importance in determining school performance.

School status of CDC-referred children without and with multiple minor congenital anomalies

Table 14.4 details the school problem grades of CDC-referred children who were or were not found to have three or more minor congenital anomalies. The children are further subdivided into those who were or were not considered clumsy by their teachers.

The difference in problem grade distribution between those who did or did not exhibit multiple anomalies is highly significant ($\chi^2 = 12.571$, 2df, p. = <0.01). In addition, children with three or more anomalies were much more likely to be considered clumsy (60 per cent) than were those with up to two anomalies (28 per cent). This difference is also highly significant ($\chi^2 = 25$, p = <0.001). In the preschool period a highly significant increase in minor neurological abnormality was found among children who had multiple anomalies (p. 104).

School status of CDC-referred children in all categories of preschool NDD

Table 14.5 details school problems for 325 CDC-referred children, attending normal primary schools, who were considered to be within normal limits or in different categories of NDD. 14 children with specific physical and neurological defects are excluded. School problems are also detailed for 287 children in control group B.

Overall, children identified as having NDD of sufficient severity to merit referral to CDC were significantly more likely to have problems in school than a matched control group ($\chi^2 = 43$, 3df, p = <0.001). The difference is of the same order for children from families with no known social disadvantage ($\chi^2 = 20.638$, p = <0.001) and for those from social classes IV and V families or those with known social problems ($\chi^2 = 17.218$, p = <0.001).

260

TABLE 14.5
School problems of CDC-referred children and control group B

	Social disadvantages	School problem grade 1		2		3		4/5		Total	
		No.	%	No.	%	No.	%	No.	%	No.	%
Preschool: Normal	No	13		1		—		—		14	
	Yes	11		2		1		—		14	
	All	24	86	3	10	1	4	—	—	28	100
Global delay/ borderline MR	No	11		12		3		6		32	
	Yes	13		14		8		13		48	
	All	24	30	26	32	11	14	19	24	80	100
Motor disorder	No	13		13		—		4		30	
	Yes	4		2		8		3		17	
	All	17	36	15	32	8	17	7	15	47	100
Speech disorder	No	46		11		5		7		69	
	Yes	17		9		4		6		36	
	All	63	60	20	19	9	9	13	12	105	100
Behaviour disorder	No	16		5		3		7		31	
	Yes	10		10		6		8		34	
	All	26	40	15	23	9	14	15	23	65	100
All NDD	No	87	53	41	25	11	7	24	15	163	100
	Yes	43	32	35	26	26	20	30	22	134	100
	All	130	44	76	26	37	12	54	18	297	100
Control group B	No	150	78	24	13	12	6	5	3	191	100
	Yes	61	63	15	16	14	15	6	6	96	100
	All	211	73	39	14	26	9	11	4	287	100

MR = mental retardation.

Within normal limits

Of the 28 children considered within normal limits preschool, 24 (86 per cent) had no problems in school, three had moderate and one had moderately severe problems. Three of the four children with school problems came from disadvantaged homes.

Global delay and borderline retardation

As might be expected, children with preschool global delay or borderline retardation experienced the most difficulties in school. Only 30 per cent were problem-free, 32 per cent had moderate problems and 38 per cent more severe problems. 14 of the 80 children were considered to be borderline retarded preschool. One had no problems in school, five had moderate problems and eight had more severe problems. On the recommendation of the Child Guidance Service, Primary 1 entrance was deferred by 12 months for all but two of these children. Of those with global delay, not amounting to borderline retardation, one-third had no problems in school, one-third had moderate problems and one-third had severe problems.

TABLE 14.6
School problems among speech-disordered CDC-referred children (N = 105) with and without behaviour disturbance

	School problem grade									
	1		*2*		*3*		*4/5*		*Total*	
	No.	%	No.	%	No.	%	No.	%	No.	%
Speech and behaviour disorder										
S.Cl. I-III, no SP	15	52	5	17	2	7	7	24	29	100
S.Cl. IV-V, or SP	7	41	3	18	3	18	4	24	17	100
All	22	48	8	17	5	11	11	24	46	100
Speech disorder only										
S.Cl. I-III, no SP	31	78	6	15	3	7	—	—	40	100
S.Cl. IV-V, or SP	10	53	6	31	1	5	2	11	19	100
All	41	70	12	20	4	7	2	3	59	100
Total population * (%)	73		15		7		5		100	

*Children attending normal primary schools at age 6½-7½ yrs; S.Cl. = social class; SP = social problem.

Motor disorder

After global delay, children with a principal preschool problem of motor disorder had the most problems in school. 32 per cent had moderate problems and 32 per cent more severe problems. Only 36 per cent were problem-free in spite of the fact that this was the only category of NDD, other than cerebral palsy and specific conditions, in which frequency was unaffected by social factors (p. 67).

Seventeen children presented initially at CDC with a motor problem but later moved into another clinical category (p. 126). 16 of these children were attending normal primary schools and one was in special education. Only three of the 16 were problem-free at school, five had moderate problems and eight more had severe problems.

Behaviour disorder

Of children with preschool behaviour disorder, 40 per cent were problem-free in school, 23 per cent had moderate problems and 37 per cent more severe problems, which were more often educational than behavioural.

Speech disorder

Children with a principal preschool problem of speech disorder had the lowest incidence of school problems: 60 per cent were problem-free, 19 per cent had moderate and 21 per cent had more severe problems.

There was a striking difference in school performance among those with preschool speech disorder only and those who had had additional problems of behaviour (p. 148) as shown in Table 14.6. Distribution of school problem grades for children with speech disorder only is very close to that of the total population of 4004 children (see Table 13.2, p. 223) and significantly different from the distribution for speech-disordered children who had additional behaviour disturbance (χ^2 = 12.589, 3df, p = <0.01). This is not due only to the excess of children from disadvantaged homes amongst those who had additional behaviour disturbance. Children with no known disadvantage in the speech and behaviour group were significantly more likely to have school problems than those with speech disorder only (χ^2 = 11.393, 3df, p = <0.01). There is a similar but less striking trend for disadvantaged children but this is not statistically significant.

Children who had speech and behaviour disturbance preschool were much more likely to be described as clumsy by their teachers (40 per cent) than were those who had speech disorder only (15 per cent). This difference is highly significant (χ^2 = 8.527, p = <0.01). On preschool examination children with associated behaviour disturbance were significantly more likely to show doubtful or abnormal minor abnormal neurological signs than were those without behaviour disturbance and the former were also more likely to be clumsy in gait and/or hand function preschool (p. 149).

SCHOOL STATUS OF CHILDREN WITH SUSPECTED PRESCHOOL NEURODEVELOPMENTAL DISABILITY

As described in Chapter 4 (p. 72), development screening folders were recalled after the school entrance medical examinations and 203 children were found to have had delays or disorders on screening sufficiently suspect to merit review or referral to CDC. When school questionnaires were received it was discovered that development screening folders for some children had not been sent in after school entrance. On scrutiny of these folders, at a later date, it was found that review or referral had or would have been requested for an additional 20 children.

Of these 223 suspect children, 206 were attending Dundee primary schools at six and a half to seven and a half years. In 124 instances the child had been reviewed by the screening doctor or health visitor and thought to be within normal limits. In 82 instances either the child was not seen again before school entry or NDD was still present, but had not been identified by diagnostic assessment when the child was last seen. In addition, 24 children were referred to CDC but did not attend; questionnaires were received for 21 of these.

Table 14.7 gives details of school problems for the three groups of children whom we wished to see at CDC, for children who did attend CDC and for the total population of 4004 children other than those listed above. CDC attenders with specific physical and neurological defects are excluded since no child, resident in the city before five years, was identified as having any of these problems after school entry.

The distribution of school problems among children who did not attend appointments made at CDC was little different from that of children in the total population who were not suspected of having NDD before school entry. Children who did not attend comprised 5 per cent of all those referred to CDC and it could be that parents were correct in thinking attendance unnecessary.

In contrast, others who were suspected of having NDD on the basis of develop-

TABLE 14.7
School problems among CDC-referred children, those with suspected NDD who were not seen, and others in the total population

	School problem grade									
	1		2		3		4/5		Total	
	No.	%	No.	%	No.	%	No.	%	No.	%
Suspected NDD:										
Did not attend CDC	15	71	4	19	2	10	—	—	21	100
Thought to be WNL	62	50	30	24	19	15	13	11	124	100
Not identified	33	40	19	23	20	25	10	12	82	100
Attended CDC	144	46	78	24	38	12	56	18	316	100
Total population* other than above	2674	77	463	13	203	6	121	3	3461	100

*Children attending normal primary schools at age 6½-7½ yrs; WNL = within normal limits.

ment screening results had a much higher frequency of moderate or more severe problems in school than did children in the total population who were not suspect. The frequency of moderate or more severe school problems among these suspect children was of the same order as that of CDC attenders, with the 'thought to be within normal limits' subgroup having rather fewer school problems (grades 3 to 5) and the 'not identified' subgroup having rather more problems than CDC-referred children. In addition, CDC had wished to see seven of 12 children transferred to special education from normal school (p. 266).

It is reasonable to suppose that, overall, the preschool problems of children with suspected NDD who were not referred to CDC were less serious than the problems of those who were, particularly as NDD was not confirmed at later review or screening in 60 per cent of cases. The proportions of disadvantaged children amongst those who did or did not attend were very similar. The relationship of severity of preschool and school problems has been demonstrated, thus it might be expected that school problems would be less frequent in the group of children who did not attend CDC. That they are not suggests that preschool intervention may have played a part in reducing frequency and severity of school problems among children who did attend CDC.

READING SCREEN OF 1974-BORN CHILDREN

Table 14.8 details the distribution of reading quotients (RQs) of 134 children with preschool NDD confirmed at CDC, 92 children with suspected NDD whom CDC wished to see, 54 children with NDD confirmed at hospital clinics, 136 control group B children and of the total population of 1995 1974-born children taking part in a reading screen (p. 239).

Children with preschool NDD identified at CDC did significantly worse on the reading test than did control children selected from the same schools ($\chi^2 = 23.445$, 4df, p = <0.001). Children with suspect NDD who were not assessed also did signifi-

TABLE 14.8
1974-born children screened for reading. Reading quotients for children with identified or suspected NDD preschool, control group B and the total population

Reading quotient	CDC referred		CDC wished to see		Hospital referred		Control group B		Total population*	
	No.	%	No.	%	No.	%	No.	%	No.	%
≤79	19 (7)**	14	6	6	4	8	3	2	84	4
80-89	27 (8)	20	19	21	7	13	15	11	210	11
90-99	34 (3)	26	21	23	10	18	30	22	367	19
100-109	31 (2)	23	21	23	15	28	50	37	583	29
≥110	23 (1)	17	25	27	18	33	38	28	751	37
Total	134	100	92	100	54	100	136	100	1995	100

*All 1974-born children screened for reading, ** in parentheses, Primary 1 deferred.

cantly worse than control group B children (χ^2 = 10.392, 4df, p = <0.05). However, there was no significant difference in distribution between those who were or were not referred to CDC (χ^2 = 5.882, 4df, p = >0.30). It might be expected that, in general, children who were referred would tend to have more severe preschool NDD and more severe reading difficulties than would those who were not referred. For example, Primary 1 entrance was delayed by 12 months for 21 referred children on the advice of the Child Guidance Service and these children had only been reading for two and a half terms, whereas all suspect children whom we wished to see had been reading for five and a half terms. That referred children did not show more reading retardation may again indicate a benefit of preschool identification and intervention.

The distribution of RQs among hospital-referred children did not differ significantly from that of the total population of reading-screened children. The majority of children with NDD confirmed at hospital clinics had minor or moderate speech disorders which are associated with a lower incidence of school problems than other categories of NDD (p. 262). In addition, the social class composition of hospital-referred children was close to that of the general population of Dundee-born and resident children with more children having fathers in social classes I to III and fewer having fathers in social classes IV and V than either CDC-referred children or children in control group B (p. 67).

CHILDREN IN SPECIAL EDUCATION

By the last term of what should have been Primary 2, 52 1974/5-born children (1.3 per cent) had been recommended for or were already in special education. One other child (CDC-referred) had died after entry to special school. 39 1973-born children (1.9 per cent) had been recommended for or were in special education at the same point 12 to 24 months earlier. The numbers in special education on account of severe mental retardation, physical handicap, sensory disability and behaviour

TABLE 14.9
1973 and 1974/75-born children in special education

	CDC referred	Hospital referred	CDC wished to see	Other	Total 1974/75	per 1000	Total 1973	per 1000
MR mild	11		3		14	3.5	16	7.7
severe	11				11	2.8	7	3.4
MR mild/PH	3			1	4	1.0	2	1.0
PH	2				2	0.5	2	1.0
Deaf/blind	3	3			6	1.5	3	1.5
Behaviour disorder								
Residential school	2				2 }	3.2	3 }	3.9
Day school	3	2	4	2	11 }		5 }	
Language unit		2			2	0.5	1	0.5
Total	35	7	7	3	52	13.0	39	19.0

MR = mental retardation; PH = physical handicap.

disorder were very similar in the two periods, but the number of mildly retarded children in special education was reduced by more than one-half for those born 1974/75 (Table 14.9). This does not appear to be due to any change in educational policy. It is possible that preschool identification, with placement in the assessment class and Primary 1 deferment, may have enabled some mildly or borderline retarded children born 1974/75 to enter and remain in normal school.

Of the 52 1974/75-born children, 35 were referred preschool to CDC and seven to hospital clinics. In seven cases preschool screening results had been sufficiently suspect for CDC to wish referral but this had not been achieved. Two children were not suspected of having problems preschool and one previously normal child sustained severe brain damage in a road traffic accident after school entry. Overall, 38 children had been admitted to special education on school entry and 14, who entered normal primary schools, were transferred to or recommended for special education before the end of Primary 2. Some details of these children are given.

Three children were transferred to a school for the mildly mentally retarded. One girl from an extremely deprived family was screened at home by the health visitor in the first year of life when developmental progress could be assessed only by history. At two years the child attended the clinic for screening. She failed all items in the adaptive and speech sections and was reported as having only three words, 'Mamma', 'Dadda' and 'Ta-ta'. No response was made to a request for referral. At three and a half years the health visitor reported that speech was still very poor but that the mother would not accept referral to CDC. She was referred to the Child Guidance Service from school in the first term of Primary 2 when intelligence quotient (IQ) on the McCarthy scales was found to be in the mid-50s.

Another girl was followed up for 15 months in the hospital infant clinic, initially on account of a big head. Rate of head growth was normal but the infant showed dystonic signs throughout the first year and at 15 months was functioning no higher than a 12-month level in any area of development. At 15 months she was referred to a children's medical outpatient clinic because of two short-lived fits.

Health visitor screening at two and a half years reported that she had only a few single words and hand function was clumsy. Referral to CDC was not requested as the child was still attending hospital and said to be 'satisfactory in neurological and general development'. Three-year screening was still suspect. At age five years she suffered a sudden onset of cerebellar ataxia of doubtful origin, possibly due to viral infection. She entered normal school at five and a half years and within two months was referred to the Child Guidance Service by the school as 'totally unable to cope'. On the McCarthy scales she appeared to be functioning at a four-year level and on the Wechsler scale appeared borderline retarded after making allowance for clumsiness.

One boy from a good home attended the clinic for most screenings. At two years he failed all adaptive items and no speech was heard. The screening doctor passed him as 'normal but unco-operative'. Failures at three-year screening were attributed to 'poor concentration'. The doctor stated her intention of reviewing the child at three and a half years and a request was made for referral then but he did not return. He was referred to the Child Guidance Service from school in the first term of Primary 2 when IQ on the Stanford-Binet scale was found to be in the low 60s.

Four suspect children whom CDC had wished to see preschool were transferred from normal school to the small group teaching situation available in the school for maladjusted children. One girl from a middle-class home had only a few single words at two years with clumsy hand function and tremor. Referral was requested after the review planned by the screening doctor for two and a half years. She did not return for this or for three-year screening. The health visitor was asked to carry out screening at home and refer if still slow. The child was seen at three and a half years and speech was still much delayed. The health visitor chose to refer the child to the hospital speech therapy department where attendance was irregular and soon ceased. She was referred to the Child Guidance Service by the school in her second term on acount of disruptive and disobedient behaviour and lack of educational progress. On the Wechsler scale she appeared to be functioning overall within the normal range, but with specific difficulties in language, very poor concentration and short-term memory and considerable behaviour disturbance.

Review or referral was requested for two boys from disruptive homes who were suspect on screening at two years. In one case, delay and behaviour disorder was not confirmed at subsequent screening. Thereafter he was taken into care because of maternal neglect and returned to his mother a few days before school entry. The other boy left the city before attendance at CDC was achieved. He returned six months before school entry and was admitted to day nursery where disturbed behaviour was noted but no action taken. Both boys were referred to the Child Guidance Service from school on account of anti-social behaviour and failure to make educational progress in spite of much individual attention.

A third boy appeared to have developmental and behavioural problems on home screening at three and a half years. Unfortunately the screening card was not sent in until one year later, shortly before school entrance. He attended nursery school and was noted there to have considerable problems of behaviour but no action was taken. He was referred to the Child Guidance Service in Primary 2 on account of behaviour problems and marked immaturity.

Two other boys, who were transferred to the school for maladjusted children, were not identified as having problems before school entry. The one was taken into care at three and a half years following non-accidental injury and fostered out of the city. He was assessed at CDC at that age (in order to provide a report for the Court) and was considered to be developmentally normal with only mild behaviour disturbance. He returned to Dundee and entered school there at six years. Soon after he was referred to the Child Guidance Service on account of marked attention seeking and encopresis.

The other boy attended day nursery from four months until school entry. At three-year screening he was reported to be a normal child both developmentally and behaviourally. This does not concur with the nursery report which indicated that, from 18 months, his behaviour had become more and more difficult. He was referred to the Child Guidance Service in his first term on account of marked aggression. This is the only child in special education whose evident preschool problems were not appreciated on screening.

Four children who attended CDC were transferred from Primary 1 to special education.

Two, described elsewhere (p. 122), were recognised preschool as being mildly retarded but were enrolled in normal schools by their parents. Both were transferred to special education when, after a trial period, it became evident to parents that they were not making any educational progress.

One boy, referred to CDC after three-year screening, was of borderline intelligence with more marked delay in speech and overactive behaviour. Nursery class placement was found but the child seldom attended. He was eligible by date of birth to enter school before five years. The parents were entirely resistant to the suggestion that Primary 1 entrance should be deferred, as they were to all other efforts to help the child. He proved unable to cope with the educational requirements of normal school and was transferred to a school for the mildly retarded.

The other boy was referred to CDC after two-year screening, carried out in day nursery, on account of slow development and aggressive behaviour. He was found to have good intelligence and his unmarried mother strenuously denied any problems of behaviour. She declined to visit CDC again. He was re-referred one year later because of continuing aggression in another day nursery. On this occasion mother agreed to clinical psychology help, but only one appointment was kept. Subsequently the child was removed from the nursery and again mother declined further offers of help in spite of prolonged social work intervention. He was referred to the Child Guidance Service in his first term on account of anti-social behaviour both in and out of school. He was completely avoided by other children in class and playground because of his aggressive actions and, in class, his overactivity caused severe disruption. On the British Abilities Scale (Elliot *et al.* 1983) he appeared to be well above average in intelligence but with severely disturbed behaviour. He was transferred to a school for maladjusted children.

The examples quoted emphasise that detection of preschool problems, by screening or by other means, is of little value if no action is (or can be) taken about the problems detected.

Summary

Of 446 children referred to CDC preschool, 377 remained in the city at age six and a half to seven and a half years.

Preschool severity grading and early school status

Highly significant correlations were found between preschool severity gradings and school problem grades, with a rather higher correlation for children with no known social disadvantage than for children from disadvantaged homes. In 39 (12 per cent) educational progress and school behaviour were very different from what had been anticipated. Some details are given about these children.

Preschool neurological findings and motor dysfunction

A highly significant excess of clumsiness, observed by teachers, was recorded for children who were neurologically doubtful or abnormal on preschool examination.

Preschool neurological status and early school problems

Children from homes with no known disadvantage, who had been neuro-logically doubtful or abnormal preschool, had a significant excess of school problems as compared with those who were neurologically normal. This was not evident in those children from disadvantaged homes.

School status of CDC-referred children with multiple minor congenital anomalies

CDC-referred children who had exhibited three or more minor congenital anomalies had a highly significant excess of school problems. They were also much more likely to be considered clumsy than were children with up to two anomalies.

School status of CDC-referred children in all and in different categories of pre-school NDD

After excluding those with specific physical and neurological defects, CDC-referred children had a significant excess of school problems as compared with control children. This was apparent in children with no known disadvantage and in those from disadvantaged homes.

Global delay and borderline retardation These children had the most problems in school, 32 per cent having moderate and 38 per cent severe problems.

Motor disorder Only one-third of these children were problem-free, one-third had moderate and one-third more severe problems. A high incidence of school problems was also found among those children who presented initially with a motor disorder but later moved into another clinical category.

Behaviour disorder   23 per cent had moderate and 37 per cent more severe problems, which were more often educational than behavioural.

Speech disorder   60 per cent were problem-free, 19 per cent had moderate and 24 per cent more severe problems. Children who had speech disorder only were little different from the total population. Those who had associated behaviour disorder had a marked increase in school problems and in reported clumsiness.

School status of children with suspected preschool NDD
Children with suspected NDD, who were not referred for assessment, had a much higher frequency of school problems than did children in the total population who were not suspect. The frequency was similar to that recorded for CDC-referred children.

Reading screen of 1974-born children
Children with preschool NDD confirmed at CDC and children with suspected NDD, who were not assessed, did significantly worse on a group reading test than did control children. The distribution of reading quotients amongst hospital-referred children did not differ from that of the total population of reading-screened children.

Children in special education
By the end of the second school year, 1.3 per cent of 1974/75-born children had been recommended for or were already in special education, compared with 1.9 per cent of those born 1973. The difference was accounted for by a reduction in the number of mildly retarded children by more than one-half.

Of 52 1974/75-born children in special education, 42 were identified preschool and seven were suspect but not assessed. 38 children were admitted to special education on school entry and 14 were transferred from normal primary school. Some details about the latter are given.

REFERENCE

Elliott, C., Murray, D. J., Pearson, L. S. (1983) *British Ability Scales.* Windsor: National Foundation for Educational Research—Nelson.

CHAPTER 15

Conclusions

DEVELOPMENT SCREENING OR HEALTH SURVEILLANCE?

The changing pattern of paediatric practice in recent years was described by the Court report (Great Britain: DHSS 1976) as follows: '. . . the emphasis in childhood illness is changing. With the prevention or more effective treatment of many infectious diseases, the major health problem affecting children to-day is no longer acute episodic illness but, increasingly, malformations, chronic illness, physical and mental handicap, psychiatric disorder and ill-health arising from family stress and breakdown'. Holt (1977) also stressed the increasing attention paid to developmental disorders: 'The preoccupation of doctors with acute illnesses, especially infectious diseases and nutritional disorders, and the sequestration of a small number of specialist paediatricians in hospitals to investigate and treat complex problems, led to little attention being given to child development . . . This situation is changing. Child development is now at last receiving the attention that it should have received in the past.'

In considering this new emphasis on child development as a component of health care, the Court report deliberately avoids the use of the term 'development screening' because it '. . . firmly rejects the notion of a developmental screening programme for children in favour of a programme of health surveillance', which would include monitoring developmental progress of all children as well as oversight of health and physical growth, providing advice and support to parents and treatment and referral of the child, infectious disease prophylaxis and participation in health education and training in parenthood. Health surveillance was conceived in the context of a major reorganisation of primary health care, with specially trained general practitioner paediatricians (GPP) and child health visitors (CHV) taking over responsibility for health surveillance. It was proposed that community child health doctors, who at present are most closely involved with development screening, should either be absorbed into general practice as GPPs or, if not aspiring to (or not eligible for) that rôle, should work exclusively in the developmental and preventive aspects of child health in association with group practices. They would then be known as child health practitioners (CHP).

Response to the Court report was ambivalent. On the one hand it was hailed as 'a splendid statement of the needs of children and of policy goals' and on the other as 'an unsatisfactory practical guide to the organisation of health services and to the improvement of child health' (Alberman *et al.* 1977).

Having in general rejected the practical implications of the Court report, the Royal College of General Practitioners (1982) has, more recently, returned to the concept of health surveillance for all children to be carried out by family doctors in a document entitled 'Healthier Children—Thinking Prevention'. However, it seems unlikely that these new proposals, which involve financial incentives and additional funding, can be implemented nationwide at a time of economic stringency. We are left with the more immediate option of an expansion of development screening, as practised already in many parts of the country, or the decision that this is an unjustifiable drain on limited resources.

DEVELOPMENT SCREENING—IS THIS A USEFUL EXERCISE?

One potentially valuable aspect of development screening, which was not considered in the Dundee study, is the opportunity to provide guidance on child rearing and child development. It has been suggested (Alberman *et al.* 1977) that screening and subsequent surveillance might lead to a loss of confidence and self-reliance in mothers. However, such evidence as is available suggests that when good developmental surveillance and guidance programmes exist, attendances are high (Curtis Jenkins *et al.* 1978), and that mothers are appreciative of and make good use of this type of service (Hart *et al.* 1981).

Alberman and her colleagues (1977) concluded that an expansion of screening for developmental delay, sensory defects or psychological problems, with subsequent surveillance, would be unjustifiable without first evaluating:
(1) the usefulness of screening in picking up particular defects;
(2) whether as a result action would be taken;
(3) how far such action would contribute to a measurable alleviation of handicap.
These important questions are considered below.

Detection of defects by screening and prevalence of NDD

The authors quoted above do not say what is meant by the word 'handicap'. The Court committee defined handicap as 'a disability which for a substantial period or permanently, retards, distorts or otherwise adversely affects normal growth, development or adjustment to life' (Younghusband *et al.* 1970). The committee calculated that 6 per cent of children up to four years will be moderately or severely handicapped by either physical (somatic), visual, hearing and communication or learning disabilities. This is much higher than the frequency (1.9 to 2.2 per cent) of what was considered to constitute handicap in Dundee (p. 199). Our study did not include all children with somatic problems, although it is known that no child born 1974/75 required special education or deferment of Primary 1 entrance (these were categorised by us as 'handicapped') on account of physical conditions other than neurological and sensory defects, which were counted in.

Mittler (1978), commenting on the Warnock report (Great Britain: Committee of Enquiry into the Education of Handicapped Children and Young People 1978), concluded that finding children with special needs before they reach school age 'must surely be one of our aims for the future'. He considered that many children with mild or moderate learning difficulties could be identified before the age of five and that preschool provision should be made for the 20 per cent of children reckoned to have developmental delay and/or social disadvantage.

In Dundee, 4 per cent of preschool children, included in the screening programme, were identified as having moderately severe, severe, or very severe NDD and a further 5 per cent as having only moderate NDD. 73 per cent of these neurodevelopmental and behavioural problems came to light as a result of development screening. 27 per cent of problems was already known, having been recognised at birth or in hospital following an acute episode which caused the diability (these two categories included the great majority of those children with severe mental retardation and most of those with physical handicaps), or identified following referral from sources other than the screening programme. Most children in the latter group were referred with speech delays or disorders in the year before school entry.

We concluded that very severe disabilities were likely to be identified without the aid of screening but that screening was an effective means of identifying less severe disabilities which were later shown to have educational implications. We reject the narrow concept of screening as being concerned only with the detection of more severe disabilities.

Our study also suggests that there exists, in the preschool population a body of pathology that is largely unrecognised and untreated by either primary care practitioners or hospital-based consultants.

Actions to be taken

Detection of disability without subsequent action could be positively harmful if this caused or exacerbated parental anxiety and family stress. Suspicion aroused on screening is only the first stage in the process of assessment and management. Facilities for detailed developmental assessment, continued surveillance and ongoing advice and support are a basic minimum, without which it is doubtful that expansion of screening programmes should proceed.

The amount of work generated by the problems detected on screening is insufficiently appreciated. After excluding children whose problems appeared minor or transitory, the investigation and management of the problems (often multiple) of other research-group children referred to CDC required 3.6 actions per child, apart from paediatric consultation and surveillance. These included correspondence, telephone calls and time-consuming discussions with medical, educational, psychological and therapy collegaues. In addition, social agencies were closely involved with 23 per cent of families. In one-half of these cases, referral to a social agency followed identification of NDD.

Effectiveness of actions taken

Evidence that treatment of severe handicaps leads to an improvement in the child's functioning is limited. Developmental stimulation programmes for Down's syndrome children do appear to effect some long-term improvement (Aronson and Fallstrom 1977). Wright and Nicholson (1973) were unable to demonstrate functional improvement in young children with spastic quadriplegia after intensive physiotherapy, although there was some evidence that treated children were happier and more socially aware than untreated children, and that their parents needed less help and support from other sources. Even if therapeutic measures are ineffective in the alleviation of severe handicaps, there is general agreement about the benefits of early identification, continuing explanation to and support of families, with advice to parents on skilled handling and such facilities as are locally available. This has been well demonstrated in Exeter (Brimblecombe 1974, Rubissow *et al.* 1979). In the USA, intensive early intervention programmes with young children and their severely socially deprived families resulted in normal functioning at seven years in the majority of cases, compared with a high frequency of mild or borderline retardation among control children from similar families (Garber and Heber 1977).

However, we would maintain that the main rôle of development screening is the detection of less severe neurodevelopmental and behavioural problems which are likely to have long-term, if less obvious, effects on the child's functioning. There was no doubt that research-group children with preschool NDD detected on screening were much more likely to have problems in the first two years of schooling than were those whose screening results did not suggest any delay or disorder. In addition, there was evidence that intervention programmes reduced both the numbers of children considered to need special education on account of mild mental retardation and the numbers expected to have significant problems in school, particularly those coming from disadvantaged backgrounds and those with evidence of motor dysfunction.

On the overall evidence of the Dundee study it appears that the provisos laid down by Alberman and colleagues (1977) can be met and that development screening of total populations could be a useful exercise.

DEVELOPMENT SCREENING PROGRAMMES

Who should do screening?

Family doctors

The Court committee were firmly in favour of family doctors being responsible for health surveillance, including the monitoring of development. No other option was considered. The Royal College of General Practitioners (1982) working party report argues persuasively for the same approach, but without recognising the need for the specialised training fundamental to the recommendations of the Court report.

The Royal College of General Practitioners working party proposed a set of screening examinations 'carefully selected to be simple, practical, quick and efficient', which were believed to be within the competence of family doctors without further training. The examination schedules are comprehensive and well-chosen, as are the practical suggestions about separate children's sessions for implementation of health surveillance. However, an important section, 'Finding the Time: the Arithmetic of Child Surveillance', reveals an alarming lack of appreciation of what is involved. Figures are given for an average family doctor with 463 children on the list. Five routine examinations are recommended for the under-fives and it is calculated that review or follow-up examinations would be required for 10 per cent. Other members of the health team could be expected to refer about one additional child weekly and one handicapped child would need review each week. In addition, about 20 per cent of appointment slots should be kept free for accommodation of children with special problems. No argument can be made with this careful breakdown. The report then goes on to suggest that 10 minutes per child is adequate for routine surveillance, and that the work load could be encompassed in one weekly two-and-a-half-hour children's session including follow-up, and more detailed review of children with complicated problems. An experienced developmental paediatrician would be hard-pressed to complete even the basic routine examinations in so short a time. The idea that more detailed assessment, with provision of necessary advice and support for parents of children with disabilities, could also be accommodated in the 10 minutes allotted for follow-up and review is totally unrealistic.

The calculations make no allowance for those (most likely to be in need of surveillance) who do not attend for screening. Different studies have shown non-attendance to range from 11 to 40 per cent, with a higher proportion of developmental problems amongst non-attenders (Robson 1978).

The report minimises the problems of the increasing number of inner-city families (whose children are again in great need of surveillance) who have difficulty in getting on to the list of any family doctor. 'These are not the areas with flourishing group practices, purpose-built health centres and thriving primary care teams who know where they are going, but those where we may find a disproportionately large number of elderly doctors, working solo or in small partnerships, probably from unsatisfactory premises and lock-up surgeries and over-using the deputising services' (Alberman *et al.* 1977, see also London Health Planning Consortium 1981).

Our study convinced us of the importance of some central monitoring system to review take-up of screening, and to provide checks on the competence of those implementing the programme and advice for less experienced screeners about children who appear to need further review or referral. The position of family doctors, as independent contractors, does not lend itself to this sort of monitoring.

Across the country there are already a number of family doctors who have developed a special interest in child health and development and whose programmes of health surveillance stand as models. Some of these are described elsewhere (p. 37). It is likely that this number will increase. Nevertheless, it is probable that the majority of family doctors have neither the experience or motivation to take over sole responsibility for developmental surveillance. As one distinguished proponent of health surveillance in general practice conceded, 'great problems of education lie ahead if general practitioners are to be brought into this field on any large scale' and 'the considerable problem of changing attitudes to (primary) care of both patients and doctors must be faced' (Curtis Jenkins 1977).

Health visitors

The Court report suggested six routine examinations for all children in the first five years of life. The first two (at birth, six to 10 days) would be conducted by the doctor providing initial obstetric or paediatric care; at six weeks, two and a half to three years and four and a half to five years by GPP or CHP; at seven to eight months and 18 months by CHV. The health visitor's review of development would place special emphasis on hearing and vision at seven to eight months and on mobility, manipulative skills, hearing, early language and social relationships at 18 months. The health visitor would also screen non-attenders at home at six weeks; arrangements for non-attenders at other ages are not discussed. The responsibility put upon health visitors of detecting defects and disorders from after age six weeks until two and a half to three years is considerable. However, the committee envisaged that health visitors would have special knowledge and skills. It was also recommended that they should work within geographical areas.

Curtis Jenkins (1978) considered that surveillance must be carried out by specially trained doctors, for which reason he and his community child health colleagues 'have not delegated any part of the examinations to health visitors, nurses or other professionals'. In other programmes (*e.g.* Barber 1982) all screening is carried out by health visitors and physical examination by doctors.

In 1967 O'Donovan and Moncrieff devised a battery of screening tests, extracted from Sheridan (1960), designed for application by health visitors in well-baby clinics. This drew an immediate response from Sheridan (1967) herself who warned of the 'many hidden pitfalls which beset those who attempt to design simplified developmental testing scales of the pass/fail type'. Sheridan stressed that 'however simple the procedures themselves may appear, interpretation of the child's manner of response in the testing situation (especially in the age range 15 to 30 months) is sometimes exceedingly difficult and requires a sound background of paediatric knowledge as well as the basic principles of child psychology'. For this reason she had tried to make it clear that not only was her schedule intended for the use of doctors, but that considerable experience was needed before the full implication of this 'clinical paediatric tool' could be appreciated. She concluded 'I am only too glad to further the adoption of adequate developmental screening programmes, but I have learnt from melancholy experience that the whole enterprise is much more complicated than at first sight it appears to be'. The training of health visitors in child development has undoubtedly increased and deepened over the past 15 years. Nevertheless, Sheridan's strictures may have continuing relevance today, especially to family doctors intending to increase their involvement in child health surveillance.

In Dundee, health visitors were responsible for screening non-attenders including many high-risk children from disadvantaged homes. In retrospect we feel that these children, more than those who attend clinics regularly, should be screened by doctors. This might entail community child health doctors going into homes for that purpose and/or the appointment of one or more specialist health visitors, with the skills and time to work towards clinic acceptance among these non-attending families.

Community child health doctors

There is general agreement (not least amongst community doctors themselves) that there still exists in community child health a proportion of doctors who are as untrained and unsuitable as many family doctors to undertake development screening and surveillance. 'The readiness of health authorities to employ clinical medical officers in their preschool and school health services who are manifestly incompetent for the work has been near disastrous for these services' (Whitmore *et al.* 1979). Nevertheless, the training programmes proposed (British Medical Association 1982) and continuing discussion among those in community child health, indicate that more than other groups, it is the doctors in the preschool and school health services who see children in educational and environmental as well as in developmental and health terms, who are already closely involved with local social work and educational facilities and who, at the present time, could be the only group capable of providing development screening and subsequent surveillance for all children in geographical areas, particularly those in deprived inner city districts. As Whitmore and his collegaues pointed out when considering these densely populated urban areas where the need for comprehensive health care is most urgent: 'General practice does not accept any obligations to offer health care to those who do not seek it, nor does it show any sign of restricting its services to geographically defined populations.'

The Royal College of General Practitioners working party report (1982) quotes with approval the work of Bax and colleagues (1980) from an inner city area. This study is considered to be especially important because of the finding that 20 per cent of children attending area health authority child health clinics had significant problems and, in particular, that an excess of respiratory tract infections, developmental delay and behavioural problems were interrelated. Adverse social findings (particularly maternal stress) were closely correlated with the health and behaviour of the child. The working party comments on the value of the arrangements made for the children concerned and notes the appreciation of parents for the services offered.

However, it would be difficult to implement the type of child health surveillance described here, and which the working party commends, in other than a local child health clinic setting. Routine examinations of 250 children were encompassed within a weekly session extending from 13.30 to 18.30 hours, but the majority of clinic visits were not for routine examinations. Other clinic sessions were conducted on a walk-in basis and parents were encouraged to come as often as they wished. One-half of mothers had considerable social, housing or marital problems, often associated with depression and anxiety or with difficulties in coping with their babies (Hart *et al.* 1981). Elsewhere (Bax and Hart 1976), it is stated that these mothers attended family doctors with their children almost exclusively because of infective illness and that developmental and behavioural problems were seldom presented. These authors (1981) conclude their description of the work of a child health clinic thus: 'We hope that our experience strikes an optimistic note for those working in the community child health service. We hope the familiar criticism of children's clinics will soon be a thing of the past.'

How should screening be done?

How many screening examinations?

The Court committee recommended six routine surveillance examinations from birth to four and a half to five and a half years (immediately before school entry) as described above. The Royal College of General Practitioners working party report agreed with this schedule.

In Dundee six screening examinations were done at eight, 20 and 39 weeks, 15 months, two and three years. The first screenings were carried out by health visitors and the five subsequent screenings by doctors. 15 minutes was allowed for each examination. In practice, time available was longer as non-attendance at any particular examination approached 30 per cent, leaving more time for those who did attend. In restrospect we feel that the time allotted for each screening was inadequate and accounted, in part, for the tendency of some clinic doctors to place undue reliance on mothers' histories. Facilities for further assessment were readily available for children born during the research years. This may have discouraged some doctors from themselves proceeding to further review of suspect children and recall of those whose screening examinations were incomplete or otherwise unsatisfactory. In our local situation a reduction in the number of examinations to four (health visitor at eight weeks, clinic doctor at nine months, 18 months and two and a half to three and a half years) as suggested by the Grampian preschool health surveillance feasibility study group (Robinson 1982), would allow more time for individual examinations and follow-up. With only three examinations after eight weeks it would be the more important to ensure complete cover at each examination age with routine review of those whose screening examinations were unsatisfactory or suspect.

The composition of screening examinations

In Dundee, the eight-week examination, carried out by the health visitor, included some observations on posture, some measures of social awareness and comments on handling, feeding, sleeping and contentment. Practical problems of management were discussed. Few defects or disorders were detected at this age as the great majority of children with obvious disabilities (or considered to be at risk of developing these) were being followed up in the hospital infant clinic. However, the eight-week examination provided a useful introduction to the screening programme. Since health visitors are, in any event, seeing infants of this age at clinic or in the home, completion of a screening schedule should not be too time-consuming and this screening age should be retained.

A doctor examination at nine months (39 weeks) should include tests of hearing and vision, examination for squint and the presence of minor abnormal neurological signs as well as assessment of gross and fine motor skills, vocalisation, evidence of general alertness and, what Sheridan (1967) calls, 'social forthcomingness'. The doctor should already be informed about any social problems known to the health visitor. At this age most sensory and physical handicaps and significant developmental delay due to innate rather than environmental factors should be evident.

278

In view of the long-term significance of motor delay or disorder, special emphasis should be placed on this aspect of development at 18 months. It is not enough to accept a history of satisfactory function. This must be exhibited. Motor skills are affected far less by environmental factors than are other developmental skills (Neligan and Prudham 1969) and delayed motor development should seldom be attributed to social disadvantage. By 18 months fine hand manipulation, comprehension and use of speech and spontaneous play behaviour should also be clearly demonstrable and children who are falling behind in any of these areas kept under review.

At two and a half to three years the main emphases should be on language and behaviour. By this age the effects of an impoverished environment are very obvious and complete social details are essential. It is to be hoped that the mother will, already, have received advice about talking to her child and joining with him or her in stimulating play activities, but this is the age for considering placement in play group or nursery class well before the child has to face the new world of school. Again, those children who cause any concern to parent or screener should be seen again at three and a half to four years, if not before.

CHILDREN AT RISK AND WITH SPECIAL NEEDS

Pre- and perinatal hazard

The concept of children 'at risk of developing disabilities' has concentrated on those who are judged to have suffered some pre- or perinatal insult. The stimulus came largely from Sheridan (1962). She recommended that special attention should be paid to infants and young children considered to be 'at-risk' because of adverse environmental influences and slow postnatal development as well as those with a high-risk pre- or perinatal history. Subsequently, the emphasis was increasingly placed on pre- and perinatal factors. For example, Oppé (1967) suggested a modified list which included only genetic or early intra-uterine factors, pre-, intrapartum and immediate postnatal status.

There is a vast body of publications dealing with the long-term effects of low birthweight and other perinatal hazards and general agreement that these factors do have an effect on later development. In Dundee, the effect of perinatal factors on function at school age was small. This may be due, in part, to the good antenatal, obstetric and neonatal services available locally, but we were not convinced that a considerable increase in these services nationwide would substantially reduce the frequency of handicapping conditions or the problems of children in normal school (p. 208).

Social disadvantage

There is an apparent contradiction in the Court committee's attitude to the identification of children considered to be at risk on account of social disadvantage. In one section the report states, 'We have wished to avoid a categorisation of children ''at risk'' on account of selected social factors . . . This might limit concern inappropriately to certain groups of children at the expense of others', and later on, 'We recommend as a priority that specialists in community medicine, area nurses and joint planning teams should take steps to identify children living in socially disadvantaged families (and particularly neighbourhoods in which there may be a high concentration of such families) and examine the possibility of . . . improving and supplementing primary health care services for these children.'

The Black report (Great Britain: DHSS 1980) produced irrefutable evidence about the deleterious effects of social deprivation on the survival, growth, development and health of children and on the provision and use of preventive services. The report concluded that early childhood is the period of life at which intervention could most hopefully weaken the continuing association between health and class and called for the abolition of child poverty as a national goal for the 1980s. Owing to restricted circulation, described by Court (1981) as 'a deliberate attempt to prevent serious discussion of health issues of urgent concern', this report was not readily available. More recently, the findings and conclusions of the research group have been published elsewhere (Townsend and Davidson 1982) with additional specialised information and research results published since 1980 and a discussion of how major developments of social and economic structure during 1980/81 might affect the arguments of the report.

There is no doubt that disadvantaged children have special needs and those who undertake development screening and surveillance must have relevant background information in order to interpret screening and assessment results and to advise on appropriate management.

Our finding of a close relationship between social circumstances and school performance repeats what has been well-established already. Nevertheless, the majority of children, recognised as disadvantaged, had reached a satisfactory educational standard and had no outstanding problems of behaviour at six and a half to seven and a half years. Some children in control group B (nearly all girls) had no problems in school in spite of very unfavourable preschool circumstances.

There is no justification in our study for the attitude that socially disadvantaged children can be expected to fail and every reason for further research into the reasons why the gap between potentially normal advantaged and disadvantaged school children increases with age and into methods of modifying environmental influences at home and in school (Rutter and Madge 1976).

Motor dysfunction

The predominance of motor dysfunction in the frequency of school problems was more surprising. It appears that motor-disordered children are at high risk whatever the social background and that this intrinsic problem can render the child more vulnerable to adverse extrinsic circumstances. These children require on-going surveillance preschool.

Non-attenders

Children who do not attend for screening and children with preschool NDD who are non-attenders at clinics and do not take up educational facilities offered, constitute a group with special needs. Our success in dealing with this problem was limited (p. 214).

Cooper and Lynch (1976) studied the 25 per cent non-attendance rate at a general paediatric outpatient clinic; non-attendance was persistent in one-third. It was found that children who persistently failed to attend not only had multiple medical problems but also came from families with diffuse social problems. The authors suggest that follow-up might well be more successfully carried out in the community with help from the health visitor and social worker and that a united effort by both community and hospital sources is likely to be much more successful than unco-ordinated attempts to make parents and children attend a variety of different agencies. A similar approach was recommended by Stacey (1980) who wrote: 'With the increased emphasis on personal responsibility and in the individualistic philosophy of our society we tend to say, ''What is the matter with these people that they do not come to use our services?'' rather than asking ''What is the matter with our services that these people do not use them?''.'

A discussion document (Tyson 1980) prepared by the Children's Committee, whose members include representatives from health, education, social work and voluntary agencies, urged professionals to recognise that parents are the central people in the lives of their children, to focus their support on schemes involving parents, to make their services geographically and psychologically more accessible and to take their services more often to where the client is, in mother and toddler group, play group and home.

WHAT COMES AFTER DEVELOPMENT SCREENING?

Further assessment and investigation

Children in Dundee primary schools, who were suspect on preschool screening, were more than three times as likely to have problems of education and behaviour in school at six and a half to seven and a half years than were children who were not suspected of having any significant delay or disorder on screening. On this basis we concluded that preschool NDD merits full assessment and investigation of all the factors, both intrinsic and extrinsic, that underlie the multiple problems which many children exhibit. Turning the problem of language delay over to the speech therapist, without elucidating and dealing with other co-existing problems, is not in the best interest of either child or therapist.

Hospital referrals may be unavoidable (*e.g.* for ophthalmic or auditory investigations), but our experience suggests that a busy children's medical outpatient department does not provide the relaxed and informal environment that facilitates the elucidation and discussion of developmental and behavioural problems. It is also difficult to provide continuity of supervision by one paediatrician as is illustrated by the case of one research-group child, who presented at age 14 months with locomotor delay and abnormal neurological signs and later developed problems of speech and behaviour. He attended hospital at six-monthly intervals until age five years three months during which time his progress was supervised by eight different doctors. Children with NDD are not ill and referral to hospital may generate unnecessary anxieties in parents. Similarly, referral to a unit recognised as dealing in the main with handicapped children can cause acute anxiety to parents of children with less serious impairments.

There are considerable advantages in a referral unit for children with NDD being perceived as a consultative facility for those with any neurodevelopmental or behavioural problems (from the least to the most severe), in having this unit sited in the community rather than in hospital premises and in combining assessment and investigation with on-going management and therapy. In some areas hospital-based consultant paediatricians are prepared to go into the community to fulfil this rôle. In others, joint hospital/community paediatric appointments are being created. However, there are not nearly enough consultant paediatricians to cover the needs of the 10 to 12 per cent of preschool children with moderate or more severe NDD. In many areas there exist senior community child health doctors who have the necessary experience already. If the training proposals of the Community Health Doctors' Sub-Committee (British Medical Association 1982) for senior clinical medical officer (career grade) are implemented, this number will increase.

Management

Management of preschool NDD should be as much concerned with social and environmental as with medical causes. A great deal depends on the extent to which the doctor, responsible for co-ordinating management, is already closely involved with health visitors, day nursery staff, social workers, nursery class teachers as well as with medical colleagues, psychologists and therapists. Certain basic local amenities are also essential, particularly preschool placements. This was recognised 10 years ago by the then Secretary for Education who supported a massive increase in nursery education, as recommended by the Central Advisory Council for Education (Great Britain: Department of Education and Science 1967), on the grounds that, 'if a child has any handicap—a reading difficulty, a difficulty in talking or a difficulty in being with other children—the earlier you can spot it, identify it and deal with it, the most chances you have of overcoming it . . . Nursery education should give a child a much better command of language right from the start' (Margaret Thatcher, April 1973). Unfortunately, governmental priorities appear to have changed in the last four years.

In Dundee, which is a rather poor industrial city, preschool facilities are good and appropriate placements were found for almost all children with special needs.

A broad-based survey carried out in 1977 indicated that preschool provision was available for 36 per cent of children (Bone 1977). Both the use of and the desire for these facilities were class related, with nearly twice as many children in social classes I and II benefiting from day provision as those in social classes IV and V and, conversely, nearly twice as many parents in social classes IV and V expressing an unmet desire for these services as those in social classes I and II. This survey also looked at provision of services on the basis of children's needs, using the same sorts of criteria as those which constitute priority needs for admission to day nurseries, such as handicap, developmental delay or behaviour disorder in the child, social deprivation and maternal depression. On these criteria, 36 per cent of children were considered to have priority needs for day placements but these were available for less than one-third. Since 1977, provision has been subjected to further contraction as a result of public spending cuts. In the absence of such facilities paediatricians and community child health doctors are well placed to co-operate with local pressure groups calling for these amenities.

The discrepancy between the widespread recognition of the influence on child health and development of adverse social factors and the apparent reluctance to call for measures to ameliorate family poverty, is well-stated in two comments on the Court report:

> Where health-care professionals are clearly appraised, as the Court committee was, of the social causes of disease, it seems proper that those in the NHS [National Health Service] who recognise the consequences of bad social conditions should act as a strong pressure group to try to get these remedied. Sadly all the report could find to say was 'Adverse social conditions will doubtless be with us for many years'. So they will if strong atttempts are not made to change them (Stacey 1980).

> The report is eloquent on the special needs of children in inner cities, slums, social classes IV and V, single-parent families, ethnic minorities and others. It is sad that the Committee did not exert its influence in support of any concrete social policies that might reduce inequality of opportunities for health . . . The dozens of detailed recommendations on health care compared with the generalities about social reform, could create a wholly misleading impression of the capabilities of medicine and of what we know about helping children to be fit for the future (Alberman *et al.* 1977).

REFERENCES

Alberman, E. D., Morris, J. N., Pharoah, P. O. D. (1977) 'After Court.' *Lancet,* **2,** 393-396.
Aronson, M., Fallström, K. (1977) 'Immediate and long-term effects of developmental training in children with Down's syndrome.' *Developmental Medicine and Child Neurology,* **19,** 489-494.
Barber, J. H. (1982) 'Pre-school developmental screening: the results of a 4-year period.' *Health Bulletin,* **40,** 170-178.
Bax, M., Hart, H. (1976) 'Health needs of preschool children.' *Archives of Disease in Childhood,* **51,** 848-852.
—— —— Jenkins, S. (1980) *The Health Needs of the Pre-school Child.* London: Thomas Coram Research Unit, University of London.
Bone, M. (1977) *Pre-School Children and the Need for Day Care. OCPS Social Survey Division Report.* London: HMSO.
Brimblecombe, F. S. W. (1974) 'An Exeter project for handicapped children.' *British Medical Journal,* **4,** 706-709.
British Medical Association. Community Health Doctors' Subcommittee (Chairman: K. Dalzell) (1982) *Career Structure and Training for Community Health Doctors.* London: BMA.
Cooper, N. A., Lynch, M. A. (1979) 'Lost to follow-up. A study of nonattendance at a general paediatric outpatient clinic.' *Archives of Disease in Childhood,* **54,** 765-769.
Court, S. D. M. (1981) 'Inequalities in health.' *Archives of Disease in Childhood,* **56,** 161-162.
Curtis Jenkins, G. H. (1977) 'Surveillance of pre-school children in general practice.' *In:* Drillien, C. M., Drummond, M. B. (Eds.) *Neurodevelopmental Problems in Early Childhood.* Oxford: Blackwell Scientific Publications.

—— Collins, C., Andren, S. (1978) 'Developmental surveillance in general practice.' *British Medical Journal,* **1,** 1537-1540.

Garber, H., Heber, R. (1977) 'The Milwaukee Project: indications of the effectiveness of early intervention in preventing mental retardation.' *In:* Mittler, P. (Ed.) *Research to Practice in Mental Retardation. Vol. 1.* Baltimore: University Park Press.

Great Britain: Committee of Enquiry into the Education of Handicapped Children and Young People. (1978) *Special Educational Needs. Report of the Committee* (Chairman: H. M. Warnock). London: HMSO.

—— Department of Education and Science (1967) *Children and their Primary Schools. Report of the Central Advisory Council for Education* (England), 2 vols., (Chairperson: Lady Plowden). London: HMSO.

—— Department of Health and Social Security (1976) *Fit for the Future. Report of the Committee on Child Health Services* (Chairman: S. D. M. Court). London: HMSO.

—— (1980) *Inequalities in Health. Report of a Research Working Group* (Chairman: D. Black). London: HMSO.

Hart, H., Bax, M., Jenkins, S. (1981) 'Use of the child health clinic.' *Archives of Disease in Childhood,* **56,** 440-445.

Holt, K, S. (1977) 'Some thoughts on developmental screening.' *Child: Care, Health and Development,* **3,** 275-282.

London Health Planning Consortium (1981) *Primary Health Care in Inner London. Report of Primary Health Care Study Group* (Chairman: E. D. Acheson). London: DHSS.

Mittler, P. (1978) 'The needs of the under fives.' *Special Education,* **5,** 12-13.

Neligan, G., Prudham, D. (1969) 'Norms for four standard developmental milestones by sex, social class and place in family'. *Developmental Medicine and Child Neurology,* **11,** 413-422.

O'Donovan, M., Moncrieff, A. (1967) 'Developmental testing by health visitors.' *Medical Officer,* **18,** 294-295.

Oppé, T. E. (1967) 'Risk registers for babies.' *Developmental Medicine and Child Neurology,* **9,** 13-21.

Robson, P. (1978) 'Screening for children. Developmental paediatrics.' *Royal Society of Health Journal,* **98,** 231-237.

Robinson, H. G. (Chairman) (1982) *Pre-school Health Surveillance Feasibility Study Report.* Aberdeen: Grampian Health Board.

Royal College of General Practitioners (1982) 'Healthier children—thinking prevention.' *Report from General Practice,* **22.**

Rubissow, J., Jones, J., Brimblecombe, F., Morgan, D. (1979) 'Handicapped children and their families: their use of available services and their unmet needs.' *In: Mixed Communications, Problems and Progress in Medical Care. Twelfth Series.* Oxford: Oxford University Press for Nuffield Provincial Hospitals Trust.

Rutter, M., Madge, N. (1976) 'Intellectual performance and scholastic attainment.' *In: Cycles of Disadvantage: A Review of Research.* London: Heinemann.

Sheridan, M. D. (1960) *Developmental Progress of Infants and Young Children. Ministry of Health Reports on Public Health and Medical Subjects. No. 102.* London: HMSO.

—— (1962) 'Infants at risk of handicapping conditions.' *Monthly Bulletin, Ministry of Health and Public Health Laboratory Services,* **21,** 238-245.

—— (1967) 'Developmental testing procedures.' *Medical Officer,* **18,** 318-319.

Stacey, M. (1980) 'Realities for change in child health care: existing patterns and future possibilities.' *British Medical Journal,* **280,** 1512-1515.

Townsend, P., Davidson, N. (1982) *Inequalities in Health. The Black Report.* Harmondsworth, Middlesex: Penguin.

Tyson, M. (Chairman) Working Group of the Children's Committee (1980) *The Needs of the Under-Fives in the Family.* London: Children's Committee.

Whitmore, K., Bax, M., Tyrell, S. (1979) 'Clinical medical officers in a child health service.' *British Medical Journal,* **1,** 242-245.

Wright, T., Nicholson, J. (1973) 'Physiotherapy for the spastic child: an evaluation.' *Developmental Medicine and Child Neurology,* **15,** 146-163.

Younghusband, E., Buchall, D., Davie, R., Kellmer Pringle, M. L. (1970) *Living with Handicap.* London: National Bureau for Co-operation in Child Care.

DEVELOPMENT SCREENING
AND THE
CHILD WITH SPECIAL NEEDS